Virilio and Visual Culture

Critical Connections

A series of edited collections forging new connections between contemporary critical theorists and a wide range of research areas, such as critical and cultural theory, gender studies, film, literature, music, philosophy and politics.

Series Editors
Ian Buchanan, University of Wollongong
James Williams, University of Dundee

Editorial Advisory Board

Nick Hewlett
Gregg Lambert
Todd May
John Mullarkey
Paul Patton
Marc Rölli
Alison Ross
Kathrin Thiele
Frédéric Worms

Titles available in the series

Agamben and Colonialism edited by Marcelo Svirsky and Simone Bignall
Laruelle and Non-Philosophy edited by John Mullarkey and Anthony Paul Smith
Badiou and Philosophy edited by Sean Bowden and Simon Duffy
Virilio and Visual Culture edited by John Armitage and Ryan Bishop

Forthcoming titles

Rancière and Film edited by Paul Bowman
Butler and Ethics edited by Moya Lloyd
Stiegler and Technics edited by Christina Howells and Gerald Moore

Visit the Critical Connections website at
www.euppublishing.com/series/crcs

Virilio and Visual Culture

Edited by John Armitage and Ryan Bishop

EDINBURGH
University Press

© editorial matter and organisation John Armitage and Ryan Bishop, 2013
© the chapters their several authors

Edinburgh University Press Ltd
22 George Square, Edinburgh EH8 9LF

www.euppublishing.com

Typeset in 11/13 Adobe Sabon
by Servis Filmsetting Ltd, Stockport, Cheshire, and
printed and bound in the United States of America

A CIP record for this book is available from the British Library

ISBN 978 0 7486 5445 1 (hardback)
ISBN 978 0 7486 5444 4 (paperback)
ISBN 978 0 7486 5446 8 (webready PDF)
ISBN 978 0 7486 5448 2 (epub)
ISBN 978 0 7486 5447 5 (Amazon ebook)

Contents

Acknowledgements

John Armitage and Ryan Bishop would like to thank: Ian Buchanan, for prompting the initial discussion concerning *Virilio and Visual Culture*; Carol MacDonald and Jenny Daly, our editors at Edinburgh University Press, for their sensible advice and support throughout our editorship of the book; Paul Virilio and the nine other contributors to the volume for their knowledge of Virilio's work and visual culture as well as for their willingness to contribute to the book and for their professionalism; and especially Joy Garnett, for her virtuoso painting, which adorns the cover of *Virilio and Visual Culture*.

John Armitage is grateful to Professor Lynn Dobbs, former Dean of the School of Arts and Social Sciences at Northumbria University, for providing him with extended research leave during 2012 to complete this volume and to Joanne Roberts for her continuing love and support.

Ryan Bishop would like to thank Bashir Makhoul and his colleagues at Winchester Centre for Global Futures in Art, Design and Media, including Jonathan Harris, Sean Cubitt, Jussi Parikka, August Davis and Stefanie Van de Peer, along with many others for their exquisite collegiality and inspiration. Many thanks also go to my father, Steve Bishop, for witty daily chats, my daughters Sarah and Sophia, for their constant joy and surprise, and finally to Adeline Hoe for her love and daily care. Without all of the people mentioned, none of this would have any meaning.

Figures

Contributors

John Armitage is Professor of Media Arts at Winchester School of Art, University of Southampton, UK.

John Beck is co-editor of *American Visual Cultures* (2005) and author of *Dirty Wars: Landscape, Power and Waste in Western American Literature* (2009). He is Reader in American Literature and Culture at Newcastle University, UK.

Ryan Bishop is Professor of Global Arts and Politics and co-director of Winchester Centre for Global Futures in Art, Design and Media, Winchester School of Art, University of Southampton, UK.

Benjamin H. Bratton is Associate Professor of Visual Arts at the University of California, San Diego, USA, and Director of the Center for Design and Geopolitics at the California Institute of Telecommunications and Information Technology.

Jordan Crandall is an artist, theorist and performer based in Los Angeles, USA. He is Associate Professor in the Visual Arts Department at University of California, San Diego. He is the 2011 winner of the Vilém Flusser Theory Award for outstanding theory and research-based digital arts practice, given by the Transmediale in Berlin, Germany. He is currently an Honorary Resident at the Eyebeam art and technology centre in New York, where he is continuing the development of a new body of work that blends performance art, political theatre, philosophical speculation and intimate reverie. The work, entitled *Unmanned*, explores new ontologies of distributed systems – a performative event-philosophy in the form of a book and a theatrical production.

Gair Dunlop makes artworks which explore the interconnections of people, places and technologies. Such artworks investigate and play with different eras of discovery, social change and propaganda. His core interest is how dreams of progress affect people and the places they live. Project materials include archive, contemporary and absurdist visions of technology and entropy. He is based in Scotland, UK, and is course director of Time Based Art and Digital Film, Duncan and Jordanstone College of Art and Design, University of Dundee. His website is: www.atomtown.org.uk

Joy Garnett is a painter and media artist who lives in Brooklyn, New York City, USA. Her paintings, based on found images of explosive events, locate instances of the apocalyptic sublime in mass media culture. Her social media performances examine the intersections of our digital and material worlds. Her work has been exhibited at the Milwaukee Art Museum, MoMA P.S.1 and the Whitney Museum of American Art. She is the Arts Editor for the scholarly journal *Cultural Politics*, published by Duke University Press.

Ian James completed his doctoral research on the fictional and theoretical writings of Pierre Klossowski at the University of Warwick in 1996. Since then he has been a Fellow and Lecturer in French at Downing College, University of Cambridge, UK. He is the author of *Pierre Klossowski: The Persistence of a Name* (2000), *The Fragmentary Demand: An Introduction to the Philosophy of Jean-Luc Nancy* (2006), *Paul Virilio* (2007) and *The New French Philosophy* (2012).

Caren Kaplan is Professor of American Studies and affiliated faculty in Film Studies, Cultural Studies, and Science and Technology Studies at University of California Davis, USA. She is the author of *Questions of Travel: Postmodern Discourses of Displacement* (1996) and the co-author and co-editor of *Introduction to Women's Studies: Gender in a Transnational World* (2001/2005), *Between Woman and Nation: Transnational Feminisms and the State* (1999) and *Scattered Hegemonies: Postmodernity and Transnational Feminist Practices* (1994) as well as two digital multimedia scholarly works, *Dead Reckoning* and *Precision Targets*. Her current research focuses on aerial views and militarised visual culture.

John W. P. Phillips is Associate Professor in the Department of English Language and Literature, National University of Singapore, Singapore.

Tania Roy is Assistant Professor in the Department of English Language and Literature at the National University of Singapore, Singapore. Her main research interest involves extrapolations of the Frankfurt School for a critical account of 'alternative' modernities, with special reference to the post-colonial. She is currently completing a book-project on Theodor Adorno's conceptions of late-style for a discussion of Indian modernism in, and after, the twentieth century. She has articles published or forthcoming on aesthetics and political violence in India with historical reference to national allegory in R. Tagore; and on the status of contemporary visual art after liberalisation in the work of Dayanita Singh and Vivan Sundaram.

Chris Turner is a translator and writer living in Birmingham, UK.

Paul Virilio is Professor of Architecture Emeritus, École Spéciale d'Architecture, Paris, France. He is the author of, most recently, *The University of Disaster* (2010), *The Futurism of the Instant: Stop-Eject* (2010) and *The Great Accelerator* (2012). He lives and works in La Rochelle.

Aesthetics, Vision and Speed: An Introduction to Virilio and Visual Culture

John Armitage and Ryan Bishop

We might add that rejection of visual (audiovisual) conformism would also tend to rule out establishing some kind of *optically correct politics* which could cause the manipulation of sight by future mass communication tools quickly to take on totalitarian overtones. (Virilio 1997: 97)

The Visual as Perpetual Contestation

Paul Virilio's major contribution to contemporary European thought has been to demonstrate that questions of visual culture are not only academic and cultural, aesthetic, historical, critical, philosophical and anthropological questions but also extremely important political questions. For Virilio, visual culture does not simply provide ways to understand the visual or examine images; it offers primarily a critical site of theory and contemporary cultural action and intervention, where relations of power in this field of study are both established in everything from film studies and psychoanalytic theory to gender studies, queer theory, television and video game studies, comics, the traditional artistic media of painting, advertising and the Internet, and potentially disturbed. Virilio's initial ways into these areas of power relations that constitute the visual cultural scene and its usual analytic topics are odd and oblique, which provide them with their intellectual purchase, emerging as they do from his work as an urbanist interested in technology, speed and the military. These larger forces, according to Virilio, are the primary influences on and shapers of visual culture, with the standard areas of enquiry being mere effects of them. Virilio reminds us that the battlefield is primarily a visual and sensory domain: perception as aiming and targeting, hiding and uncovering, and that urban centres result from paths of movement and means of defence, all of which responds to and alters the visual field. The visual domain, in Virilio's theoretical work, no matter how it manifests itself, is always concerned with movement, speed, time, the built environment, technology and their complex interactions, resulting in the constantly increasing militarisation of all aspects of daily life.

Virilio is an unusual intellectual, in the sense that his work on visual media and their various components have made a difference both to academic debates over visual culture and to the field's cultural versatility and the range of politicised objects contained under the term visual culture (see Garnett and Armitage 2011). *The Aesthetics of Disappearance* (2009a), for example – for many Virilio's most innovative and influential published project on visual events – increasingly turns up on the bibliographies of visual cultural studies courses around the globe. An important development in Virilio's thinking and writing, this book examines, among other things, those gaps in perception caused by technologically produced movement and speed, resulting in 'picnolepsy' which is a form of perception emergent from absences and lost snippets of time. Finding overlaps between the fundamentally different philosophers Descartes and Bergson, Virilio claims that for both thinkers consciousness or thought emerges from duration. It's 'our duration that thinks, the first product of consciousness would be its own speed in its distance of time, speed would be the causal idea, the idea before the idea' (2009a: 32). Virilio thus brings his preoccupations with speed in relation to temporality and its influence on apperception and consciousness into the heart of visual culture, marking this as an important but decidedly oblique examination of visual studies, which makes it somewhat like picnolepsy itself in that the study emerges from gaps in the field's general perceptive apparatus.

Despite having widespread influence and notwithstanding his centrality to the field, Virilio remains something of a visual culture outsider, by choice and by dint of the eclectically challenging demands he places on it. He claims to be not a revolutionary but a revelationary philosopher (Virilio 2009b: 43; Virilio and Richard 2012: 71). He is not persuaded by the belief that the intellectual can mobilise people; rather, the role of philosophy is to critically engage the material and intellectual conditions of possibility for change. Thus millennial thinking, which can become a rationale for various forms of social change, for example, comes repeatedly under his scrutiny: to prepare for the apocalypse or the end of the world, for Virilio, is to concentrate on 'a concept without a future' (2009b: 43). On the one hand, this is because Virilio does not believe that there is such a thing as *the* end of the world in the sense of 'One "boom" and there is nothing left' (2009b: 43). On the other, it is because he does not believe that there is a quick intellectual or philosophical fix to visual and cultural questions concerning the end of the world, or for that matter, a way of fixing it for good as a concept *with* a future. Apocalypse, however, means revelation or revealing as in lifting the veil, and thus Virilio cheekily separates what cannot be easily separated and what indeed constitute an inherent paradox, for apocalypse cannot be thought without revelation. His revolutionary/revelationary formulation contains an assumption that pulses throughout his thinking: that humanity is the end of things and that it is through our mortality, our ends, that we have consciousness at all. Visual culture, he argues, is a site not only of ongoing struggle but also of revelation that can never be guaranteed by either his deeply held religious faith (Virilio is a practising Catholic) or by his own intellectual work. In this sense, his intellectual contribution to visual culture and, in particular, to our understanding of vision technologies, has not simply been to expose the cultural politics of media, perception and human visual capabilities; it has also been to reveal that visual culture is never reducible to the cultural politics of vision technologies.

For Virilio, the investigation of visual culture entails revealing the techno-scientific methods and desires, creations, taxonomies, articulations and, above all, relations of power that subsist within visuality at any given instant so as to think about how alternative cultural visionaries, or perhaps 'marginal groups', might obtain or win, however provisionally, cultural space from the dominant groups associated in particular with the study and development of techno-science (Virilio and Brausch 1993; Virilio and Richard 2012: 22). This is an enormously multifaceted process, full of potential pitfalls, and Virilio, we and our contributors deliberate how Virilio has theorised and practised this approach in greater detail in the 12 chapters that follow. For now, though, it suggests a way of thinking about Virilio's philosophy of electronic media, techno-science, images and critical theory, not as a set of linear and internally consistent, static ideas involving visual culture through which we can move book by book, chapter by chapter, line by line, but as part of an ongoing and necessarily incomplete process that is always historically, visually, and technologically contingent. In this sense, Virilio's own writings, his entire corpus, constitute a singular and single body of work and thought, ever evolving and varying but always concerned with these same issues and struggles.

Virilio's thinking on the production and dissemination of technological images forms part of a response to imaginary and real cultural and political developments concerning how such images work and what they do at precise moments in contemporary technological history (e.g. Virilio's [1989] focus on World War I, cinema and the 'logistics of perception' in the early 1980s). As Virilio might put it, he is not merely interested in the ideas that technological images represent or the reality they purport to depict. He is interested in why technological images were like they were in World War I, or why questions about technological mediations and extensions of visual experience are like they are in the twenty-first century. Additionally, he is concerned with how that 'why' of a specific intersection of time, space, speed, and technology manifests in images that influence and affect almost every dimension of human experience (Virilio 2012: 38–9). For Virilio, visual culture is a process over which we must struggle to theorise and practise, rather than a static object such as traditional art history we can simply describe or provide a grand, overarching theory of; visual culture, from this perspective, functions more as a verb than a noun, more of a landscape of events than a field.

In this context, the position of the intellectual in visual cultural studies is, as Virilio puts it, revelationary. Talking about the question of apocalypse in 2007, Virilio pointed not to 'the end of the world', which he doesn't 'give a damn about' but to the 'finitude of the world' (especially for each cognisant individual) and to the revelationary role of the visual cultural critic in the face of 'the idea of revolution'. What, then, has Virilio's visual cultural studies to offer somebody who wants to know if they should take up his profound beliefs about the apocalypse and especially if that means 'the end of the world is a concept without a future' (Virilio 2009b: 43)? The joke embedded in Virilio's pithy formulation is indicative of his multidimensional engagements with the visual, for he is always deadly serious while at the same time, rather like Jean Baudrillard (see, for example, Bishop and Phillips 2009), aware of humour's efficacy to illuminate complex ideas and entrenched thinking. Virilio makes his point here by saying that the end of the world is something of a cliché and thus has no intellectual future while also underscoring the futility of millennial or apocalyptic thinking: for the end of the world would indeed be the end of a future (and thus an idea *without a future*).

Nonetheless, Virilio emphasises that the apocalypse does elicit intellectually and politically significant visual and cultural questions but mostly in relation to how it constrains and delimits strategies for thinking otherwise. The apocalypse, he argues, is also a question not so much of the end of the world or of a concept without a future but also a contestation of whose revelation gets represented and whose revelation does not. As with Baudrillard, a comparison Virilio himself makes in this regard, his interest in the end is that, as mortals, all we can ever experience is the end of things. This, therefore, is a site at which the advance of his religious faith, of his own studies, is becoming a revelationary perspective, but it is not one solely bounded by his religious faith. It is a site at which he not only seeks to understand today and tomorrow, but also, by way of revelation, to surpass our traditional understanding of the idea of 'revolution', cosmogony and astronomy. Unless we operate in this tension between cosmogony, astronomy and the ideological idea of revolution (used in a punning fashion that collapses politics and astronomy), we won't know what visual cultural studies can do *as* visual and critical studies, cannot do or can never do; but also what visual and cultural studies *has* to do, what alone it has a privileged capacity to do (Virilio 2009b: 43). The apocalypse, he proposes, is not solely about the reality of attempting to understand today and tomorrow, of going beyond our perhaps outmoded understanding of the idea of revolution; it is also about the visual and cultural politics of representation, of 'ways of seeing' (Berger 1972), the failure of the idea of the ideological revolution (e.g. the catastrophe of those who have been looking for, or are waiting for, *the* revolution, those who, as Virilio [2009b: 43] puts it, 'have chosen the wrong planet') and the awaiting of an ultimate transcendental revelation (through working with this specific vision, this specific narrative, of revelation).

What our example of the apocalypse points to is Virilio's (2009b: 43) sense of both the limitations and the relevance of intellectual work on visions of finitude and his commitment not just to visual cultural studies as opening up to us a 'new type of thought' but also as a significant and serious field concerned with post-phenomenological theorisations of the gaze and 'iconology' (Mitchell 1987), art history, critical theory and, as we have seen in the case of Virilio himself, religion inspired studies (see, also, for example, Morgan 2001). That said, Virilio returns consistently to visual culture as a site of contestation manifesting the larger concerns of urbanisation, technology, militarisation and speed as inextricably intertwined phenomena. Visual culture, for Virilio, then is as political and as quotidian, as concerned with the micro-cosm as the macrocosm.

Exploded View: Virilio and Visual Culture

> So here we have an important revolution. Video images, info-graphic images, they are all *images that speak*. It's similar to what I said about the vision machine – giving sight to a machine without a gaze, sight without seeing, and giving speech to an image without humans: we are here faced with developments that can only disturb art's voices of silence for good. (Paul Virilio in Virilio and Lotringer 2005: 36)

Anybody writing a book about post World War II French intel-lectual life, and who started by looking for some representative academic figure to connect its numerous tendencies and stages regarding the study of images, would find him- or herself early on turning to Paul Virilio. In the 1950s Virilio played a pivotal role within research on the image of the 'Atlantic Wall', a system of permanent field and other fortifications built by the Germans from 1940 to 1944 after the defeat of France. This system is more than 4,000 km long, stretching along the European coast of the Atlantic Ocean from Denmark to the Spanish frontier. Virilio's research on the Atlantic Wall was the start of a long journey that has had him scanning the visual culture of the western French coasts for the rest of his life (e.g. even today, in retirement, Virilio lives in La Rochelle, a French city and port in western France, on the Bay of Biscay), research and imagery that, according to him, sought to reclaim what John Beck (2011) calls the 'concrete ambivalence' of the military bunker and to offer an alternative cultural and highly politicised image of the destruction and oppression wrought by the Nazi defence systems of World War II (Virilio 1994a).

In the 1960s Virilio founded with the architect Claude Parent

Figure 1.1 Church of Sainte-Bernadette-du-Banlay, Nevers, France
(2006). Architects: Claude Parent and Paul Virilio, 1966. Photograph
by John Armitage.

the Architecture Principe group, the review bearing the same
name, and the theory of 'the function of the oblique', which
issued in the construction of two major works: the Church of
Sainte-Bernadette-du-Banlay in Nevers in 1966 (Figure 1.1) and
the Thomson-Houston centre of aerospace research in Vélizy-
Villacoublay in 1969 (Virilio and Parent 1996a, 1996b). The function of the oblique, according to Virilio, is to resist the horizontal
and vertical assumptions operative in architectural practice in the
middle and later parts of the twentieth century. This entails their
resistance as well to the general tendency toward architectural
facilitation of ease and efficiency. Instead, Virilio and Parent wish
to ground architectural practice in the body, forcing consideration
of the corporeal in opposition to the more generalised erasure of
it by larger trajectories of social, economic and labour practices:
architecture as *memento mori* in the name of geopolitics and geometrical politics.

By the 1970s, Virilio emerged not only as professor, workshop
director and director of studies at the École Spéciale d'Architecture

in Montparnasse, Paris, but also as one of the leading exponents of various new academic fields involving architecture and philosophy, war, archaeology, museology, art, military strategy, technology, geopolitics, speed, transportation and ecology, all of which led to a sustained engagement with imagery and the theorisation of visual cultural studies (Virilio 1976, 1990, 2006).

In the 1980s he emerged as one of the most prolific and radical intellectuals in debates over the complex socio-cultural effects of cinematics, over the place of Continental philosophy within the humanities and 'critical space', conflict, the perception of figural artefacts, the accelerated cultural development of the advanced societies, vision technologies, ideas of progress, automation and those post-industrial production systems now routinely associated with the increased and rapid expansion of the stimulation of visual experiences, such as surveillance cameras in public spaces, machinic vision and imagery, ubiquitous circulation of visual data and other related issues (Virilio 1989, 1991, 1994b, 2005a, 2009a). Throughout his various writings across a myriad of topoi, he consistently operates with an assumption about contemporary European and American culture as resultant from and in a civilisation of the optical, that it is optics that are at stake in many contemporary cultures. Similarly, civilisation, for Virilio, operates as a synonym for militarisation. The struggle for optics – for the visual/audio-visual field – constitutes a struggle of world formation, knowledge production and power at every level of existence.

Meanwhile, since the 1990s and the 2000s, Virilio's influential writings on the Gulf War and technology, 'polar inertia', the Kosovo War, the 'landscape of events', the 'information bomb', al-Qaeda's attack on the World Trade Center in New York City and the Pentagon Building in Washington DC on 11 September 2001, fine art, fear, accidents, the city, terror, 'grey ecology', the university, the 'instant', the 'accident', the screen as 'third window', and pervasive visual and cultural acceleration, combined with the ever growing confirmatory evaluation of his studies within the academy have earned him global recognition as a preeminent figure in visual cultural and image studies today (Virilio 1995, 1997, 2000a, 2000b, 2000c, 2000d, 2002a, 2002b, 2003a, 2003b, 2005b, 2007a, 2007b, 2009b, 2010a, 2010b, 2012; Virilio and Lotringer 2005, 2008; Bishop 2004). In a word, few others enjoy the same prestige (especially across such a wide range of issues and conceptual formulations in so many different kinds of media) as Virilio within the realm of visuality and visual cultural studies.

Nonetheless, Virilio himself would cast doubt on any characterisation of his intellectual career that ascribed to it any kind of initiatory centrality within accounts of visual cultural or image studies and the ongoing militarisation of contemporary culture and visual images (Armitage 2003; Bishop and Phillips 2010). Given his take on the field as emergent, inchoate and contingent, as well as inseparable from a number of material and immaterial phenomena not usually associated with visual studies, his eschewal of centrality seems perfectly logical. Virilio is a part of visual culture but apart from its mainstream manifestation. Thus, he lays no claim to an origin – much less the authority of any asserted origin – within visual cultural studies. After all, didn't early work on visual cultural studies emerge somewhere at that moment between when John Berger (1972) published his seminal *Ways of Seeing*, which – partially as a response to Kenneth Clark's BBC television series *Civilization*, which represented a more traditionalist view of the Western artistic and cultural canon – criticises traditional Western cultural aesthetics by raising questions about hidden ideologies in visual images, and Laura Mulvey's (1975) decisive essay 'Visual Pleasure and Narrative Cinema', first published in the influential British film theory journal *Screen*? (See, inter alia, Mirzoeff 1999, 2002; Dikovitskaya 2005; Morra and Smith 2006; Grau 2011.) In that instant contemporary visual cultural studies was born; and it emerged principally from Jacques Lacan's (1978, 1991) theorisation of the unconscious gaze (Sturken and Cartwright 2007). Yet, while Virilio often wants to talk about the history of visual cultural studies, he definitely does not want to talk about it in the same way as, for example, Lacan or Slavoj Žižek (2010) since he 'does not have a psychoanalytic background or training' or 'have very much to say in this respect' (Virilio and Armitage 2001a: 178).

These remarks present researchers into, readers and indeed editors of Virilio's writings on visual culture with a specific difficulty: that is, how – and certainly whether – to construct an intellectual description of Virilio's writings on seeing, how to write clearly about his often complex writing on, for instance, photography, how to foreground his significance for visual culture without reproducing him as an expert on everything from the visual culture of orbiting satellites during the Kosovo War to one of the inventors of the study of new media in art (Rush 2005)?

Strangely perhaps, given our and Virilio's remarks above on imaging and so on, possibly the best way of producing an academic explanation of his writings on photography, digital manipulations, computerisation, etc. is to start with a reflection on his use of first-hand experience. Direct – as opposed to virtual – experience would appear wholly appropriate here because it is the first-person narrative wherein he repeatedly and somewhat unfashionably reflects on and indeed privileges the authority and centrality of his own, defiantly urban, subjectivity (e.g. he often refers to himself as an 'urbanist'; see, for instance, Armitage 2001; Virilio and Brausch 2011). Far from simple skyline gazing, however, Virilio has suggested that deliberating and speaking about, say, the visual culture of the city in terms of his actual experience allows him to be authoritative concerning, for example, the title of his most recent book-length interview on the war-torn city and other related topics, *The Administration of Fear*, which is 'a direct echo of the title of Graham Greene's well-known book, *The Ministry of Fear*' (Virilio and Richard 2012: 13; Greene 2001 [1943]). As Virilio puts it in response to a question posed by his interviewer on the conflict-ravaged city, Bertrand Richard:

As you know, the novelist portrays London under the devastation of the German *blitz* in the Second World War. Greene's protagonist fights members of the Fifth Column, Nazis disguised as ordinary Londoners fighting a merciless war against the British *from the inside*. I lived through *the ministry of fear* as a child in Nantes after witnessing the Debacle; the Fifth Column, which had been formed during the Spanish Civil War, was omnipresent in everyone's thoughts and conversations. (Virilio and Richard 2012: 13–14)

From World War II to today, Virilio constantly uses his own actual and pivotal childhood experiences of fear in the battle-destroyed city as a strategy for theorising images, urbanism and even luminosity, not to explore his own or our increasingly virtual lives and alter-identities as de-centred conceptions, but in order to present what he calls (and in absolute earnestness) his real, 'first-hand experience of the *Blitzkrieg*, the lightning war':

Nantes, 1940: one morning, we were informed that the Germans were in Orléans; at noon, we heard the sound of German trucks rolling through the streets. We had never seen anything like it. We had been living with memories of the First World War, a conflict that stretched out endlessly in time and between the positions occupied by the combatants – a war of attrition. Thirty years later, it only took a few hours for our city to be *occupied*. (Virilio and Richard 2012: 14)

In general though, Virilio's immediate experience of the speed of modern warfare offers a means of 'blitzing' what he might call the 'lightning wars' of a visual cultural studies currently and perhaps mistakenly centred on virtual reality that should, arguably, be focused on the infinitely more important topic of the accelerated occupation by the military–industrial–scientific complex of the mass media, of television and of the visual domain generally (Armitage 2012: 95–116). Important to this formulation, it must be noted, is the historical *Blitzkrieg* as well as speed and illumination, the rapidly changed cityscape brought about by swift military intervention and military technology violently imposed into urban space and lit briefly for an instant like the flash of a camera. The speed-determined context of the appearance of an image also constitutes its disappearance, and as such, speed becomes that which establishes not only our relationship to time and space but also our relationship to the visible and the invisible. The image, too, is but another projectile.

Born in Paris in 1932, Virilio grew up in what he describes as a Breton (mother) – Italian (father) family that was trying to come to terms both with the German occupation of France that was simultaneously physical (material) and mental (immaterial) and with an environment dominated by terror (Virilio and Richard 2012: 14). He has portrayed his childhood within this atmosphere of dread as one of German occupation and French preoccupation. His family felt estranged from and afraid of their immediate locality because of the seemingly unidentifiable 'everyday' 'events' of war and the shrinking timeframes within and between human lives, fighting, famines and epidemics and their own former relatively peaceful world. An increasingly politicised student of the unlimited, saturated and ever-expanding nature of the visual aspects of World War II, Virilio was, then, as now, unsympathetic towards the restrictions, stresses and claustrophobia of visual existence during wartime. Franco-German cultural relations grew more and more tense when his family and their compatriots suffered under German observation and terrorism after the lightning war, a terrorism that not only accelerated an already frightful world, which was characterised by what he (2005c: 27–30) has called elsewhere 'cold panic' but also created specific policies for the orchestration and management of a new visuality of culture based on fear. These policies resulted in a prevalence of visual propaganda, such as the Nazi-published magazine *Signal* aimed at the French population and pro-Vichy regime posters with their startling design and graphic statements (Virilio and Richard 2012: 38).

Keen to get away from the visual and other wartime experiences of Nantes, the city he and his family had been evacuated to from Paris for the duration of World War II, Virilio returned to the French capital and became a craftsman in stained glass in the early post-war years and, up until his retirement in 1997, when he moved to La Rochelle, he was based in Paris for almost 50 years. The frequency with which he has returned to document his early childhood cultural experiences in France during World War II, particularly in his many published contemporary interviews, indicates their important formative impact on his subsequent observations and thinking, most notably perhaps in terms of his intellectual preoccupation with the visual culture of the state and nationality, security, ideology and democracy in wartime as legitimate fields of study (see, for example, Virilio and Petit 1999; Armitage 2001). He often refers to himself as 'a war baby' and the effects of the rise of fascism brought into his urban setting by tank, gun and mortar remain formative in all of his theorisation.

Consequently, visual cultural studies, classically defined by Nicholas Mirzoeff (2002: 3) as being 'concerned with visual events in which information, meaning or pleasure is sought by the consumer in an interface with visual technology', takes on a wholly different character when seen from the standpoint of Virilio's formative years during the German *Blitzkrieg*. If Virilio has been integral to the founding of a particular field of visual culture in France and elsewhere – a field which includes his 'true theoretical brother in arms' (Winthrop-Young 399–412), the late German literary and media historian Friedrich A. Kittler (see, for instance, Kittler 2009), who focuses on the materiality of visual and media technologies – then that is in part owing to the insights offered by his militarised, technological relationship to prevailing ideas involving the German occupation of France by way of visual and other media-related apparatuses. Machines such as Germany's Panzer command tanks which, unlike the Allied command tanks, contained radio equipment for use by Panzer unit commanders

(McCarthy and Syron 2003), making them mobile multimedia platforms deployed for destruction, power and control. Virilio's background as a dumbfounded evacuee from Paris placed him at a mesmerised militarised angle to the phenomenon of the German occupation of France (see, for example, Virilio and Brausch 2011: 6–10; Virilio and Richard 2012: 15). Certainly, he has recently said of his refusal to stop reflecting on speed that his is a sighting of the world from the perspective of the accelerated German occupation of France during World War II, a sighting replicated today in the fear produced by the technological 'progress' of digital television and the Internet. It is with this kind of watchful and wary eye that he views the 'dromosphere', the technological realm of speed, which has become the standard-bearer of innovation and technological advance:

> I am convinced that just as speed led to the Germans' incredible domination of over continental Europe in 1940, fear and its administration are now supported by the incredible spread of real time technology, especially the new ICT or new information and communications technologies. (Virilio and Richard 2012: 16)

It is this viewpoint on the speeding technological 'progress' of the dromosphere that, in an earlier period of his career, allowed him to challenge some of the most taken for granted aspects of contemporary techno-cultural life in the advanced societies, while opening it up to the submerged question of 'the propaganda of progress' (Virilio and Armitage 2009). Viewed within this context, his importance as a thinker of image making, aesthetics and the vital completion of visual works by their cultural reception has a lot to do with his status as a critical media philosopher and historical theorist but equally with the way he draws into question new visual technological creations and developments like the iPhone and Facebook together with ideas associated both with the genealogies and trajectories of techno-scientific cultural domination, as well as placing them within the larger IT and techno-science landscape (see, for instance, McQuire 2011). One of the characteristics of Virilio's current work is its refusal of the *propaganda* of progress (while simultaneously not eschewing the ideal of progress itself as an Enlightenment goal) that reproduces and circulates in France and other countries all of the often fluid traits of occupation: physically, visually, culturally and mentally

(Virilio and Richard 2012: 38; Virilio and Goldmann 2012). The propaganda of progress regularly emerges as uncritical techno-science cheerleading, a juggernaut of entrenched public discursive positions that he wishes to slow significantly. He is not a Luddite, which he has sometimes been charged with, he is 'awake' before technology, conscious of it, engaged with it and battling it.

After settling back in Paris to do advanced work on stained glass, painting, stage set design and movie posters, Virilio finally deserted his initial vocation in the materiality of the fine, performing and plastic arts in the late 1950s, feeling that he could not attend in purely aesthetic or material terms to the political and urban, military, organisational and territorial questions that were beginning to preoccupy him (see, for instance, Virilio, Joubert and Carlut 2001; Virilio and Brausch 2011: 68–9). Importantly, this was also the era in which Virilio became involved in the Atlantic Wall work, pioneering research that, among other things, argued for a more visual conception of the cultural politics of the littoral and a more 'oblique' conception of the cultural politics of the theory and practice of architecture. An important element of this early work on bunker architecture is his encounter with it as ruins. Photographing these structures of defence against the mightiest militaries of the mid-twentieth century in toppled disrepair helped Virilio towards his first theorisations of the accident and its import in historical thought and collective amnesia as an integral dimension to the propaganda of progress.

Throughout his time as co-founder of the Architecture Principe group and as co-editor of its review of the same name, Virilio sustained himself economically by, first, becoming an indispensable addition to Claude Parent's architectural practice as a 'discussion partner' and by, second, bringing both the Church of Sainte-Bernadette and the Thomson-Houston Aerospace projects to Parent's practice (Parent, Scalbert and Mostafavi 1996: 51). This indicated the start of a combined architectural and teaching career that would reach over some 30 years, a career looked upon by many as a fundamental feature of Virilio's contribution to the field of the contemporary cultural politics of architecture, the built environment and visual culture generally (see, for example, Leach 2000; Sharr 2011).

Between 1969 and 1997 Virilio worked in architectural education at the École Spéciale d'Architecture. All the same, he remained a famous intellectual all through these years and editor, with Jean-

Marie Domenach and Paul Thibaud, of the review *Esprit*, a French literary magazine founded on the principles of 'personalism', a philosophical school of thought centred on the uniqueness of the human person in the world of nature, specifically in relation to animals (James 2007: 90; Mbacke Gueye 2011). 'Personalism', though, does not place the human at the centre of the world or universe, a gesture that Virilio calls truly apocalyptic. Distinct from many other critical thinkers whose writings on images circulate almost exclusively among an academic select few, Virilio's writings on architecture, the unceasing flow of representations and the swirl of Marshall McLuhan's (1962, 2001) 'global village' have appealed to a much wider postmodern audience, and his ideas have been disseminated on video, television, radio and the Internet, as well as in the print media not only of today's university presses from Minnesota to Princeton to Semiotext(e) but also in, among many others, *Cause Commune* and *Traverses*, *Libération*, *L'Autre Journal*, *Critique* and *Les Temps Modernes*. As Virilio himself has observed, he has always wanted his authorial self as it were to be active rather than contemplative, to extend his thoughts on images, progress, paintings and so on, far beyond those texts he himself has written; he is as much a painter as a teacher, and an activist as much as a writer or an observer of cultural events (Virilio and Brausch 2011: 66–7).

Despite a lifetime teaching at the École Spéciale d'Architecture, it is notable that Virilio has time after time also worked outside traditional university institutions. Prior to moving to the École Spéciale d'Architecture, he was a city planner and essayist in Paris, researching the representation and the dominant expressionist style of military space: a unique position in France or anywhere else in the 1960s. He then moved to Architecture Principe, where he was collaborator and critic-in-chief with Claude Parent between 1963 and 1968, when Virilio and Parent disbanded Architecture Principe after disagreeing over the merits of the May 1968 student protests. These protests incorporated the first wildcat general student strike ever, thus bringing the French economy to a virtual standstill. Virilio not only supported the student protests but also actively participated in them, while Parent described the political actions as 'idiotic' (see Parent, Scalbert and Mostafavi 1996: 57). Though Virilio does not see himself as a revolutionary philosopher, he does see himself as a revolutionary citizen, bound to protest civil injustice at all turns. That said, it is very difficult to separate out the thinker engaged in visual studies from an oblique, culturally/intellectually critical perspective from the private activist Virilio has been for decades.

One of the most distinctive aspects of Virilio's innovative work at Architecture Principe and beyond was not the production of its modern architectural review, the modernist theory of the oblique function or even the construction of a church and a research centre but the production of research on the architecture of everything from apartment buildings to shopping malls in various intellectual groups: a sustained engagement and dialogue in a collective and collaborative manner with the civic and private architecture that was radically altering the post-war cityscape of Paris and the rest of France (itself metonymic of internationalist styles and assumptions). For example, Virilio led the L'Espace critique group, which featured, among other colleagues, his close friend Georges Perec, the modern novelist and author of the influential *Species of Space* (1997). Here, then, ideas concerning structural design and projects involving bunkers and anthropology, exhibitions, museums and the visual arts were not founded or owned by individual intellectuals, but developed cooperatively, as in the case of Virilio's foundation with Alain Joxe of the Interdisciplinary Center for Research on Peace and Strategic Studies at the Hautes Etudes en Sciences Sociales in Paris in 1979 (see, for instance, Joxe 2002). The collective social agenda carried the critique of the May 1968 barricades beyond that particularly painful moment of thwarted radical change into other, less threatening but no less important sites of resistance as articulated in the built environment.

In the 1970s and 1980s, Virilio published numerous articles and books contending with the contemporary effects of technology on the organisation of space, a cultural theme that has remained consistent in his writings until the present day. *Bunker Archeology, L'Insecurité du territoire, Speed & Politics: An Essay on Dromology* and *Popular Defense & Ecological Struggles*, for example, are all unconventional essays on conflict and buildings, political beliefs, the armed forces, transportation, technological communication, the occurrence of political resistance, and their appearance and/or disappearance in the collective visual field. Established in the 1970s, his writings on modern vision thus largely discarded the customary secluded limitations of the university press text, heading instead by way of the aesthetic and socio-cultural effects of cinema and broadcast media to a dispersed community of editors, visual and architectural reviews, cultural newspapers, modern monthlies, and their philosophically inclined readers in the visual arts and humanities across France and beyond. His cultural texts remain open in the sense that they do not discriminate between applied visual research into the crisis in the notion of physical dimensions undertaken on request of the Minister of Equipment and Housing and highly theoretical historical research into the use of cinematographic and other visual techniques used during the two world wars (Virilio 1989, 1991). Both elements of the spectrum remain not only equally important but, more crucially, unavoidably interrelated. His is not a strategy of social change or hierarchy-breaking in and of itself; rather it is an intellectual strategy that of necessity entails social change and challenges to institutional power and entrenched discursive formulations.

At this point we might note that Virilio's technological and visual horizons are less negative than without end when it comes to studying the links between speed and the cultural and political development of modern and postmodern societies, between critical boundaries and the discovery of new existential and organisational territories and, above all, between the technologisation of the visual and the huge number of machines that are currently and systematically discouraging the use of human-centred visual culture through the propaganda of progress. Talking of the incentives behind his somewhat Heideggerean shift to 'the question concerning technology', Virilio has drawn attention to the appeal of a more open, interdisciplinary, alternative way of conversing with people, in both academic and in non-academic ways, about the technologies of film and broadcast media as 'both the best and the worst' of what techno-scientific image making has to offer, a proposition which he has not only 'always believed' but which also serves some of his artistic and historical, social, cultural and political aspirations regarding the visual culture of totalitarianism, citizenship and architecture (Heidegger 1978; Virilio and Brausch 2011: 30–1). In diverse ways Architecture Principe and the question concerning technology have allowed Virilio to break with the more technophilic, post-industrial aspects of the production of the present in order to connect with wider interdisciplinary cultural fields, political studies and perceptual formations beyond, for instance, the world of *The Vision Machine* (Virilio 1994b).

Time, Space, Acceleration, Visuality

What I'm trying to show is the really powerful character of the images that are produced everywhere around us and that no one is analysing. Because images have become munitions. Their delivery and impact have the same speeds as the impact of a bullet. The arms of the future will much more resemble a TV than a mortar. (Paul Virilio in Armitage 2001: 119)

Virilio's research at Architecture Principe and on issues regarding vision technologies in particular has of course developed out of numerous collaborative projects on the visual with others, such as his programme directorship of the International College of Philosophy, founded in 1983 by Jacques Derrida, François Châtelet, Jean-Pierre Faye and Dominique Lecourt in an effort to re-imagine the teaching of philosophy, inclusive of the philosophy of the visual arts, in France. However, within his writing and interviews on post-industrial cultures and their visual regimes, Virilio characteristically, and rather behind the times some might say, assumes the modern first-person singular 'I' instead of the more postmodern collective first-person 'we' or possessive 'our' of contemporary academic research on imagery. For example, the opening sentence of his *Polar Inertia* (2000a: 1), his collection of essays on the development of remote control, digital and cinematic technologies and the human environment, reads: 'I still remember my astonishment, ten years ago, when I saw video screens replacing mirrors on Paris Metro platforms.' In this sense, the displaced and shocked child that witnessed the Nazi invasion of Nantes remains solidly the phenomenological subject of apperception and engagement at the centre of Virilio's work, even as that subject is increasingly fitted out with a battery of teletechnological prostheses.

While the following twelve chapters are structured around Virilio's important ideas concerning the visual culture of photography, imaging, the Internet and the like, and while it is important to remember their occasionally collective contexts of production, equally, to forget their individual, personalist, not to say idiosyncratic contexts of production would also be forgetful of the very hyper-individualist spirit in which much of his research on global visual culture was and is produced and practised (see, for instance, Caren Kaplan's interpretation in Chapter 5 of *Desert Screen: War at the Speed of Light* [Virilio 2002a], the latter of which is a collection of Virilio's singularly subjective and idiosyncratic reports on the transformations wrought by postmodern visuality during the 1991 Gulf War for *Libération, L'Expresso, Die Tageszeitung*, etc.). Many of Virilio's historical ideas and contemporary publications discussed below emerge out of, and were made possible by, group work with others on advisory boards for modern art exhibitions and book series centred on visual culture. But by far the greater part of his thoughts on visual culture surface from, and were and are set in motion by, his individual writings on postmodern visual experience without others. *The Art of the Motor* (1995) and *Open Sky* (1997), for example, were both not only written individually but also alongside *Strategy of Deception* (2000b), *A Landscape of Events* (2000c), *The Information Bomb* (2000d) and *Ground Zero* (2002b) in an extraordinarily inventive period during the 1990s and 2000s. In what follows we and our contributors will be as concerned with the hypermodern work of Virilio the hyper-individualist as with the collaborative author and interviewee Virilio, a fact that might underline the danger of regarding him as one of the authoritative originators of visual cultural studies but not as the authoritative originator of visual cultural studies as the art of fear (Armitage 2000; Virilio 2003a).

Virilio's refusal to eschew the leading role of the agent provocateur appears almost deliberately engraved in the very form of his art exhibition activities and publications on visual culture, such as the *Unknown Quantity* (2003b) exhibition at the *Fondation Cartier pour l'art contemporain* in 2002–3 and *City of Panic* (2005b), which favour the postmodern blockbuster art exhibition *and* the durability of the book, even if the latter book is composed of highly speculative cultural essays previously published elsewhere; the independence and status of single-authored texts like *The Original Accident* (2007a) appear alongside of and in dialogue with the comparative anonymity of group work. Just as the distribution of his work across a range of media and types of intellectual productions indicates a desire to conflate academic and public discourses, Virilio as solo author and collaborator collapses divisions one might think solidly entrenched by his personalist and individualist theoretical positioning. However, manifesting the most basic structuralist articulation of subjectivity, Virilio positions the self as knowable only in opposition to the others that it is not.

It is perhaps no accident that, so far, Virilio has neither opposed the production of two comprehensive readers, of anthologies of his writings, nor resisted opportunities to participate in seemingly hundreds of interviews (Der Derian 1998; Armitage 2001; Redhead 2004). In other words, while it may well be Virilio's 'opinion' that 'those who seek celebrity today' must understand that they have to remain 'unknown' or 'anonymous' to become a celebrity, such as his favourite examples of Henri Michaux (1997) and Thomas Pynchon (1997), the fact of the matter is that we readers are faced with an almost viral proliferation of photographs of and interviews with Virilio (Virilio and Goldmann 2012: 63). In sum, it is difficult not to conclude that Virilio is the world's worst recluse alive today. Yet such interviews, particularly the book-length interviews like *Grey Ecology* (2009b), do not inflict upon his thinking a false unity in works such as *Art as Far as the Eye Can See* (2007b) as help to clarify their complex contemporary visual and cultural contents, myriad articulations and multiple strands of influence and connection.

Even so, increasingly, Virilio's preference is for *all* forms of intellectual production on visual representations, inclusive of the book, the interview, the essay, the journal article and even the DVD (Virilio and Paoli 2008), which, arguably, are strategic features of his theorising of visual culture in such texts as *The University of Disaster* (2010a) and *The Futurism of the Instant: Stop–Eject* (2010b). This strategy allows him to constantly revise, update, retract and elaborate upon his theoretical ideas and to intervene in current issues relating to visuality and media events in the daily press, philosophical periodicals, critical academic journals concerned about developments in techno-science, and art exhibition catalogues before turning his newspaper articles and so forth into book-length theoretical studies of the visual, which take much longer to produce and publish (see, for instance, Virilio and Depardon 2009). Read collectively – indeed almost as if updates of a single body of work, rather as a website archives and updates itself (an analogy he would likely abjure) – Virilio's dispersed books, essays, interviews, DVDs and art exhibitions do not add up to a complete or finished 'Virilian' position on spectatorship or looking, the gaze or human observation, surveillance or visual pleasure but are full of contradictions, discrepancies and U-turns (Armitage 2012: 8–9, 117–21). This is not a flaw, but rather an essential part of the process of engaging with the unsettled and ever-changing conditions of contemporary visual experience, visual literacy and visual culture. If he is to remain 'awake' in the face of this site of contestation, then he will also need to be fleet and responsive as well as contemplative and considered, thus ensuring an engagement with the field of perception until he can no longer do so.

For readers stumbling upon Virilio's writings on visual culture for the first time, however, such vitality, and indeed inevitable contradiction and repetition, can bring its own set of difficulties along with its benefits, rather like being dropped *in medias res* into an intellectual and critical picaresque of monological rants, warnings and ululations. The diffusion of Virilio's thoughts on visual media across an extensive assortment of languages and media presentations, many of which can be hard to obtain, in conjunction with his continuous reconsideration of important positions on his 'philosophy of vision', light and 'the forms presented to searching eyes' throws up specific challenges to readers eager to keep up with Virilio's prolific writings on visual culture (Virilio 2012: 38). One of the most important purposes of *Virilio and Visual Culture* is to assemble a text that focuses on his major ideas concerning contemporary vision technologies in particular through the numerous phases of his intellectual career. Its goal is not to map out the growth of his modern and postmodern views and discourses but to aid readers in placing his specific modern and contemporary writings within the wider intellectual, visual, cultural and historical contexts in which they were and are being produced while also staking out intellectual and theoretical positions in conversation with his own.

In the chapters that follow, Virilio will be seen arguing that in postmodern visual culture there is no authentic 'zero time' uncontaminated by the 'illusions' of contemporary culture (see Chapter 2): and our other contributors will be observed contending that there is no time free of ecological considerations (see Garnett, Chapter 3); no visual abstraction without contemporary aeriality and aspect perception (see Beck, Chapter 4); no desert wars untouched by the limits of genuine knowledge (see Kaplan, Chapter 5); no phenomenon untainted by its capacity for appropriation as a weapon, not even light (see Phillips, Chapter 6); no postmodern human body empty of the history and art of Auschwitz (see Roy, Chapter 7); no aesthetic perception devoid of the illusions of time, seeing, politics and movement (see Bishop, Chapter 8); no event unaffected by the events of others (see Crandall, Chapter 9); no face uncorrupted by the figureless aesthetics of 'sacred humanism' and 'the accident of art' (Virilio and Lotringer 2005; see Armitage, Chapter 10); no image without information and no information without image, and no cosmographic mapping without secretion (see Bratton, Chapter 11); no acceleration without its relics (see Dunlop, Chapter 12); and no postmodern present unaffected by the productions, debates and endless redefinitions of the subject and concepts of visual culture (see James, Chapter 13). Each chapter thus defines and explores the moves in Virilio's thoughts on such important issues and the theories surrounding them as time or perception to indicate what are, in effect, his enduring projects rather than his completed positions on visual culture.

In this sense, *Virilio and Visual Culture* has two basic aims. On the one hand, it seeks to offer a comprehensible overview of Virilio's ideas about the history and development of the image and of technological representation over the past half century. On the other hand, it seeks to employ his ideas to provoke implicit questions about currently emergent orthodoxies, such as the effort to generate a sociology of visual culture or a social theory of visuality (Jenks 2007). For, as is well known, sociology is a discipline that Virilio loathes with a passion bordering on fanaticism (see, for example, Virilio and Armitage 2001b: 35). Here, then, the idea of visual cultural studies as a united, self-sufficient discipline or suite of official theories is subject to cultural and political critique. To contemplate the story of Virilio's own vocation concerning the appearance and experience of visual cultural studies is not to summon up the 'real meaning' of what the subject 'really is', or should be. Quite the reverse, it points to what is possibly lost in the disciplinary and institutional reduction of the discipline of visual culture to a series of perhaps humanities-based or sociological founders, to established cultural studies texts, or to important yet traditional ideas derived from art history.

This is a cultural and political issue that Virilio, we and our contributors return to over and again and in greater detail in the following chapters of this book, with the intention of disputing, deliberating and, in the end, transforming the ever more 'hyper-interactive' concept and interdisciplinary field of visual culture into a different, Virilian-inflected, terrain of enquiry and study which thrives on the singularity of fear and the uncertainty of civil dissuasion, the risks of the administration of fear and the simultaneously random yet increasingly submissive nature of our mediated everyday lives. 'In early 2010, in France', for example, Virilio recently informed Bernard Richard, 'the Milgram experiment of 1963 was repeated to reveal the frightening docility of individual television viewers towards the commands of the host in a documentary called *"The Game of Death"*' (Virilio and Richard 2012: 92–3). The increasingly mediated variation of this classic psychological experiment highlights, for Virilio, a shift of the locus of authority from institutional relations to mass media relations, with a repetition, intensification and diffusion of power and control mechanisms no less effective for their apparent objective and anonymous sources. As his (Virilio and Richard 2012: 92–3) contemporary appreciation of the visual culture of the television programme is still a theory for the future, rather than a well-defined existing branch of learning, *Virilio and Visual Culture* aspires to be of assistance in delineating, explicating and at times challenging Virilio's conception of the visual culture of militarised media and panicked images, rather than offering it as an accomplished theory or specific discipline where 'Graham Greene's *Ministry of Fear* has once again taken up active – and interactive – service' (Virilio and Richard 2012: 93).

References

Armitage, John (ed.) (2000), *Paul Virilio: From Modernism to Hypermodernism and Beyond*, London: Sage.

Armitage, John (ed.) (2001), *Virilio Live: Selected Interviews*, London: Sage.

Armitage, John (ed.) (2003), Special issue on 'Militarized Bodies', *Body & Society* 9(4).

Armitage, John (2012), *Virilio and the Media*, Cambridge: Polity.

Beck, John (2011), 'Concrete ambivalence: Inside the bunker complex', *Cultural Politics* 7(1): 79–102.

Berger, John (1972), *Ways of Seeing*, London: Penguin.

Bishop, Ryan (2004), '"The vertical order has come to an end": The insignia of military C3I and urbanism in global networks', in Ryan Bishop, John Phillips and Yeo Wei-Wei (eds), *Beyond Description: Space Historicity Singapore*, London and New York: Routledge, pp. 60–78.

Bishop, Ryan and Phillips, John (2009), 'Baudrillard and the evil genius', in Ryan Bishop (ed.), *Baudrillard Now: Current Perspectives in Baudrillard Studies*, Cambridge: Polity, pp. 28–46.

Bishop, Ryan and Phillips, John (2010), *Modernist Avant-garde Aesthetics and Contemporary Military Technology: Technicities of Perception*, Edinburgh: Edinburgh University Press.

Der Derian, James (ed.) (1998), *The Virilio Reader*, Oxford: Blackwell.

Dikovitskaya, Margaret (2005), *Visual Culture: The Study of the Visual after the Cultural Turn*, Cambridge, MA: The MIT Press.

Garnett, Joy and Armitage, John (2011), 'Virilio and visual culture: On the American apocalyptic sublime', in John Armitage (ed.), *Virilio Now: Current Perspectives in Virilio Studies*, Cambridge: Polity, pp. 200–33.

Grau, Oliver (2011), *Imagery in the 21st Century*, Cambridge, MA: The MIT Press.

Greene, Graham (2001 [1943]), *The Ministry of Fear*, London: Vintage.

Heidegger, Martin (1978), 'The question concerning technology', in David Farrell Krell (ed.), *Martin Heidegger: Basic Writings*, London: Routledge, pp. 307–42.

James, Ian (2007), *Paul Virilio*, London: Routledge.

Jenks, Chris (2007), *Visual Culture*, London: Routledge.

Joxe, Alain (2002), *Empire of Disorder*, New York: Semiotext(e).

Kittler, Friedrich (2009), *Optical Media: Berlin Lectures 1999*, trans. Anthony Enns, Cambridge: Polity.

Lacan, Jacques (1978), *Seminar Eleven: The Four Fundamental Concepts of Psychoanalysis*, New York: W. W. Norton and Co.

Lacan, Jacques (1991), *The Seminar of Jacques Lacan: Freud's Papers on Technique 1953–1954 Book I*, New York: W. W. Norton and Co.

Leach, Neil (2000), 'Virilio and architecture', in John Armitage (ed.), *Paul Virilio Live: From Modernism to Hypermodernism and Beyond*, London: Sage, pp. 71–84.

Mbacke Gueye, Cheikh (2011), *Ethical Personalism*, Berlin: Ontos Verlag.

McCarthy, Peter and Syron, Mike (2003), *Panzerkrieg: The Rise and Fall of Hitler's Tank Divisions: A History of the German Tank Division in World War II*, London: Robinson.

McLuhan, Marshall (1962), *The Gutenberg Galaxy: The Making of Typographic Man*, Toronto: University of Toronto Press.

McLuhan, Marshall (2001), *Understanding Media: The Extensions of Man*, London: Routledge.

McQuire, Scott (2011), 'Virilio's media as philosophy', in John Armitage (ed.), *Virilio Now: Current Perspectives in Virilio Studies*, Cambridge: Polity, pp. 92–114.

Michaux, Henri (1997), *Darkness Moves: An Henri Michaux Anthology, 1927–1984*, Los Angeles: University of California Press.

Mirzoeff, Nicholas (1999), *An Introduction to Visual Culture*, London: Routledge.

Mirzoeff, Nicholas (2002), 'What is Visual Culture?', in Nicholas Mirzoeff (ed.), *The Visual Culture Reader*, London: Routledge, pp. 3–13.

Mitchell, William T. (1987), *Iconology: Image, Text, Ideology*, Chicago: University of Chicago Press.

Morgan, David (2001), *The Visual Culture of American Religions*, Los Angeles: University of California Press.

Morra, Joanne and Smith, Marquard (eds) (2006), *Visual Culture: Critical Concepts in Media and Cultural Studies* (4 vols), London: Routledge.

Mulvey, Laura (1975), 'Visual pleasure and narrative cinema', *Screen* 16(3): 6–18.

Parent, Claude, Scalbert, Irénée and Mostafavi, Mohsen (1996), 'Interview with Claude Parent', in Pamela Johnson (ed.), *The Function of the Oblique*, London: Architectural Association, pp. 49–58.

Perec, Georges (1997), *Species of Space and Other Pieces*, trans. John Sturrock, London: Penguin.

Pynchon, Thomas (1997), *Gravity's Rainbow*, London: Vintage.

Redhead, Steve (ed.) (2004), *The Paul Virilio Reader*, Edinburgh: Edinburgh University Press.

Rush, Michael (2005), *New Media in Art*, London: Thames and Hudson.

Sharr, Adam (2011), 'Burning Bruder Klaus: Towards an architecture of slipstream', in John Armitage (ed.), *Virilio Now: Current Perspectives in Virilio Studies*, Cambridge: Polity, pp. 46–67.

Sturken, Marita and Cartwright, Lisa (2007), *Practices of Looking: An Introduction to Visual Culture*, Oxford: Oxford University Press.

Virilio, Paul (1976), *L'Insécurité du territoire*, Paris: Stock.

Virilio, Paul (1989), *War and Cinema: The Logistics of Perception*, trans. Patrick Camiller, London: Verso.

Virilio, Paul (1990), *Popular Defense and Ecological Struggles*, trans. Mark Polizzotti, New York: Semiotext(e).

Virilio, Paul (1991), *The Lost Dimension*, trans. Daniel Moshenberg, New York: Semiotext(e).

Virilio, Paul (1994a), *Bunker Archeology*, trans. George Collins, Princeton: Princeton Architectural Press.

Virilio, Paul (1994b), *The Vision Machine*, trans. Julie Rose, London: British Film Institute.

Virilio, Paul (1995), *The Art of the Motor*, trans. Julie Rose, Minneapolis: University of Minnesota Press.

Virilio, Paul (1997), *Open Sky*, trans. Julie Rose, London: Verso.

Virilio, Paul (2000a), *Polar Inertia*, trans. Patrick Camiller, London: Sage.

Virilio, Paul (2000b), *Strategy of Deception*, trans. Chris Turner, London: Verso.

Virilio, Paul (2000c), *A Landscape of Events*, trans. Julie Rose, Princeton: Princeton Architectural Press.

Virilio, Paul (2000d), *The Information Bomb*, trans. Chris Turner, London: Verso.

Virilio, Paul (2002a), *Desert Screen: War at the Speed of Light*, trans. Michael Degener, London: Continuum.

Virilio, Paul (2002b), *Ground Zero*, trans. Chris Turner, London: Verso.

Virilio, Paul (2003a), *Art and Fear*, trans. Julie Rose, London: Continuum.

Virilio, Paul (2003b), *Unknown Quantity*, trans. Chris Turner and Jian-Xing Too, London: Thames and Hudson.

Virilio, Paul (2005a), *Negative Horizon*, trans. Michel Degener, London: Continuum.

Virilio, Paul (2005b), *City of Panic*, trans. Julie Rose, Oxford: Berg.

Virilio, Paul (2005c), 'Cold panic', trans. Chris Turner, *Cultural Politics* 1(1): 27–30.

Virilio, Paul (2006), *Speed and Politics: An Essay on Dromology*, trans. Mark Polizzotti, New York: Semiotext(e).

Virilio, Paul (2007a), *The Original Accident*, trans. Julie Rose, Cambridge: Polity.

Virilio, Paul (2007b), *Art As Far As the Eye Can See*, trans. Julie Rose, Oxford: Berg.

Virilio, Paul (2009a), *The Aesthetics of Disappearance*, trans. Philip Beitchman, New York: Semiotext(e).

Virilio, Paul (2009b), *Grey Ecology*, trans. Drew Burk, New York: Atropos.

Virilio, Paul (2010a), *The University of Disaster*, trans. Julie Rose, Cambridge: Polity.

Virilio, Paul (2010b), *The Futurism of the Instant: Stop–Eject*, trans. Julie Rose, Cambridge: Polity.

Virilio, Paul (2012), *The Great Accelerator*, trans. Julie Rose, Cambridge: Polity.

Virilio, Paul and Armitage, John (2001a), 'The Kosovo W@r did take place', trans. Patrice Riemens, in John Armitage (ed.), *Virilio Live: Selected Interviews*, London: Sage, pp. 167–97.

Virilio, Paul and Armitage, John (2001b), 'From modernism to hyper-modernism and beyond: An interview with Paul Virilio', trans. Patrice Riemens, in John Armitage (ed.), *Virilio Live: Selected Interviews*, London: Sage, pp. 15–47.

Virilio, Paul and Armitage, John (2009), 'In the cities of the beyond: An interview with Paul Virilio', trans. Patrice Riemens, in Brigitte van der Sande (ed.), *OPEN 18: 2030: War Zone Amsterdam: Imagining the Unimaginable*, Amsterdam: NAi Publishers-SKOR, pp. 100–11.

Virilio, Paul and Brausch, Marianne (1993), 'Marginal groups', *Diadalos: Berlin Architectural Journal* 50 (December): 72–81.

Virilio, Paul and Brausch, Marianne (2011), *A Winter's Journey*, trans. Chris Turner, Calcutta: Seagull.

Virilio, Paul and Depardon, Raymond (2009), *Native Land: Stop Eject*, Paris: Fondation Cartier pour l'art contemporain.

Virilio, Paul and Goldmann, Sacha (2012), 'Celebration: A world of appearances', *Cultural Politics* 8(1): 61–72.

Virilio, Paul, Joubert, Dominique and Carlut, Christiane (2001), 'Paul Virilio', in John Armitage (ed.), *Virilio Live: Selected Interviews*, London: Sage, pp. 121–7.

Virilio, Paul and Lotringer, Sylvère (2005), *The Accident of Art*, trans. Michael Taormina, New York: Semiotext(e).

Virilio, Paul and Lotringer, Sylvère (2008), *Pure War*, trans. Philip Beitchman, Brian O'Keefe and Mark Polizzotti, New York: Semiotext(e).

Virilio, Paul and Paoli, Stéphane (2008), *Paul Virilio: Penser La Vitesse: Un Film de Stéphane Paoli*, DVD, Paris: Arte Editions.

Virilio, Paul and Parent, Claude (1996a), *Architecture Principe 1966 and 1996*, trans. George Collins, Besançon: Les Éditions de L'Imprimeur.

Virilio, Paul and Parent, Claude (1996b), *The Function of the Oblique*, trans. Pamela Johnson, London: Architectural Association.

Virilio, Paul and Petit, Philippe (1999), *Politics of the Very Worst*, trans. Michael Cavaliere, New York: Semiotext(e).

Virilio, Paul and Richard, Bertrand (2012), *The Administration of Fear*, trans. Ames Hodges, New York: Semiotext(e).

Winthrop-Young, Geoffrey, 'Hunting a whale of a state: Kittler and his terrorists', *Cultural Politics* 8(3): 399–412.

Žižek, Slavoj (2010), *Everything You Wanted To Know About Lacan But Were Afraid to Ask Hitchcock*, London: Verso.

2

The Illusions of Zero Time
Paul Virilio

'Painting cannot deceive us since it does not have about it the genuine hue of light', wrote Schlegel in his nineteenth-century work *Die Gemählde* (see Schlegel 1996: 33 [Trans.]). What are we to say today of the deception wrought by the live television image except that it possesses this 'genuine hue' thanks to the light-speed of wave optics – a genuine hue that is simply the 'real time' of TV transmissions, which lights up the reality of the scenes observed.

Where pictorial representation could not claim to match the effects of immediate lighting – since every past pictorial figure is inscribed in 'recorded time' – televisual presentation, thanks to the techniques of live coverage, possesses this light of immediacy, this sudden verisimilitude that painting, photography and even cinema lacked completely – whence the emergence of a last 'horizon of visibility', as soon as the optical depth of the human environment is reduced.

Currently, though the televised event certainly *takes place*, it nonetheless makes us aware of its ultimate limit, that of the absolute speed of light. Human beings are now no longer merely putting the relative speed of the animal or the machine to work; they are using the speed of the wave-packets of the electromagnetic domain, without even noticing that here they run up against an insuperable barrier, which is no longer the barrier of sound or heat, such as is encountered by supersonic or hypersonic vehicles, but the barrier of light, the last frontier of an energy intensity that forever limits human action and perception. In fact – and we forget this too often – if the event takes place here and now, it also takes place 'in the light' of a positive or negative acceleration. For example, the chance meeting of two passers-by who greet each other on the pavement is not of the same nature as the unexpected encounter in which two slow-moving motorists wave to each other as they pass on the road that runs alongside that pavement. Let us now imagine that we greatly speed up the two vehicles that are passing here and now: the meeting and greeting of the two parties simply would not take place, for want of sufficient apperception time; and the relative invisibility of the two motorists would not be due to a ghostly absence of bodies, but simply to an absence of the necessary time for their reciprocal apprehension.

The event of the meeting of the pedestrians on the pavement or the passing of the motorists driving down the avenue take place here and now, admittedly, but they also take place *en lumière* – in light – or, as the colloquial expression has it, *en vitesse* – at speed, at a speed relative to the rate of travel of the various moving bodies. Conversely, if the two interlocutors communicate thanks to interactive technologies – in 'real time' – it is the absolute speed of the waves that will facilitate their face-to-face encounter, and will do so whatever the intervals of time or space actually separating them.

In this case, the event does not take 'place'. Or, more exactly, it takes place twice: the unity of time and place is split between the transmission and reception of the signals – here and there at the same time – thanks to the wizardry of electromagnetic interactivity. The problem of the 'televisual horizon' of the fleeting encounter remains, however, unresolved. If the trans-appearance of the appearances of the co-present interlocutors is comparable to – if not indeed analogous with – the trans-appearance of the pedestrians or motorists mentioned above, the terminal of their reciprocal perception is different. The horizon of the pedestrians brushing up against each other is the end of the street and that of the motorists who pass at low speed is the view down the avenue: the vanishing point of the urban horizon limits the zone of their actual meeting.

On the other hand, in the case of the TV viewers co-present in front of their screens, the horizon isn't the 'depth of the image' but its delimitation, the frame of the screen, the framing of the programme and, above all, the length of time granted to their conversation before the TV screen falls silent and opaque once more. 'The televisual horizon' is, therefore, solely the horizon of the programme's present and of the real-time reception of the televised encounter, a present moment defined precisely by the framing of the viewpoints of the two TV viewers and, above all, by the time-period set for their face-to-face dialogue.

'To define the present in isolation is to kill it', wrote Paul Klee.

Isn't this the wrong that telecommunications technologies are committing here, by isolating the present from its 'here and now' in favour of a commutative elsewhere that is no longer the site of our concrete presence in the world, but merely of a discrete and intermittent telepresence? The real time of telecommunications does not stand opposed, then, as is generally claimed, simply to the past – to 'the recording' – but to the present and its very nowness – an optical switching between the real and the figurative that refers back to the physical observer present here and now, the only persistent factor in an illusion in which the body of the witness becomes the sole element of stability within a virtualised environment. The focusing of the gaze of the film-viewer, ocular witness of the small-scale optical illusion that results merely from retinal persistence, gives way, then, to this polarising of the body of the TV viewer, who is witness to the grand electro-optical illusion of a conversion of the whole world's reality into waves, with the persistence on-the-spot of the witness's body coming to complement the persistence of the ocular system. We have here the inertia of the body as the apparent product of this generalised influx of (optical, sound) information, in which everything converges and is concentrated on the being who is attentive to the instantaneous passage of images and sounds, the screen becoming suddenly a last horizon of visibility, a horizon of accelerated particles that stands in for the geographical horizon of the expanse in which the television viewer's body still moves.

Visible or deep horizon? For the inhabitant of this tight little planet, the question of the optical depth of the real environment repeats today the question of the direct, customary transparency of materials, adding to it, however, the enigma of that indirect trans-appearance which is a product of the capacities of the 'active' optics of the indirect light that comes, in its turn, to illuminate the human milieu, like the direct light of the sun or the direct light of the magic of electricity that lit up and revealed our surroundings, thanks to the properties of the 'passive' optics of the various corrective materials, such as air, water or the glass of the lenses in our spectacles! As everyone knows, there can be no apparent speed without a horizon, without a terminal. Has the frame of the TV screen become for us a real horizon, a horizon 'squared'? That square which is nothing but a 'cube' that hides itself in the two dimensions of the reductive, fragmented image of the televised sequence. The question remains to be answered.

As has been noted, the irruption at this century's end of an indirect horizon, a product of the appearance of a 'third interval' of the light kind (zero sign) alongside the traditional intervals of space (negative sign) and time (positive sign), leads to the unexpected invention of a last perspective, in which the depth of real time wins out over the depth of territorial real space. The indirect light of signals now brilliantly illuminates the world of sensory experience by momentarily reducing the optical depth of our planet to zero. To the spatio-temporal deformations of distance and time, due to the very rapidity of transport and the physical movement of persons, is added the intermittency of these appearances that are instantaneously transmitted over a distance . . . Interactive techniques that promote an unremarked occurrence, the sudden cyberneticisation of geophysical space, of its atmospheric volume, and not just – as had been the case since the invention of the first automata – of the object or robotised machine; the establishment of control over the geophysical environment in which the piloting of the instantaneous *rapprochement* of places might be said to supplant the piloting of the vehicles that still move about there . . . the telescoping of the near and the distant, the expanse of the world suddenly becoming thin – 'infra-thin' – thanks to the capacities for optical amplification of appearances in the human milieu.

'The true observer is an artist. He divines the significant and knows how sensitively to select the most crucial elements from out of the strangest, most fleeting mixture of appearances', wrote Novalis (2007: 219 [Trans.]). There can be no better description, I believe, of the energy of observation, an energy in images or, more exactly, in information. If speed is not, strictly speaking, a phenomenon, but the relationship between phenomena (relativity itself); if speed serves to see, to conceive and not solely to move about more easily, then the German poet has perfectly described the kinematic optics of that gaze which strives to select the essential from the ephemeral movement of phenomena. This is, moreover, what computer scientists today call 'imaging capacity'.

Like the microprocessors involved in CGI, the human eye is a powerful instrument for analysing the structures of the visible, capable of apprehending the optical depth of events very rapidly (in 20 milliseconds), to the point where it seems necessary today to add to the two usual types of energy – potential energy (latent) and kinetic energy (actual) – a third and last type: kinematic (informational) energy, without which, it seems, the relativistic character of our observation would disappear, once again uncoupling the observer from the observed, as was the case in the past, in the pre-Galilean era.

But let us leave aside this unnecessary historical regression to return to the technologies of real time. Having succeeded in disseminating electro-optical images and electro-acoustic sounds at the limit speed of elementary particles – together with telemetric signals that make not only tele-audition or television possible but also tele-action – the scientific laboratories, with support from their respective governments, are now tackling the improvement of the very resolution of the television image, so as to speed up this indirect transparency and further increase the optical amplification of the natural environment. We should remember that the human gaze divides up both space and time. Ocular objectivity therefore performs a relativistic feat, adding to the limits of the field of vision and the succession of sequences the temporal *découpage* of the rhythmics of the image. To speak, then, of acts of the discriminating gaze is no empty notion: or, if it is, then the relativity of the visible is itself merely a perspectival hallucination!

The pursuit of a high-definition television and of a high-fidelity tele-audition are bound up, therefore, with the scientifically controversial question of observed energy. As soon as contemporary physicists convinced us that the observer is inseparable from the thing observed, it became legitimate to enquire about the objective plausibility of this 'observed energy' that underpins all measurement in the field of the experimental sciences. Observed energy or energy of observation? The question remains. This does not, however, prevent us from producing today, through research into high-definition, a live television image whose imperfections ought to be imperceptible to the naked eye, the resolution of the electronic image becoming greater than the resolution of human vision – to the point where the image becomes more real than the thing of which it is only, in fact, an image. This is a literally stupefying phenomenon, made possible by, among other things, an acceleration from 25 to 50 images per second, the subliminal limit of human perception being 60 images per second.

In this way, the optical amplification of our natural environment is emerging at this century's end as a final frontier, as a last 'horizon' of human technological activity. Improving the precision of tele-observation today is analogous to what the conquest of territory or the expansion of empires was yesterday, the recently popularised term *glasnost* being in no way innocent. Shortly after the events in Eastern Europe in December 1990, a representative of a country bordering on the EEC exclaimed at Strasbourg, 'If they abolish borders, they'll also have to abolish distance. Otherwise we'll have big problems in the peripheral areas.' To understand what is currently at issue politically, we ought, in my view, to turn this statement around. If, in fact, distance is abolished (and with the recent development of telecommunications this has been achieved), then we'll also have to do away with borders – not just the political borders of the nation-states, to be replaced by federal or confederal unions, but also the 'aesthetic' borders between the things around us – and replace them with a final temporal limit: that of the acceleration of the optical commutation of the appearances of a world that is wholly telepresent 24 hours a day, 7 days a week; we'll have to speed up the – as yet intermittent – thinning of the optical depth of the horizon of visibility of a planet overexposed to the technologies of interactivity, in the same way as the time distances involved in physical travel have been shortened since the transport revolution. In other words, we'll have to further increase the intensity of light from this second sun that illuminates the full reaches of our territories, the way meteorological satellites already provide us with knowledge of their climates.

This would mark the end of the external world, of that *mundus* of immediate appearances that still made physical movement necessary, that still required the negotiation of an interval in space or a certain lapse of time – these 'negative' and 'positive' intervals being singularly devalued by the absolute-speed-of-light interval, the (zero) interval of those waves responsible for the television broadcast, which throw into question not just the philosophical notion of 'present time' but, most importantly, that of 'real instant'. For many of us, the risk or nearness of death lend each moment of life greater intensity and depth. Conversely, should we not intuitively realise that these new electromagnetic technologies, in lending greater 'depth' to the moment, are ruining us and literally killing us? – the so-called 'real' moment of television only ever being the instant of the sudden disappearance of our immediate consciousness, and the ceaseless deepening of the intensity of the present moment only ever being carried out to the detriment of that 'intuition of the instant' dear to Gaston Bachelard.

With the teletechnologies of the video-signal, we are no longer talking about a 'minor illusion', such as the one that frightened the audience at the Lumière brothers' film *L'Entrée du train en gare de La Ciotat* in 1895, but an emancipatory 'grand illusion', the illusion of the very presence – right here – of the ends of the earth: a telepresence just as unsettling as that of the locomotive charging towards the audience at the first screening of a cinema film. Whereas the relative speed of the shots that make up the photogram merely produced the apparent movement of the Lumière brothers' film, the absolute speed of the videogram shows up the apparent proximity of the opposite ends of the earth in a move that goes to the limits of visibility, since the purely mechanical parading of sequences at a rate of 17 or 24 images per second gives way to the electronic raster of the video image moving at 25, 30 or 50 images per second. Killing the immediate present is possible, then, only on the express condition of also killing the TV viewer's mobility in space – merely for the debatable gain of a pure and simple on-the-spot mobility. Isolating 'the present' consists, above all, in isolating 'the patient', in isolating her definitively from the active world of the sensory experience of the space around her in return for a mere 'image-feed' – in other words, for a return to the inertia of her body, to an interactive corporeal clinch.

Moreover, we may note that the 'global village' Marshall McLuhan hoped for has not come about; we have, rather, poles of inertia at which the present world is frozen within each of its inhabitants. This marks a return to the zero point of the origin of a peopling of the Earth that relates not so much to its territorial expanse and to the urbanisation of the real space of our planet, as to the urbanisation of real time, its mere appearances and the intermittent eclipsing of the interlocutors we have all become.

'Truly the light is sweet, and a pleasant thing it is for the eyes to behold the sun. But if a man live many years, and rejoice in them all; yet let him remember the days of darkness; for they shall be many. All that cometh is vanity.' So wrote the author of the book of Ecclesiastes (11: 7–8 KJV). How will things stand in the future with this sweet light of morning, when the indirect light of the wave optics of television cameras has definitively supplanted the direct light and geometrical optics of the sun's rays? Shall we put the daylight in a museum, and let in only the indirect light of reality's control screens?

If this really were the case, crypts and subterranean darkness would become superfluous, since shadows would no longer be cast by the sun lighting up the external landscape, but by that 'virtual reality' that is renewing our inner lives from top to bottom.

Simulators, virtual reality helmets, video-surveillance monitors – these are all signs of optical light coming to its end and of the furtive dawning of what is now an electro-optical light, in which the virtual will soon take the place of the visual and the audio-visual, thus putting an end to the Romantic analysis of Schlegel's *Die Gemählde*, since the real-time representation of sensory appearances *will* be able to deceive us, thanks to the very speed of light, the limit-speed of an electromagnetic radiation that will abolish the importance of the transparency of day and replace it simply with this trans-appearance of appearances instantaneously transmitted from remote locations. With speed liberating us from cosmic light, this is the paradox of a technical acceleration that suddenly runs up against the time-barrier, the barrier of that 'real time' of a media ubiquity that only ever operates to the detriment of the naked eye's gaze. In this, the virtual vision machine accomplishes what the arts of painting or sculpture had only ever been able to hint at from the quattrocento onwards, with the invention, first, of perspective, then of *chiaroscuro* and with Galileo's telescope prefiguring the television of the future. So here we are, then, at the very last museum, the Museum of the Sun! The museum of that light in which the horizon of appearances has bathed since the dawn of time.

Museum of the Rising Sun, symbol of the Land of the Morning Calm, of that Far East which still lives by the breaking of the astronomical day and which tomorrow, in common with all the rest of us, will have to bury itself, enshroud itself in the luminous shadows of the obscurantism of a virtual reality, in which cybernetic space will win out, once and for all, over the expanse and geographical depth of the World.

Translated by Chris Turner

Acknowledgement

John Armitage, Ryan Bishop and Chris Turner would like to express their thanks to Paul Virilio and the editors of *L'Esprit* for permitting the translation and publication of this chapter, which first appeared in French in January 2000.

References

Novalis (2007), *Notes for a Romantic Encyclopaedia*, Albany, NY: State University of New York Press.

Schlegel, August Wilhelm (1996), *Die Gemählde: Gespräch*, edited by Lothar Müller, Amsterdam/Dresden: Verlag der Kunst.

3

Towards a New Ecology of Time
Joy Garnett

Painting in the Dromosphere

Virilio's ideas about the 'dromosphere', by which he means our accelerated techno-culture with its closure or 'pollution' of distances and the contamination of space-time by real-time, are relevant to recent developments in visual culture, particularly and perhaps unexpectedly with regard to contemporary painting. Virilio's insights point us past illusions or delusions of 'progress' and toward the dreadful and dread-filled prospect of a daily reality by which we remain enslaved to an agenda of undiluted speed. According to Virilio, such a programme of hyped acceleration has a built-in downside in the form of the inevitable, unavoidable and infinitely repeatable catastrophic accident.

Pondering this real-time enslavement to the closure of distances coupled with the prospect of collectively experienced disasters, Virilio enjoins us to search for a corrective. This is the significance of a 'grey ecology', his poetic term for processes that engender alternatives to what he has identified as our current apocalyptic condition, one in which we are forced to deny anything that does not take place in an absolute present (Virilio 2009).

Interestingly, the accident enjoys some play in discourses apart from Virilio's discussion of techno-culture. In modern and contemporary art – where the latter increasingly privileges a dematerialised, conceptually driven art over art rooted in the physical realm – the accident has contributed to, and even embodied the creative process. This is certainly the case in modernist mythology, especially in the realm of painting, though this is a narrative that has long been strenuously critiqued, if not entirely abandoned. This narrative describes the first great American art moment of the mid-twentieth century, Abstract Expressionism, and its hero, the iconic 'artist-genius'. Consistent with this mythology, the lone artist-genius, (usually an angst-ridden white male), when confronted with a blank canvas, spontaneously and 'ingeniously' ejects his creation, whole from his psyche, which, though drug and alcohol addled, and on the verge of self-annihilation, nevertheless mimics the godhead itself by performing and painting primordial acts of creation. The importance of the technology of painting itself is minimised; instead the 'genius' narrative privileges the hand, the brush, the lexicon of splash, stain, pour or drip of viscous and dilute paints, and any flat substrate that holds them, usually stretched canvas. While this technology is indeed a pared-down version of the age-old technology of painting in Western culture, the idea of painting as an explosive, spontaneous, ego-driven creative event, inclusive of 'happy accidents' was a revolutionary departure from all that came before; it emphasised not pre-existing 'texts' or schools of thought, or conventions of an optical or symbolic nature, or even insider art historical conversations, but instead, the notion of a purity of impulse, of spontaneity (and hence brilliance) of the human gesture itself. This important linkage of artistic merit and 'quality' to spontaneity, and, hence, to a speedy if not instantaneous creation, is unprecedented in Western art, with the possible exception of its precursor, Impressionism, and it resonates unexpectedly with Virilio's thoughts about speed, the dromosphere, the accident and the loss of the poetics of the ephemeral to the dictates of real-time.

In light of the technological accelerations taking place since the 1950s, including the Internet, the spontaneity and relative 'speed' of Action Painting and Abstract Expressionism is interesting not least because of its now obvious relative *slowness*, and its necessary attachment to the material world through the human body itself.

This shift in our perspective wrought by new communications technologies allows us to see the modernist myth of spontaneity and speed in painting for what it is; it seems obvious now that processes tied deeply to the human must obey the demands of the body and its innate slowness. We might well ask: how might the art of painting, despite its late, great, failed attempt at transcending representation and hence the limitations of flesh, insert itself now, and perhaps disrupt the hyper-accelerated, dematerialised electronic surfaces and information clouds that dominate our age? Can the outmoded notion of a gestural painting become

Figure 3.1 Joy Garnett, *Predator 1* (2011). Silver acrylic; oil on canvas, 18 × 18 inches. Courtesy the artist.

useful in unexpected ways, as we attempt to make sense of our runaway will to accelerate beyond the boundaries of the human body and its ecosystems? Moreover, can we harness this renewed understanding of the painted physical gesture in a way that will point us to the humble preservation of what is left in our culture that remains fully human (as opposed to the physical gesture as an embarrassingly obvious symbol of bravado, human as that may be), and as a step in the direction of a grey ecology?

Virilio's grey ecology calls for a renewal for humankind, one that acknowledges the dogma of acceleration as a pollutant, and moreover treats the poetics of ephemera as a sought-after, delicate and ultimately sustainable cultural process, one we cannot afford to live without. This poetics of ephemera includes activities that

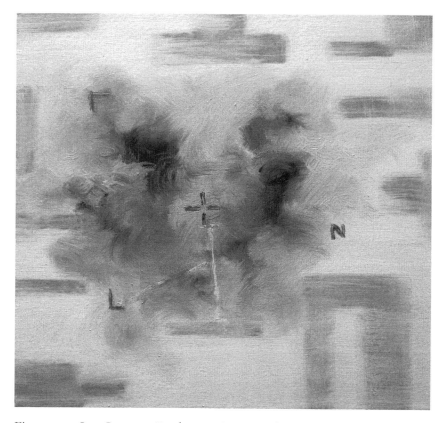

Figure 3.2 Joy Garnett, *Predator 4* (2011). Silver acrylic; oil on canvas, 18×18 inches. Courtesy the artist.

exude from the slowness and imperfection of human nature and the animal organism. From the point of view of the visual arts, one possibility of recouping this endangered poetics is through the sustained activity of painting itself, which continues to evolve within the broader visual cultural landscape despite its periodic 'death' announced by various spokespersons. Deflecting repeated attempts to sideline it critically, painting persists and flourishes, obstinately perhaps, considering the twenty-first century's technologisation on one hand, and the steady march toward demateri-alisation and virtualisation of art on the other. Painting continues to crop up at the centre of the art world as well as at its fringes; its format and methodology, varied though they may be, seem to have adapted to its particular corner of the dromosphere – our

Figure 3.3 Joy Garnett, *Predator 1* (2012). Oil on canvas, 16×16 inches. Courtesy the artist.

hyper-accelerated electronic media narrative and image world – in ways that remain unexamined and unexplained.

How is it that painting has managed to adapt, considering the radical changes in our media ecology and the overwhelming dominance of technologies that, at first blush, appear to render its practice nonsensical and moribund? This is a worthwhile direction of enquiry in light of and in spite of Virilio's overwhelming neglect of painting as a viable form in face of the dromosphere and its exigencies (Garnett and Armitage 2011b). If some feel more comfortable sidestepping the apparent un-deadness of painting, they must choose to ignore the inconvenient truth of its resilience. One could explain this attitude by acknowledging that perhaps writing about painting has been exhausted, or maybe writing about painting is too difficult for all but poets. But Virilio is nothing if not a strange poet

Figure 3.4 Joy Garnett, *Predator 2* (2012). Oil on canvas, 16×16 inches. Courtesy the artist.

of the dromosphere. Despite this neglect, the art of painting, insisting as it does on the primacy of the flesh and of the human, continues to insert itself, slowing things down for both painter and viewer, revealing meanings and sensations slowly, gradually, through what might seem to us now to be an exorbitant indulgence of time.

Painting the Apocalyptic Sublime

To paint is to resurrect the primacy of the body in a way that flies in the face of our culture's current spectrum of electronic prostheses. It posits the necessity of physical *matériel* as an inevitability that includes our own demise and death. Where the will to accelerate expresses and propels itself through technology and real-time, the desire to outstrip and outrun death resonates.

Figure 3.5 Joy Garnett, *Burst* (2010). Oil on canvas, 60×70 inches. Courtesy the artist.

Painting invigorates the eye-hand, and like certain other sustaining creative acts (cooking comes to mind), it is invariably linked to the body, even as it employs intellectual and abstract modes, and deploys or exploits contemporary technologies of speed such as the Internet.

My own agenda of painting from found military-derived imagery and image artefacts has brought me to recognise the importance of painting in a digital, electronically speeded-up environment. My process is, overall, one of appropriating and remaking documentary, scientific or technical images to my own personal, intellectual and animal needs. Conventionally, to convey their supposedly 'neutral', informational or documentary significance, these source images rely heavily on technologised modes of transmission (television; the Internet) and on (supposedly) emotionally detached, mediated contexts (techno-scientific journals; news; military documentation). Painting offers an effective means of infiltrating these contexts and subverting the dromosphere itself. The implication is that creative, abstract processes, enacted in and through the body, are analogous to processes of germination, duration and space-time consciousness in the natural and animal world, the very processes that have engendered the varied creative disciplines that have developed slowly, gradually, over millennia, throughout human culture.

The human dimension that comes to the fore in painting reveals the continuum or feedback loop that resides between tangible and virtual worlds; the pollution of one realm by another results in the relocation of instances of visceral as well as spiritual intensity. In the studio, through the viewer, and over time, the decontextualised source images become something more than fleeting, virtual representations; painting transforms them by humanising them, quite literally, through the hand and the body's interaction with paint technology, and again through the duration of reflection experienced by the viewer.

I am conscious, as a painter and consumer of Internet imagery, of having embarked upon this new ecology of time, implemented through the ambiguity and viscosity of paint, and continuous acts of Internet plunder. Despite what seems to be a dismissal on the part of Virilio, painting involves a continuous Virilian renewal – a grey or temporal ecology – sustaining as it does, numerous processes of reflection and introspection in the face of a hyper-accelerated information culture. I have referred to aspects of this renewal elsewhere (Garnett and Armitage 2011a) in discussions of the 'apocalyptic sublime', an all too human condition whereby a sharp discontinuity or gap exists between what has occurred and what is perceived, and where painting offers a means by which to agitate within these gaps, bringing them to fruition. I have become invested in parsing and repurposing images from the mass media that I experience on the Internet and throughout our image-saturated and mediated visual environment. Once torn from their original contexts and left to 'sit', such images shift and begin to resonate with new meaning; the activity of translating through painting and repurposing these images reinstills the human in them. In this way, painting positively contributes to Virilio's notion of the dromosphere, if not by reversing it, then by infiltrating it with counter-activities that rely upon and hence reinstate a sense of power and renewal through duration. It offers us a glimpse of a new ecology of time, through the reinvigorating engagement with an old, analogue, highly pliant and resilient art.

Figure 3.6 Joy Garnett, *Pink Bomb* (2011). Oil on canvas, 54 × 60 inches. Courtesy the artist.

Shown: a selection of paintings from the series 'Boom & Bust' (2010–11) and 'Predator' (2011–12), which repurpose appropriated images captured and distributed through machine vision, re-establishing them within a human – and humane – taxonomy, through painting.

References

Garnett, J. and Armitage, J. (2011a), 'Apocalypse now: An interview with Joy Garnett', *Cultural Politics* 7(1): 59–78.

Garnett, J. and Armitage, J. (2011b), 'Virilio and visual culture: On the American apocalyptic sublime', in John Armitage (ed.), *Virilio Now: Current Perspectives in Virilio Studies*, Cambridge: Polity, pp. 200–33.

Virilio, Paul (2009), *Grey Ecology*, ed. Hubertus Von Amelunxen, trans. Drew Burk, New York: Atropos Press.

4

Strangers to the Stars: Abstraction, Aeriality, Aspect Perception

John Beck

'Give me truths', wrote Ralph Waldo Emerson in his poem 'Blight' (1847), 'For I am weary of the surfaces / And die of inanition' (1994: 111). The poem is a scalding critique of the instrumentalisation of a natural world invaded 'impiously for gain' and the alienating consequences of this pinched yet conquering rationalism. For Emerson, as for Paul Virilio, the eye has taken on 'the function of a weapon' (Virilio 1989: 3) with the power to capture and command, yet such authority is not without cost, as Emerson's assessment of the impoverishment that comes with full spectrum dominance suggests: 'Our eyes / Are armed, but we are strangers to the stars' (1994: 112). The act of looking here is an act of aggressive appropriation that, in opposition to commonplace assumptions about seeing and believing, does not yield truth but only a debilitating emptiness. What is perceived, Virilio concludes, in terms of a military optics Emerson would have recognised, is already lost (1989: 4).

Eleven years after the publication of 'Blight', Nadar made the first aerial photograph from a balloon over Paris; two years later, in 1860, James Wallace Black produced the first aerial photograph in the US, 1,200 feet above the streets of Emerson's Boston. While aerial reconnaissance from balloons was first used during the American Civil War, it was with World War I that aerial photography for military purposes properly emerged, the vertical aerial image instantiating the optical domination of the flattened and estranged surface world anticipated in 'Blight'. Reading aerial reconnaissance photographs required highly trained interpreters who, like Emerson's 'young scholars, who invade our hills, / Bold as the engineer who fells the wood / And travelling often in the cut he makes' (1994: 111), parse representations of an environment that has been collapsed and denatured for them alone. The closed loop created here between mode of representation and its legibility effectively, as Bernd Hüppauf argues, 'kill[s] the natural land-scape and replace[s] it with highly artificial and, within its own parameters, functional spatial arrangements' (1995: 6). In Donna Haraway's pithy formulation this assault by the God's-eye view 'fucks the world to make techno-monsters' (1991: 189).

By eliminating the horizon the aerial photographic view pro-duces an all-over visual field that, without supplementary infor-mation or the training required to travel in the cut made by the camera that felled the wood, is primarily apprehended as opaque form. In this way, aerial photographs can seem as distant and blankly non-figurative as abstract painting, as if the vertical vantage that makes the aerial view possible has collapsed and left just the flat plane of the image. While the commanding function of the aerial view, now as in World War I, is commonly used by state agencies for purposes of surveillance, control, targeting and destruction, aerial photographs are also exhibited as works of art. From Emil Schulthess, Mario Giacomelli, William Garnett and Ed Ruscha to Emmet Gowin, David Maisel, David T. Hanson and Terry Evans, aerial photography has become an established genre of art photography (Cosgrove and Fox 2010: 99–138). Beyond the functional purpose of data gathering, though, what cultural and aesthetic work might aerial photographs of this kind be expected to do? Often aerial art photography is directly engaged in a self-reflexive examination of the promise and limitations of the vertical perspective as it has been used as a mode of capture and control. Much contemporary aerial photography is concerned with issues of industrial despoliation and military concealment, with strate-gies of visibility and invisibility, display and concealment, camou-flage and surveillance.

What is also the case, though, is that in approaching the complex history of vertical imaging as a mode of domination, aerial art photography often appears to reproduce the obfuscatory strate-gies it seeks to challenge. A large part of the difficulty here lies in the meaning and purpose of abstraction and its apparent resist-ance to interpretation. In engaging with the abstracting power of the aerial view, recent photography draws attention to the ways in which abstract form has been and can be used as a form of ideological camouflage that screens from view content that is considered best hidden, such as contaminated military test sites and large-scale industrial devastation of forests and mountains.

At the same time, this critical engagement also deploys abstraction in order to interrogate its function, a kind of counter-surveillance that replays camouflaging strategies as a form of exposure, a form of showing rather than hiding. Nevertheless, the abstract image's ambiguity and indeterminacy does not make this intervention especially obvious. The slippery nature of abstraction, especially with regard to the distinctions and similarities to be made between forms of abstract visual art (painting and photography) and in terms of the conventional opposition between surface and depth, requires serious consideration in order to establish the possibility of an aerial view that might move beyond the ultimately unhelpful binary deployed by Emerson. The weariness toward 'the surfaces' announced in 'Blight', with its denigration of surface as falsehood in favour of the truth of depth, is, I want to argue here, misplaced and in need of revision. What if whatever truths there may be are in fact embodied in the surface itself? Can the hidden be a form of display? Does every act of concealment actually call attention to itself? These are some of the questions, I think, raised by aerial art photography and directed toward the history of abstraction in twentieth-century visual art and its links to the military–industrial optic of capture and command.

Is There Life on Earth?

In a 1972 article for *Engineering and Science*, in order to explain what the Mariner 9 spacecraft needed to do in order to detect possible signs of life on Mars, the astronomer Carl Sagan turned the tables and imagined how close a Martian observer would need to be in order to detect life on this planet. Beginning with thousands of images produced from weather satellites which photograph the Earth at one-kilometre resolution, Sagan found the pictures to be 'biologically uninteresting'. At one-kilometre resolution, he concludes, 'there is no sign of life – intelligent or otherwise – in Washington, Boston, New York City, Moscow, Peking, Melbourne, Berlin, Paris, London, or any other major population center' (Sagan 1972: 17). Zooming in to examine 1,800 high-resolution colour photographs produced by Apollo and Gemini astronauts at 100-metre resolution, Sagan detects some evidence of life, but only in a mere 57 images. Equipped with a knowledge of the Earth's features, it is possible to identify roads (29), canals (5), agricultural geometricising (15), jet contrails (4) and industrial pollution (4). Cities with large highway systems like Dallas–Fort Worth are easily detectable, but large cities without such systems are not. At 100 metres, then, it is possible to detect evidence of human life, but not much; beyond a kilometre the earth yields no evidence of habitation at all. Life that does not rework the environment (such as animals and trees) is even harder to see and only detectable at one- to ten-metre resolutions (Sagan 1972: 19).

In an earlier draft of these findings, Sagan concludes from the evidence that '[n]ature paints with a broad brush, but Man, with a culture far from global, is a pointillist' (Sagan and Wallace 1970: 5). It is a throwaway line, disposable enough not to make it into the published version, but Sagan's choice of metaphor is both familiar and revealing. The distance provided by the aerial perspective tends to render phenomena invisible more often than it reveals and instead what is shown are formal configurations that bring to mind the shapes and patterns of modernist painting. Refusing to yield the kind of information that close and expert interpretation of photographic data ought to uncover, the image collapses into the surface of a painterly abstraction.

Fear of Abstraction

The tendency to conflate the aerial view and modernist painting is in no small measure a consequence of the aeroplane and Cubism (especially) appearing at around the same time (Saint-Amour 2003: 349). From Gertrude Stein to John Piper, the temptation to liken the view from above to the paintings of Miró or Picasso has been irresistible (Hauser 2007: 189). Writing in 1984, however, the cultural geographer J. B. Jackson complained that it had become a lazy habit, when looking at 'large-scale organizations of man-made spaces' from the air, to compare the view of the land to familiar patterns, tapestries, floor coverings, 'or to the work of some painter: Mondrian or Fernand Léger or Diebenkorn' (1984: 141). A more detailed study of the surface of the aerial view, Jackson argues, should reveal rather than conceal what lies beneath. While it is understandable that a geographer expects to utilise photographs for data gathering rather than for aesthetic contemplation, Jackson's dismissal of the lazy habit of seeing the aerial view as if it were art is revealing of a visual sense that responds to surface primarily as form. To see abstract images as somehow in the way of the truth of the landscape says something about the powerful suspicion of surface as a veil behind which 'real' meaning hides. Is it really possible to block out the formal properties of the surface – as enemy of truth – while the buried significance is excavated by close reading? Refusal to trust the surface appearance of the image as evidence can also belie the otherwise persistent faith in photographic representation as the truth made visible: consider the unshakable misconception during the Cold War that the Soviets had masses of ICBMs hidden somewhere where aerial reconnaissance could not find them, or the more recent puzzle of Saddam Hussein's weapons of mass destruction. The paradox here is that the evidence produced by a surveillance system based on the purported 'truth' of photography is refused if it is not consistent with need.

A similar discomfort with abstraction can be seen in environmental writer Wendell Berry's preface to a volume of David T. Hanson's aerial photographs of US military–industrial despoliation, *Waste Land: Meditations on a Ravaged Landscape* (1997). Berry expects 'that some people will account for these photographic images as "abstract art," or will see them as "beautiful shapes"'. A closer look, though, Berry argues, will show that 'nothing in them is abstract and that their common subject is a monstrous ugliness' (Berry in Hanson 1997: 3). Berry is clearly resisting the optical immediacy of the image in favour of its informational, documentary, readerly function and to the extent that the image is offered as evidence of the usually unseen management of space, this is an appropriate warning against the aestheticisation and neutralisation of a consciously political form of representation. Indeed, the fact that Hanson's images are accompanied with captions and information on the sites depicted surely does suggest that the photographer is determined to avoid the absorption of the photographs into an unreflective discourse of visual beauty. Yet at the same time Berry is surely fighting a losing battle against the visual medium: form is apprehended first, everything else follows. Hanson himself explains that the aerial view 'seemed the most appropriate form of representation for the late twentieth-century landscape: an abstracted and distanced technological view of the earth, mirroring the military's applications of aerial photography for surveillance and targeting'. The aerial view, he goes on:

> realizes the Cartesian rationalization and abstraction of space that has
> preoccupied Western culture and visual art for the last three hundred

years [and] also allows for the framing of relationships between objects that may seem unrelated on the ground, and it permits access to sites with security restrictions. What otherwise cannot be pictured becomes available to the camera. (Hanson 1997: 5)

As compelling as Hanson's explanation of his practice is here, the problem is that it still relies on the negative associations of the abstract aerial view as the unequivocal sign of power. What Jackson, Berry and other commentators uncomfortable with the aerial image's capacity to awaken unreflective aesthetic responses are sceptical of is the power of the 'God's-eye view' to dissolve all critique into a diverting spectacle of abstraction. This is certainly the common reading of the emergence of aerial photography as a decisive technology during World War I, evident in Hüppauf's assessment of industrialised war 'kill[ing] the natural landscape' and replacing it with 'functional spatial arrangements'. Aerial photographs, Hüppauf continues, 'resemble abstract landscape paintings, which also reduce the profusion of details of a "natural" landscape to a "rationally" structured order' (1995: 6). Interpreting the vertical perspective as the de facto position of power in this way, Paul K. Saint-Amour argues, has meant that the horizontal view has been oppositionally situated as the subordinated site within which resistance might arise: 'the vertical is the axis of order, paradigm, symbolic function, disutility, unimpeded sightlines, and disembodied omniscience; whereas to the horizontal belong disorder, syntagm, enunciative function, utility, partial sightlines, and exposure to visibility' (2011: 246). The problem with this binary interpretation, for Saint-Amour, is that it does not allow room for 'differential qualities' within the abstract space of the aerial view itself because they have 'long been camouflaged, ignored, or misattributed exclusively to the ground' (248).

No small part of the hostility toward seeing aerial photographs as analogues for abstract painting, then, is due to the perceived impenetrability of the abstract surface as a display of authoritarian power. In fact, abstraction is more complicated than that, as Saint-Amour suggests. During World War I the photographer Edward Steichen became commander of the photographic division of the American Expeditionary Forces, his experience of aerial photography on the Western Front leading him to renounce the pictorialism of which he had been, until this point, a leading exponent. Instead Steichen became a powerful advocate of photography's capacity for sharp, unretouched realism, a move that, for Virilio, is paradigmatic of the way in which the technologies of photography and war converged in the twentieth century. This convergence transformed the battlefield and the relationship between war and art: 'The image is no longer solitary (subjective, elitist, artisanal); it is solidary (objective, democratic, industrial). There is no longer a unique image as in art, but the manufacture of countless prints, a vast panoply of imagery synthetically reproducing the natural restlessness of the spectator's eye' (Virilio 1994: 53). While it seems that the fact of photography's integration into the optics of twentieth-century industrialised warfare compelled Steichen to renounce art photography, what is revealing is Virilio's observation that 'Steichen claimed to have only been able to carry out his military mission properly thanks to his knowledge of French art (the Impressionists, the Cubists and especially the work of Rodin)' (49). It is this fusion of art and military–industrial production that comes to shape Steichen's understanding of photography, an awkward convergence marked by the fact that Steichen held on to thousands of wartime images he did not himself take yet 'exhibited and sold as products of Steichen's authorship and as his property' (Virilio 1994: 53; Sekula 1975). Transposed into the field of art, wartime aerial photography levers open some of the 'differential qualities' latent in the abstract view, even if, in Steichen's case, a lingering desire to hang on to the aura of the creative individual and the unique art object gets in the way. The resistant properties of modernist abstraction and the mechanically produced aerial view do, I think, suggest ways of thinking about the vertical perspective and its collapse of the third dimension into surface that are not reductively instrumental and rationalistic. To see how this might work involves a brush with high formalism.

Forced to the Surface

The American art critic Clement Greenberg argued in his influential early essay 'Towards a Newer Laocoon' that in order for modern painting to claim its position as an art it had to 'surrender to the resistance of its medium; which resistance consists chiefly in the flat picture plane's denial of efforts to "hole through" it for realistic perspective space' (Greenberg 2000 [1940]: 68). For Greenberg, yielding to the medium meant that painting could finally become itself and be no longer a vehicle, subordinate to illusion, narrative or any extraneous function of what Greenberg broadly terms 'literature'. Acceptance of the flatness of the picture plane and the rectangular shape of the canvas 'got rid of imitation' (68) and the apparatus of an illusionistic third dimension in favour of an interrogation of the medium as itself: brushstroke, colour, line, shape, surface. As Greenberg tells it, painting's process of resistance and surrender is one of dynamic struggle where the medium strains and pushes in order to realise itself. This is not a story of artists or movements; instead, Greenberg provides a narrative of force and counterforce, of pressure and volume and weight. In a remarkable passage, Greenberg writes that 'the picture plane itself grows shallower and shallower, flattening out and pressing together the fictive planes of depth until they meet as one upon the real and material plane which is the actual surface of the canvas; where they lie side by side or interlocked or transparently imposed upon each other' (68). This is a plastic, almost geophysical account of tectonic shift and realignment where 'real and material' things are active forces working upon one another in space and time. Under these conditions, if the painter does try to represent objects, 'their shapes flatten and spread in the dense, two-dimensional atmosphere' (68). Faced with the pressure exerted by the medium, a 'vibrating tension is set up as the objects struggle to maintain their volume against the tendency of the real picture plane to re-assert its material flatness and crush them to silhouettes' (68). As a result of this tension, like some seismic release, 'realistic space cracks and splinters into flat planes which come forward, parallel to the plane surface' (68). This push to the surface, Greenberg notes, can be accelerated by a violent puncturing of illusionistic space made by the insertion of found materials (newspaper, wood) which 'destroy the partial illusion of depth by slamming the various planes together' (68). While the artist here can push things along, the direction of events is driven by some kind of physical inexorability. In Greenberg's account, the annihilation of illusionist space is virtually apocalyptic – volcanic, catastrophic, purgative – and results in the perfect alignment of the elements: 'the pristine flatness of the stretched canvas' (68). With the universe now in order, art can get on with the business of being art.

By describing the work of the modernist avant-garde as a process of tectonic resistance and release, Greenberg positions the shifting plates of art as autonomous from individual artists, tendencies or movements. The ground of art seems to be moving all by itself, like an indifferent earth held together only by the immutability of certain physical laws. The emergence of abstraction is cataclysmic, like an earthquake or tsunami, pressing, cracking, splintering and slamming until the illusion of depth is shattered and dispersed. Imagining the extinction of perspectival space to be a consequence of the internal logic of painting – the force of the medium ultimately becoming too great to resist – allows Greenberg to position the triumph of flatness as the inevitable outcome of painting's interrogation of its own limits. Yet the death of the dinosaur is not a geophysical inevitability; as T. J. Clark points out, flatness is compelling not in and of itself but because it stands in critical relation to perspectival depth, both epistemologically (flatness 'standing for the truth of *seeing*, the actual form of our knowledge of things') and politically. As an aggressive challenge to bourgeois consumption, according to Clark, 'flatness appeared as a barrier to the ordinary bourgeois' wish to enter a picture and dream, to have it be a space apart from life in which the mind would be free to make its own connections' (1982: 152). Here, flatness is not formally inevitable but it does, as in Greenberg's formulation, stand as a material, physical barrier to subjectivist reverie: art is not an escape from the world but a confrontation with it.

The tectonic collisions in Greenberg's field of art conjure a dynamic arena somehow beyond human agency and certainly beyond human scale; this is art operating in spaces inhospitable to ordinary representation. Indeed, what is most effective about Greenberg's account of how illusion surrenders to the medium of painting is the way that, like abstract painting, the description creates an entirely non-figurative space. Greenberg's narrative provides no space in which objects could be plausibly situated; it is a field of action – of planes, extensions, force – beyond any conventional system of representation. In a later essay on post-war American abstraction, Greenberg explains that such painting has abandoned 'the representation of the kind of space that recognizable, three-dimensional objects can inhabit' (Greenberg quoted in Harrison 1993: 201). This, I think, is precisely what he is after in 'Towards a Newer Laocoon': a kind of primordial space that no one can enter and dream, upon which no fantasies can be projected, where only the imperatives of the medium itself can be said to have authority and substance. This space of abstraction is like a world before and after history, a space of refusal so profound it has voided every trace of where it might come from and what might have motivated its creation and instead appears simply as brute matter, beyond all comment.

Greenberg's story of the coming of abstraction is deliberately non-figurative in the same way that abstract painting is non-figurative; the purpose of this non-figuration lies in its relative and negative power. As Charles Harrison explains, non-figurativeness is always relative 'both to the expectations aroused by antecedent and contemporary figurative art and, once a tradition of abstract art has become established, to the extent of negation of those expectations which has so far been reached within that tradition' (1993: 202–3). If the non-figurative presupposes that the figurative is what is normally expected, the radicalism of Greenberg's description of the emergence of flatness lies in its defamiliarisation of the narrative of art history: Greenberg's non-figuration negates the conventional story of art and, to recall Clark's point about flatness, attempts to embody 'the actual form of our knowledge of things' (1982: 152). What is important here is the pressure Greenberg – and the abstract painting he describes – puts upon expectations about art, what it is for and what it can show, not to mention the simultaneous pressure exerted upon thinking about art and what that is for. The negation of perspectival space is profound and driven by, as in Clark's reading, a critical refusal of the notion of art as 'a space apart from life'. Abstraction is oppositional and instead of dreams and illusions it offers the unadorned fact of its physicality as surface.

In order to activate its own critical position, the work of abstract art, for Harrison, 'must first evoke and set in play those very functions it aims to disparage' (1993: 203). To be considered as painting the work somehow has to do what paintings are expected to do but at the same time reject those expectations. In other words, to make clear its criticality, the abstract work must call attention to what it is not; it must recall the production of illusionistic depth even as it denies this. Greenberg accepted that '[t]he first mark made on a surface destroys its virtual flatness' (1982: 8); the relationship between the mark and the surface is a kind of figure-and-ground relationship, but one that is doubly there and not there. As Harrison writes: 'An abstract painting is something standing in place of a picture, which is nevertheless not a picture *of* anything' (1993: 203).

In light of this discussion, Sagan's leap from the aerial photograph to the abstract painting may seem more irrelevant than ever, a lazy comment based solely on no more than a broad resemblance. While the horizonless, pattern-dominated aerial photograph replicates the all-over surface of the abstract painting, the two seemingly have little else in common ontologically or aesthetically. Certainly, because of their expressed interest in flying there is a clear relationship between the work of abstract painters like Peter Lanyon and Richard Diebenkorn and the aerial view, and between aerial images by photographers like William Garnett and modernist abstraction. The nature of that relationship however, may be no more than formal in the loosest sense. Yet the critical discourse surrounding modernist abstraction still provides a means of interrogating the function of abstraction in aerial photography and its relationship to issues of visibility, invisibility and power. What the art historical analysis of modernist abstraction offers is a way of thinking about forms of art as in complex, often antagonistic relationships with each other; a way of thinking about the nonfigurative that holds the formal and political in critical tension; and a means of approaching the implications of surface and depth.

Harrison's point about abstract painting is that one form of art is necessarily interpreted through its relationship to other forms. Reading aerial photographs as abstract paintings does not have to collapse the two but can allow one form to be read through the other; the abstraction of the aerial photograph appears to deliver what we expect from abstract painting but does not. Greenberg notes the doubleness in the painting's pristine surface that is nevertheless interrupted by the mark; the aerial photograph is also double in the sense that it may superficially appear to be like an abstract painting but its surface carries no marks. In this way the abstract photograph works in the opposite direction to Greenberg's painting. The absence of the mark confirms the flatness of the surface of the image; the photograph resembles a painting but is not. Yet what the aerial photograph smuggles back into the equation is precisely what the abstract painting has denied: the plausible representation of a space occupied by three-dimensional objects. At the same time, by resembling the abstract painting, the aerial photograph defamiliarises three-dimensional space enough to preserve the element of negation abstract art opened up.

Greenberg's almost non-figurative writing about abstraction as a field of contending forces gets close to achieving the paradoxical condition of a non-anthropomorphic reading of culture much as

Steichen came to be drawn to photography's hard-edged resistance to human intervention (photographs, as Roland Barthes reminds us, seem to belong to that class of images 'not made by the hand of man' [1981: 82]). The alienation effect Greenberg manages to generate here, where human agency appears as non-human physical force, is an effect often achieved in aerial photographs where distance renders evidence of human activity as indistinguishable from geophysical or biological process. Although this alienating impenetrable surface is so often the target of hostility toward instrumental rationality's classification and domination of the object world – the source of Emerson's weariness – it is here also the means of blocking the penetrating assault by perspectival rationalism. Greenberg insists on the imperatives of form as the material signs of struggle; what the aerial photograph opens up is a sense of epistemological doubt about the nature of the forms depicted in the images. Nevertheless, it is through form that the aerial photograph announces its concerns and presents its evidence. The abstract painting and the aerial photograph both raise complex questions regarding the meaning and value of surface and depth. If the surface of the abstract painting rebuffs illusionistic perspectival depth, the pristine surface of the photograph confirms the material flatness of the picture plane even as every millimetre of that surface calls out for interpretive reconstruction of a lost third dimension.

Abstraction and Homeland

On 18 May 1980, Mount St Helens, one of several volcanic peaks that dominate the Cascade Range of the Pacific Northwest, exploded after two months of intense earthquake activity and a series of weak, intermittent eruptions. In the Washington area at the time, having been awarded a National Endowment for the Arts fellowship to undertake a photographic project in the state, was Princeton-based photographer Emmet Gowin. Intent on documenting the devastation, security restrictions meant that the best way to approach the site was from the air (Reynolds 2002: 143). While Frederick Sommer's horizonless landscapes were already a big influence on Gowin's work, he had made no aerial photographs until this point, yet the Mount St Helens project would result in Gowin becoming one of the most prominent aerial photographers working in the US, and he would return to the site of the earthquake over a number of years. The Mount St Helens explosion also drew to the area landscape photographer Frank Gohlke who, like Gowin, returned numerous times through the 1980s. The scale of the disaster – 40,000 acres levelled, 20,000 additional acres of timber damaged, more than 60 people killed – meant that, as Gohlke wrote in 1985, 'Mount St. Helens is the only place on the continent where one can *see* so clearly the effects of forces comparable in scale to those produced by nuclear weapons' (2009 [1985]: 97). Gohlke's move from natural to nuclear catastrophe here perhaps reflects the political climate of the mid-1980s during President Ronald Reagan's revivified Cold War. The fear of and fascination with destruction that Gohlke admits drew him to Mount St Helens, though, is also about the American West's historical place as the double site of US natural and technological sublime.

This convergence of geophysical and historical sources of awe and dread identified by Gohlke is also not far away during Gowin's explorations of Mount St Helens. A chance flight over the Hanford Reservation in 1986, Gowin notes, 'changed my whole perception of the age in which we live' (Gowin in Reynolds 2002: 144). Originally built as part of the Manhattan Project, and home to the first full-scale plutonium reactor in the world, during the Cold War Hanford in south-central Washington expanded to nine nuclear reactors and five large plutonium processing complexes. Plutonium for most of the US nuclear arsenal was produced at Hanford, and though the site was decommissioned at the end of the Cold War it remains the most contaminated place in the United States. What emerged for Gowin in his flight over Hanford was 'a pattern of relationships and a dark history of places and events':

> Still visible after forty years were the pathways, burial mounds, and waste disposal trenches, as well as skeletal remains of a city once used by over thirty thousand people who built the first reactors and enriched the first uranium. Etched and carved into the body of the desert landscape below was a whole history of unconscious traces . . . What I saw, imagined, and now know, was that a landscape had been created that could never be saved. (Gowin in Reynolds 2002: 144)

From Hanford, which from the air exposes its history as a series of ghostly scratches and scars, Gowin began to seek out other nuclear sites, 'realities that [he] had unconsciously forgotten' (144). The power of the aerial view for Gowin here resides, as it does for Hanson, in its capacity to expose the signs simply not available to the ground-level observer, a point emphasised by Kitty Hauser in her discussion of aerial archaeology: 'once soil has been disturbed . . . that disturbance is essentially virtually ineradicable, no matter how long ago it took place' (2007: 163). Nonetheless, without the supporting paraphernalia of captions, maps or other contextualising information, such as Gowin's explanation of his investigative surveillance of sites from the air, the images are still in danger of looking like anything at all.

Discussion of aerial photographs, as we have seen in Jackson and Berry, invariably turns to this dilemma. Discussing Gowin's images of Western US military sites, environmental writer Terry Tempest Williams asks:

> Do we view each photograph as a work of art and simply enjoy the pleasure of form and texture as its own aesthetic statement? Earth becomes the artist's canvas. Or do we see this portfolio of images as a haunting documentation of place, how we have altered the land with our industrial and technological might from agriculture to recreation to national security? (2002: 126)

The answer for Williams is both; Gowin shows the earth as 'abstraction and homeland' (126). Peter Goin, another photographer of nuclear landscapes (though not aerial views), admits that '[f]ormal beauty can be a contradictory element in a photograph that comments critically on land use and land management' (1991: xxii), but it is this contradictory element that saves aerial photographs like Hanson's and Gowin's from functioning merely as decoration, since their abstract surface aligns them with the confrontational energy of modernist painting. Hanson's and Gowin's images, while carrying the awful toxic information Berry wants us to carefully see, present themselves as pure form. While this form may look like aestheticist acquiescence, it is the abstract form itself that refuses to allow us to reductively convert the photographs back into pure information as some kind of objective truth. As form the images stand apart from the instrumentality of vision expected of the camera as part of the apparatus of surveillance and disciplinary intelligence. What Berry wants us to look at we cannot see, and what he does not want us to dwell on is precisely what we do see.

Williams's identification of a doubleness in Gowin's work is important here and the terms she uses to describe that duality are also revealing, the coupling of abstraction and homeland bringing together aesthetic form and politics ('homeland' post-9/11 is an especially freighted word) as aspects of each other. What Williams is suggesting, I think, is a way of thinking about doubling as a form of simultaneous showing and hiding that speaks both to the ambiguities of abstract form evident in aerial art photographs and to the politics of surveillance and security embedded in the vertical view. Commentators who want to shut down an aesthetic response to aerial photography because it somehow occludes or dismisses any critical clout the images may carry have missed, if Williams is right, the power of such images to embody the contradictory phenomenon of a power that hides by showing itself (homeland as abstraction) and where any attempt to expose that power ends up calling attention only to itself (abstraction as homeland).

The doubleness Williams identifies in Gowin's aerial shots recalls, to return briefly to painting, a suggestive discussion by art historian Fred Orton of Jasper Johns's famous mid-1950s painting of the Stars and Stripes entitled *Flag*. What is important about Johns's work, I think, is that it stands between the poles of Greenbergian abstract formalism and the violent return of figuration in Pop Art. It is also, of course, a painting with something to say about form and politics, though exactly what is hard to read. *Flag*, then, seems to be operating in two directions at the same time in ways that are not dissimilar, at least in Orton's reading, to what I believe is going on in aerial art photography. Orton argues that the painting works by transmitting two main messages simultaneously, one about art and one about flags. For Orton, '[a]s a work of art [the painting] embodies a set of ideas and beliefs about art and aesthetics and as the American flag it embodies a set of ideas and beliefs about citizenship, nationalism and patriotism' (1994: 140). Any attempt to concentrate on the painting's 'message as a work of art', Orton continues, is 'interrupted' by its message as an American flag:

> This interruption causes doubts about *Flag*'s ontology as a work of art but not about its patrioticness. Rather, this interruption confirms the work of art's patriotic value . . . But when we try to concentrate on *Flag*'s message as the American flag, the patriotic message is interrupted by the art message . . . The meaning of *Flag*'s surface in art

must somehow be at odds – this is the character of an interruption – with its meaning as the American flag if it is not to be understood – and never has been understood in this way – purely and simply as the American flag. (1994: 140–1)

Read this way, *Flag* might be understood as functioning as a form of dazzle painting or camouflage, its surface interfering with the signals it is itself simultaneously sending. Like Wittgenstein's duck–rabbit illustration, which is used to explore the differences between seeing an image *of* a duck or rabbit ('passive' seeing) and seeing the image *as* a duck or a rabbit (interpretive seeing), seeing a flag is distinct from seeing the painting as a flag (see Wittgenstein 1968: 194–7; Bull 1999: 21–4). And, like Wittgenstein's example, *Flag* carries more than one message at once – a message as art and about flags; it is both a duck and a rabbit, and to see both requires an oscillation between the two. The two readings, as Orton suggests, do not sit comfortably together; rather, one is always interrupting the other. This is the abstraction/homeland oscillation Williams identifies in Gowin's work and which, I think, is crucial to an interpretation of aerial art photography that does not dismiss consideration of abstraction as a reactionary formalism but instead reads it as intrinsic to what the images can show and not show about power and vision.

Aspect-Dawning

The stubborn foregrounding of abstract form is most obviously present in the work of David Maisel, a student of Gowin's at Princeton and his assistant on the Mount St Helens project. After working with Gowin, Maisel went on to photograph the logging industry of northern Maine; open pit mines in the West, first in black and white, then in lurid colour; Owens Lake in Los Angeles; the Great Salt Lake in Utah; and, in negative, aerial views of LA. Maisel's work revels in the contradiction between abstract form and the overdetermined site already noted in work like Hanson's and Gowin's. The photographs from the 2005 series *Terminal Mirage* depicting the area around the Great Salt Lake in Utah, for example, supply no contextualising support beyond the title. The Great Salt Lake is one of the biggest terminal lakes in the world; it is also in the middle of the desert where mirages are common. So the title is prosaically factual at one level but also invokes the entropic sci-fi scenarios of J. G. Ballard and Robert Smithson. *Terminal Mirage* calls up an entire repertoire of tropes relating to disease and decay, duplicity and illusion, but beyond these two words, the images are left to fend for themselves.

The scale of Maisel's images is hard to discern; the square format and absence of horizon resist a reading of the surface as landscape and the colours are implausibly vivid. There must be something wrong when bodies of liquid are angry reds, purples and greens, but it is impossible to tell from the images what this chromatic excess signifies (Figure 4.1). The Great Salt Lake, as well as being terminal, is naturally rich in five major elements, each with its own colour, which seep into the water and are concentrated in the lake. Other sources of colour in the lake are species of algae and bacteria; industrial evaporation ponds for extracting salts and minerals; toxic chemical weapons waste; and contaminated wastewater ponds of the Magnesium Corporation of America. This information expands but does not resolve the information in the photograph, which sends simultaneous messages that cannot be comfortably received at the same time: it is a photograph that looks like a painting; it is a photograph of a real place; within that real place are colours that look like paint; some of those colours are natural, some are manufactured. To recall Orton, the image is sending messages as documentary and messages as art, one interrupting the other. The meaning of the photograph's surface as form gets in the way of its documentary function as a picture of the Great Salt Lake; the art message calls up an implied context within the visual history of abstract forms even as the image reports on the garish deformations wrought by natural and unnatural processes on the ground. Donna Haraway's point that the vertical view 'fucks the world to make techno-monsters' must also be modified or expanded here to include the fact that the techno-monsters have already fucked the world so that Maisel can take these photographs.

William Fox has observed that Maisel's images 'can be abstract in the extreme and run exactly counter to the intent of most aerial photography, which is to specify and identify pattern and activity in the landscape' (2009: 116). The absence of grounding information in Maisel's work may be, as Fox suggests, because 'people used to spend more time in front of his work discussing pollution than appreciating the photographs as artworks' (116), and it is probably true that if the primary function of the photographs was to deliver compelling evidence of environmental negligence then intoxicating abstractions are unlikely to work as documentation. What I think Maisel knows is that aerial abstraction is less effective as a direct truth-telling device and more about an intense oscillation between showing and hiding and the resistant and seductive properties of surface. What the Salt Lake photographs show is a mess of natural and unnatural elements, a scrambled set of codes that cannot be separated out. Painting and photography, documentary and abstraction, industry and algae occupy the same surface, exposed and concealed at the same time. When Williams writes of Gowin that his contradictory earth is both abstraction and homeland, she optimistically goes on to suggest that in the aerial views '[w]hat has remained hidden is exposed. What is largely unseen, therefore unknown, is revealed. What we thought benign becomes malignant. Our perception of the world shifts' (2002: 126). This is a dream of art's emancipatory capacity which, given abstraction's duplicitous history, is too straightforward. The shift that has taken place from Gowin to Maisel – from austere black and white to violent colour; from cool elegance to garish opacity – is a move from the possibility of exposure to the recognition that it is the condition of hiddenness that is the only thing visible in the photographs. Maisel's lake is terminal; as he explains, having no natural outlets, the 'claustrophobic, no-exit, existentialist aspect of this fact sparked my curiosity'. Furthermore, to return again to the terms of the title, 'the word "mirage" seems to describe the entire hallucinatory quality of the expanse of the Great Salt Lake, the unflinching light that illuminates it and that is reflected from its surface, and the manner in which this body of work questions the nature of sight and perception' (Maisel). There is no exposure here but there is illumination. The light is unflinching but not in a revealing way; it is hallucinatory, challenging the certainties of sight and perception.

A common experience of looking at the duck–rabbit drawing is to just see one or the other: to see the duck and not consider the possibility of the rabbit. Wittgenstein uses the term 'aspect-dawning' to describe the experience of seeing the rabbit for the first time after previously only seeing the duck. While the drawing has not changed, something is different. As Malcolm Bull explains, '[a]spect-dawning is not a matter of reclassification, but of the direct apprehension of something that did not appear to be there before' (1999: 187). The rabbit was there all along but not

Figure 4.1 David Maisel, *Terminal Mirage 9* (2003). C-Print. © David Maisel/INSTITUTE.

perceived; it was not, as Bull writes, 'insensible' because 'in seeing the duck you are necessarily seeing all that is to be sensed of the rabbit'. Rather, the rabbit is hidden because it is imperceptible. When we see the duck, writes Bull, 'the rabbit is disguised, and when we see the rabbit the duck is disguised'. Once we know there is a duck and a rabbit in the drawing, while we cannot see both at once we can 'oscillate between the various possibilities more or less at will' in order to perceive each in turn (22). When we are looking at the duck or the rabbit, then, something is disguised but nothing is concealed.

The aerial photograph is both non-figurative and figurative; it is abstraction and homeland, surface and depth, concealing and exposing, art and information. Resistance to the perception of aerial photographs as abstractions reveals a desire to maintain continuous aspect-perception, to hold the meaning of the image in place unambiguously. By visually recalling abstract painting, though, the aerial photograph opens up another aspect: the aspect of art with its history of non-figurative resistance to the penetration of the surface. This aspect-dawning means that the photograph, while unchanged, seems to show something that did not appear to be there before. The photograph is sending simultaneous messages that cannot be apprehended at the same time; something must be disguised in order for something else to be seen. Nothing is concealed, yet there is something hidden. In the end, it is not the information the photograph contains about military sites or industrial pollution that is paramount; nor is the aesthetic impact of the abstract image the most important thing. What is most compelling here is that both aspects can be sensed even when only one can be seen at a time. It is the awareness of hiddenness that the aerial photograph makes possible by generating the oscillation of perception between the indexical and the abstract.

Virilio: Hidden but Not Concealed

For Virilio, Jackson Pollock's vertically executed 'all over' paintings signify a shift from the perspectival conventions of spatial representation focused on the horizon to an outlook 'on the NADIR starting from the aerial zenith' (2007: 36). This 'scopic turning back to face the terrestrial surface' is, in Virilio's view, a consequence of aerial technology, the 'abstract world of aeroscopy celebrated by Nadar' that will, by the end of the twentieth century, end in 'the televisual MEGALOSCOPY' of real-time satellite geo-surveillance (36–7): 'Instead of observing the line that decides between Earth and sky, you observe the surface, the "support-surface", as people once contemplated the stars in the age of popular astronomy' (37). Like Sagan turning the space camera back on to Earth, the view from above renders human life undetectable at worst and at best remote and transitory. As vision is restructured by the release from the pull of gravity enabled by aerial technology, what Virilio mourns is the loss of depth and weight, of embodied experience; instead, the collapse of space represented by the horizonless surface of the abstracted ground seen from above means that the earth is no longer a support and threatens a 'fall upwards' into the abyss (1997: 2). The relationship between vision and weight is crucial for Virilio since it embeds sight in a material world of physical forces. The Renaissance geometers might have insisted on 'near' and 'far', but for Virilio, it is not 'vanishing lines converging on the horizon' that is the original reference point for sight but rather 'one bound up with the delicate balancing act of a universal attraction which imposes on us its gearing toward the centre of the Earth' (1–2). The weightless, depthless aerial view, then, not only sweeps aside the space of perspectival illusion but any substantive relation between vision and human being in the world.

The kind of alienation Virilio registers in his assessment of technology's destruction of space is a reminder of Emerson's nineteenth-century weariness (and wariness) toward surface as well as recalling those critics who are sceptical of aerial photography's capacity to produce abstract, and therefore evasive because non-figurative, versions of real despoliation and criminal damage. What the history of abstraction in painting and photography suggests, however, is a potentially more resistant view, where the violent flattening of depth made possible by the aerial scopic regime (the panoptical rationalisation and control of space) is held in productive critical tension with abstraction's art historical tradition of non-figuration as a means of defying modes of representation that aim to capture and command.

References

Barthes, R. (1981), *Camera Lucida: Reflections on Photography*, New York: Hill and Wang.

Bull, M. (1999), *Seeing Things Hidden: Apocalypse, Vision and Totality*, London: Verso.

Clark, T. J. (1982), 'Clement Greenberg's theory of art', *Critical Inquiry* 9(1): 139–56.

Cosgrove, D. and Fox, W. L. (2010), *Photography and Flight*, London: Reaktion.

Emerson, R. W. (1994), *Collected Poems and Translations*, ed. Harold Bloom and Paul Kane, New York: Library of America.

Fox, W. L. (2009), *Aereality: Essays on the World from Above*, Berkeley: Counterpoint.

Gohlke, F. (2009 [1985]), 'A volatile core', in *Thoughts on Landscape: Collected Writings and Interviews*, Tucson: Holarts, pp. 93–7.

Goin, P. (1991), *Nuclear Landscapes*, Baltimore: Johns Hopkins University Press.

Greenberg, C. (1982 [1965]), 'Modernist painting', in F. Frascina and C. Harrison (eds), *Modern Art and Modernism: A Critical Anthology*, London: Sage, pp. 5–10.

Greenberg, C. (2000 [1940]), 'Towards a newer Laocoon', in F. Frascina (ed.), *Pollock and After: The Critical Debate*, 2nd edn, London: Routledge, pp. 60–70.

Hanson, D. T. (1997), *Waste Land: Meditations on a Ravaged Landscape*, London: Aperture.

Haraway, D. J. (1991), *Simians, Cyborgs and Women: The Reinvention of Nature*, New York: Routledge.

Harrison, C. (1993), 'Abstraction', in C. Harrison, F. Frascina and G. Perry, *Primitivism, Cubism, Abstraction: The Early Twentieth Century*, New Haven, CT: Yale University Press, pp. 184–262.

Hauser, K. (2007), *Shadow Sites: Photography, Archaeology, and the British Landscape 1927–1955*, Oxford: Oxford University Press.

Hüppauf, B. (1995), 'Modernism and the photographic representation of war and destruction', in L. Devereaux and R. Hillman (eds), *Fields of Vision: Essays in Film Studies, Visual Anthropology, and Photography*, Berkeley: University of California Press, pp. 94–124.

Jackson, J. B. (1984), *Discovering the Vernacular Landscape*, New Haven, CT: Yale University Press.

Maisel, D., 'Mount Saint Helens', <http://www.davidmaisel.com/works/msh.asp> (accessed February 2012).

Orton, F. (1994), *Figuring Jasper Johns*, London: Reaktion.

Reynolds, J. (2002), 'Above the fruited plains: Reflections on the origins and trajectories of Emmet Gowin's aerial landscape photographs', in E. Gowin, *Changing the Earth: Aerial Photographs*, New Haven, CT: Yale University Art Gallery, pp. 133–50.

Sagan, C. (1972), 'Is there life on Earth?', *Engineering and Science* 35(4): 16–19.

Sagan, C. and Wallace, D. (1970), 'A search for life on Earth at 100 meter resolution', Center for Radiophysics and Space Research, Cornell University, pp. 1–27.

Saint-Amour, P. K. (2003), 'Modernist reconnaissance', *Modernism/Modernity* 10(2): 349–80.

Saint-Amour, P. K. (2011), 'Applied modernism: Military and civilian uses of the aerial photomosaic', *Theory, Culture & Society* 28(7–8): 241–69.

Sekula, A. (1975), 'The instrumental image: Steichen at war', *Artforum* 14(4): 26–35.

Virilio, P. (1989), *War and Cinema: The Logistics of Perception*, trans. Patrick Camiller, London: Verso.

Virilio, P. (1994), *The Vision Machine*, trans. Julie Rose, London: British Film Institute/Bloomington and Indianapolis: Indiana University Press.

Virilio, P. (1997), *Open Sky*, trans. Julie Rose, London: Verso.

Virilio, P. (2007), *Art as Far as the Eye Can See*, trans. Julie Rose, Oxford: Berg.

Williams, T. T. (2002), 'The Earth stares back', in E. Gowin, *Changing the Earth: Aerial Photographs*, New Haven, CT: Yale University Art Gallery, pp. 125–31.

Wittgenstein, L. (1968), *Philosophical Investigations*, trans. G. E. M. Anscombe, Oxford: Blackwell.

5

Desert Wars: Virilio and the Limits of 'Genuine Knowledge'

Caren Kaplan

> There is no war, then, without representation, no sophisticated weaponry without psychological mystification. Weapons are tools not just of destruction but also of perception . . . (Virilio 1989: 6)

> To represent is to perform division. To represent is to generate distributions . . . To represent is to narrate, or to refuse to narrate. It is to perform, or to refuse to perform, a world of spatial assumptions populated by subjects and objects. To represent thus renders other possibilities impossible, unimaginable. It is, in other words, to perform a politics. A politics of ontology. (Law and Benschop 1997: 158)

Acts of war create divisions: the separation of populations into orders of 'us' and 'them', combatants and non-combatants; distinctions drawn between wartime and peacetime and so on. Yet, war itself is utterly confounding of divisions; perceptions of time and space are altered, certainties are destabilised. Or, perhaps another way of putting it is that war's innumerable divisions and distributions make some subjects and objects possible – perceived and known – while making others impossible, unimaginable. During wartime, identities become matters of life and death. Legibility creates targets as well as safety zones. These divisions and distributions are the cost of being perceptible to the modern nation-state and its proxies. What or who cannot be perceived as possible even in the midst of relentless documentation, measurement or narration? Can those who have no part, who cannot be known – making possible the modern world of exchange, power and perception – can these subjects and objects ever become alive to possibility? Can representation ever surrender to the unimaginable, the unknowable?

69

In *Desert Screen* (2002), a series of essays on the Gulf War of 1990–1, Paul Virilio called our attention to the transformative influence of visual information technologies, in an era of 'desert wars'. In these and many other works, Virilio has argued that the innovation of televisual data along with its strategic circulation by militaries for propaganda purposes has altered the political landscape of modernity as much as the bombs falling on Iraq have destroyed infrastructure and human lives. In the 1990s, the most recent 'strategies of deception' – a pattern of disinformation – utilised by the US and its allies in the context of a brief but relentless air war were changing the contemporary battlefront yet again, sending it back to earth, even underground. In particular, Virilio singled out the desert – which seemingly provides no cover and reveals all to the 'eyes' in the sky – as the paradigmatic space of disinformation's 'known' lies. In the desert, stealth overcomes speed – the status of visibility becomes renewed as paramount; who can be detected and who can escape such identification? Above all, stealth overtakes truth; there is no possibility of 'genuine knowledge' when deception has moved beyond conventional camouflage to operational virtuality.

It can be argued that the integration of the computer and its powerful styles of communication marks the crucial difference in representational practices between earlier wars such as World War I – which ushered in an entire era of perceptual logistics – and the air war in Iraq in the early 1990s. That is, the Gulf War performed a new kind of conflict, one of total control not only over the battlefield but also over 'public representation'. In this context, 'that which is seen is already lost', or at the very least tracked, tagged, known, identified (Virilio 2002: 77). But 10 years after a second US-led Gulf War and several decades into the installation of informatics throughout commercial and military domains, the hegemony of 'electro-optic perception' now seems less totalising and more unevenly practised. In the second decade of the twenty-first century we know now that civilian aeroplanes can bring down skyscrapers and that so-called 'irregular' warfare causes even the most sophisticated drones to circle endlessly without sensing a target. The strategies devised for desert or open spaces are stymied or challenged by the urbanising or underground tactics of contemporary war (Weizman 2007; Graham 2010; Bishop 2011). But there is yet another way in which the pivotal division between a 'before' and 'after' World War I and the 1990–1 Gulf War designated other possibilities as impossible. If the continuities of air war over desert regions are made impossible in the narrative of the fields of perception generated by the 'Great War' then the ways in which empire operates through violence are rendered unimaginable. When empire's violence cannot be known, its impossible nature structures the possible. But to acknowledge empire's violence through information-retrieval or the substitution of one set of facts by another will only reiterate representation as war (Spivak 1988).

Story 1: The Possibility of Oil

Although Nature has been sparing in her gift of water to these people, she has made up for it a hundred-fold by a lavish gift of oil. South Persia is incomputably rich in the multitude of oil wells which are there. (Miller 1934: 7)

Through its hyper-generation of movement, mixing the accomplishments of the means of destruction and the means of communicating destruction, war falsifies appearance by falsifying distance. (Virilio 1989: 24)

Almost 100 years ago, the British navy phased out the use of coal and contracted with the Anglo-Persian Oil Company (now known as BP, British Petroleum – one of the largest oil companies in the world) to provide petroleum for its ships. Not long after, at the start of World War I, troops from the British Indian Army were sent thousands of miles to secure the major oil refineries at Abadan in the strategic area where the Euphrates and Tigris rivers meet to flow into the Shatt al-Arab waterway and on to the Persian Gulf. Today the nation-states of Iran, Iraq and Kuwait brush against each other in this narrow area bordering the sea, linked by rivers. In 1914, British operational maps marked these zones as 'Syrian Desert', 'Persia', 'Arabia' and 'Lower Mesopotamia'. The first war of the 'world' created by industrialised high imperialism extended itself to this specific area as an expedition to secure oil for the British military effort and soon developed its own colonial *raison d'être* – to push the Turkish allies of Germany out of the entire region of Mesopotamia. The sign of success for this goal would be the occupation of Baghdad. British strategists envisioned a quick trip north up the rivers, a few skirmishes with an enemy presumed to be inherently inferior and therefore easily overcome, and a triumphant entry into the ancient, fabled city on the Tigris River. Over the course of four years, the Ottoman forces were eventually defeated and the flag of the United Kingdom was flown in Baghdad.

Although the British were successful in both protecting the oil fields and expanding their reach far beyond southern Mesopotamia, their strategic and tactical approaches had almost resulted in a complete military catastrophe. The British navy was of little use in shallow rivers and marshland, requiring concerted support from land forces to clear both natural blockages and those created by enemy sabotage. In order to keep secret the plan to secure the refineries of Abadan, the military had decided against equipping the troops deployed from India with anything that would suggest a desert campaign. Instead, they arrived in southern Mesopotamia with uniforms and other equipment designed for use on the much colder Western or Eastern Fronts. Sent out to the Gulf on ships with metal decks that heated up like ovens, equipped with wool uniforms and single fly tents, operating in relatively open terrain that offered little shelter or strategic advantage, the British Indian Army was decimated by illness. Over 92,000 British troops out of a total deployment of 350,000 died during the campaign; many soldiers died miserable deaths from heat stroke or dysentery rather than from enemy fire (Barker 2009 [1967]: 373). The Mesopotamian Campaign's non-combat losses were considered to be so egregious that a special parliamentary inquiry was conducted near the end of the war. In addition to finding that lapses in human judgement and leadership had caused a needless number of deaths of largely Indian troops, the parliamentary commission report provided support to those who argued that aviation would have been a better investment of resources than the costly and inappropriate naval and conventional cavalry units.

The need for air power had been apparent to many; there were air squadrons in Egypt, Palestine and other areas as well as in Mesopotamia. But there were few aeroplanes and they were often not designed for the terrain or climate in which they were operating. Supplies were uneven and inadequate. Yet, the contribution of aviation to aerial reconnaissance, mapping and bombardment in Mesopotamia was indisputable (Satia 2006). Planes flew up and over flood plains, dry stretches of desert and the highest moun-

Figure 5.1 This image of Kut-al-Amara from the air frames the future of what becomes the nation of Iraq – it is also a fragment of a newly possible visual culture that begins with war and moves into innumerable avenues of everyday life. A ubiquitous view but one that divides populations into those who should and should not be bombed based on location designated by geography. It is a view that metropolitan moderns know almost by heart whether we are acutely aware of it or not, a view we make and remake endlessly.

tains. They conducted observation and transmitted information at unprecedented speeds. Aviation changed entirely the perception of distance. Thus, this new technology promised to transform not only the approach to conducting wars in the future but also the ways in which the nation-states would configure their authority over distant colonies, often via the divisional practices of representation (Figure 5.1).

Story 2: Eyes of the West

Aerial photography of the country on all fronts had been pressed on daily. There were no maps, and to fight the Turk without eliminated any chance of the co-operation on which success depended. The photographic section were developing and printing far into each night, and with the results the mapping section at G.H.Q. turned out accurate squared maps which were distributed by air on the front. (Tennant 1920: 145)

Once the general staffs began to take aviation seriously, aerial reconnaissance, both tactical and strategic, became chronophotographic and then cinematographic. (Virilio 1989: 17–18)

World War I is marked by most cultural commentators and historians as a pivot around which the entire globe turned: from older industrial practices to newer ones, from visual cultures of spectacle to surveillance, picturesque to utilitarian, local to global, discipline to control and management. Although these changes did not necessarily occur evenly or instantaneously, the general consensus is that the 'Great War' marked a divide between a 'before' and 'after', a division that became legible across modern societies. On just one register, the shift from coal to petroleum fuel for naval fleets and the enthusiastic embrace of oil-powered automobiles threw European miners out of work and rationalised the occupation of oil-producing regions on the grounds of 'security'. On yet another level, the distribution of aviation introduced not only new calibrations of speed into understandings of space but new perspectives and distinct kinds of views.

In *War and Cinema* (1989), Virilio delineates just how direct vision – unmediated viewing by the human eye – became superseded by a war machine of articulated innovative technologies. Such a transformation did not take place all at once. Through the pervasive experiential upheavals of World War I, Virilio argues, the 'old homogeneity of vision' began to be replaced by a 'heterogeneity of perceptual fields' that 'escaped' classic Euclidian visual practices (Virilio 1989: 20). 'Airborne vision' broke through the stasis of the ground war, mixing the means of communication and those of destruction into a new kind of weapon, the 'ultimate' way of seeing. Thus, while on the ground the 'vast new battlefield' of the blasted Western Front seemed to be 'composed of nothing – no more trees or vegetation, no more water or even earth, no hand-to-hand encounters', in the air 'there was no longer an above or below, no longer any visual polarity' (14, 18). In this strange new space and time of war, new tools for perception were needed and new practices for discernment – for the labour of division – were required.

Aviation holds a special place in this analysis, standing for the evolution from the sites of war as fields of perception to the operation of perception itself as techno-culture. This mix of 'chrono/camera/aircraft/weapon' becomes generalised as mobility, circulating pervasively from battlefield to homefront, from earth to sky, from war to entertainment and the arts (Virilio 1989: 19). When Virilio writes, then, in the context of World War I that 'there is no war . . . without representation', he is lamenting what he believes to be a lost world of material substance that is legible to the human eye, brought about by the transformative mobility of aviation and its sister technology, cinema. With the end of direct vision at this stage in modernity, the division between home and away is destabilised, even undone, by time and space compression. Thus, the emergent immateriality of perceptual fields derealised not only warfare but everyday life.

We can trace this regret for unmediated vision throughout Virilio's work on the visual culture of war by posing representation as a question of the division and distribution of the perceptible, making impossible some possible ways of being and knowing. Two technologies in particular assist the separation of the possible and impossible into configurations of control; the analogue reconnaissance photograph and the operational map. Both observational image and map mediate the new space and time of World War I by creating enhanced viewing practices based on the hybrid 'chrono/camera/aircraft/weapon'. The reconnaissance photograph incorporates standardisation and simplification to convey its system of truth. As James Scott has argued, the narrowing of visual elements that became endorsed by both state and industrial sciences from the late nineteenth century forward led not only to efficient managerial practices that privileged the precise measurement of uniform units of goods or objects; this selective narrowing created a 'synoptic vision' that engendered rational control and spatial order (Scott 1998: 58). This standardisation of the seeming randomness of Enlightenment encyclopaedic scholarship became a speciality of the modern science of cartography; triangulation and precise measurement by instrument replaced narrative approximations and schematic drawings collected from travellers. While maps can be understood to be 'exercises in negotiation, mediation, and contestation', the military invested in exhaustive ordnance surveys and increasingly detailed topological maps in order to produce irrefutably accurate representations (Edney 1997: 25; Hewitt 2011). During World War I, flight crews took great risks in order to shoot film that could be transmitted to cartographers who would send them new maps to use to continue to conduct reconnaissance. This circular loop of communication and representation configured control by working and reworking details as 'covers' and 'mosaic' compositions in order to generate a form of 'genuine knowledge', the possibility of truth through representation (RAF 1918; Sekula 1984; Virilio 2002: 87; Wexler 2006).

Virilio pinpoints the Battle of the Marne in September 1914 as the first event in which aerial reconnaissance as a form of camera weapon influenced the course of battle for the Allied forces, thereby creating passionate advocates for air power among a certain cadre of the military command (Virilio 1989: 17). This recognition of heroic aerial observation in the very earliest days of the war on the Western Front makes possible the narrative of air power as a teleological inevitability, situating the camera weapon as military high-tech while marking the decisive temporal break between pre- and post-war visual culture. It also makes other narratives or representations impossible. Thus, for example, from the very beginning of the war the British Royal Flying Corps was operating aerial reconnaissance in the regions derogatorily referred to as 'sideshows' – the theatres of war 'other than those of the Western and Eastern Fronts in Europe' and consisting, in the main, of Gallipoli, German East Africa, Salonika, North-East Italy, Palestine and Mesopotamia (Mead 1983: 111). Narratives of air power in World War I are almost exclusively concerned with the Western Front and, occasionally, with the Eastern. The role of air power in the so-called 'sideshow' regions is impossible to 'fit' into the narrative of the Western Front's air war because it is primarily a story about European empire and colonisation rather than a dualistic battle between ethnically 'white' German soldiers on one side and their British, French and US counterparts on the other (Omissi 1990). It also cannot participate in the mythologies of 'aces', 'dog-fights' and other well-known, even beloved, tropes that accompany the histories, both popular and academic, of air war on the Western Front. RFC pilots in Mesopotamia fought their German counterparts in the air and strafed the German/ Ottoman bases. But the distances and perceived alterity of the terrain and climate were unlike the Western Front to a significant degree (Thomas 1920: 350). The stories do not sync. Although air power played a significant role in the arenas of war outside of Europe, the very separateness of the colonial context (with its racialised biopolitics and orientalised representations) makes aviation's advances there nearly impossible to figure in most contemporary accounts. The logistics of perception in Mesopotamia are configured by Western eyes that shift not only from direct to mediated vision through the deployment of the 'chrono/camera/aircraft/weapon' but from the possibility of half-empty maps to the impossibility of anything other than total surveillance through modern cartography.

A 'world' war needed an almost unimaginable number of maps and images that depicted the emerging divisions of wartime. Aerial reconnaissance images were rushed to cartographic units and fresh maps were supplied in so-called 'air packets' to flight crews for further surveillance and to identify targets. The air packets were composed of numbered, individual square sheets placed in chronological order in an envelope. Placed end to end, the square maps could comprise a long strip of territory. The cover sheet provided a key to terms, symbols and abbreviations; a new lexicon that transposed old and new iconography. While aerial surveying in Europe was undertaken to edit and correct existing maps, the entire Middle East was regarded as missing the 'framework upon which military mapping could be hung' (Collier 1994: 100). Mesopotamia, in particular, was viewed as needing the most work, thereby becoming a 'perfect' laboratory for new state-of-the art cartographic techniques such as strip-mapping and methods of linking information from both vertical and oblique imagery (Figures 5.2 and 5.3).

Story 3: Desert War

The beauty of the flight back was ethereal; the morning clear and cold, the sky cloudless . . . High up in that wonderful dawn it seemed that the airplane was stationary, the movement so smooth; one sang for the very joy of living, and the song harmonised with the rhythmic hum of the engine. Far below the nullahs and trenches occupied by the enemy were disclosed by the charcoal fires on which they cooked their coffee. The situation was as plain as draughts on a board; it all seemed so simple. (Tennant 1920: 57–8)

For men at war, the function of the weapon is the function of the eye. (Virilio 1989: 20)

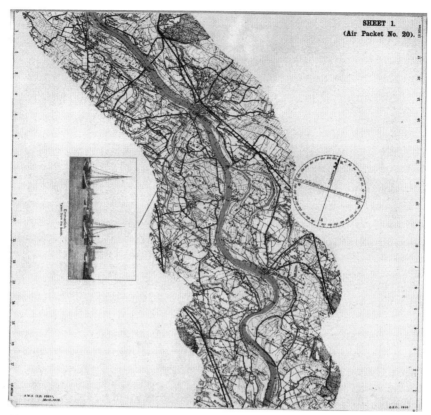

Figures 5.2 and 5.3 In these figures, two riverside cities are displayed
c.1915–16: Emmerich, behind the lines in Germany on the Western
Front; and Kut-al-Amara, about half-way up the Tigris between Basra
and Baghdad. The European view is densely inscribed to assist the pilot
or observer in identifying landmarks and sites in close proximity. It is
an image that represents density of population, among other things. An
inset detail view of the harbour with ships under sail adds a picturesque
element. The Mesopotamian map is clear of much detail; some ruins,

Virilio's enquiry into the logistics of perception helps us to understand the growing tension between direct and mediated vision
as the camera weapon becomes increasingly dominant; bringing
distant objects closer while maintaining remoteness, moving at
unprecedented speeds while producing the effect (and the imagery)
of stillness. The images produced by this amalgam of technologies,
people and modes of perception generate an enigmatic, vintage
aura across the stretch of nearly 100 years. But at their moment

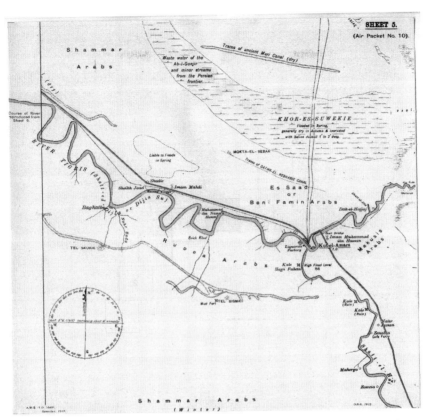

a few towns, ancient canals and flood plains are noted along with the one road deemed 'passable for wheeled traffic'. Graphic, simple and unadorned with 'picturesque' inset views, the Mesopotamian air packet marks the beginning of systematic surveying and charting of a region identified as a future resource. Empty spaces remain to be filled in as needed with information needed for the extraction of resources and control of variable elements such as restive populations, floodwaters, new infrastructure, etc.

of creation they were an 'up-to-the-minute' iteration of modernity, the state of innovation at the service of a military–industrial complex thundering into profitable being. Aerial reconnaissance photography separated subjects and objects into what could be observed through a state-of-the-art optical lens, made visible through chemical emulsions on the photographic plate. The tactical task was to observe and designate enemy locations but the strategic implications were nothing less than changing the maps of the territory. This remapping established with brutal simplicity 'who' and 'what' and 'where' in order to make possible control of an area otherwise blank, unknown.

The costs for the British of a battle within its own military branches over strategies, tactics and technologies were paid, heavily, in the case of Kut-al-Amara. Between December 1915 and April 1916, the British were under siege in the town, having fallen back in their first push to take Baghdad. Kut-al-Amara became a signal disaster for the British; forced to surrender and sent on an infamous death march, the starving troops became seen by the public at home as martyrs to the cause of empire. To some ambitious politicians (like the relatively young Winston Churchill), the siege and fall of Kut-al-Amara demonstrated the terrible vulnerability of ground troops dependent on land and water for logistical support. They joined a powerful avant-garde in political, military and scientific circles to argue for the rational development of air power: eliminate dependency on the gunboats bogged down in Mesopotamian sand-bars; reduce the number of troops needed on the ground (fewer to transport, feed, clothe and bury). Patrols could take place by air with greater powers of surveillance, reconnaissance could be conducted more scientifically, supplies could be delivered in more timely and cost-saving ways, and war could be waged at greater distance with infinitely fewer casualties on the side of empire. Above all, the credo of air control in colonial spaces that promoted mapping while enacting aerial bombardment and machine-gun attack simply segued from World War to Mandate period as the war wound down (Satia 2006). If the fall of Kut became a rallying cry for a new kind of military under the sign of nationalist fervour, air control offered a lower-cost, efficient solution, especially for desert terrain.

Therefore, aerial patrol of Mesopotamia, which had commenced with the arrival of the first air squadrons in the spring of 1915 and continued throughout the war, was never dismantled. In 1920, when the League of Nations divided the defeated Ottoman Empire according to the Treaty of Sèvres, the British were 'awarded' Mesopotamia and a civil government was installed to administer the territory. The Mandate divided territory, designating Middle Eastern countries as 'independent' while establishing European 'administrative' oversight; a practice that endured for 12 years until 1932. This structure of nominal independence experienced as military occupation, as the possibility of self-rule that is simultaneously impossible, was not embraced uniformly by the population of the Mandate territories. 'Arab riots', as British history has termed them, continued throughout the Mandate period. In their often violent effort to gain control over the people of Mesopotamia, the British relied on the 'chrono/camera/aircraft/weapon' that had been so useful during World War I, refining and expanding its techniques to generate a visual repertoire for modern management.

Story 4: Desert Screen

Farther on I came up with the rear party on the march. Flying along about ten feet from the road I mowed down seven with one burst of machine-gun fire; it was sickening; they had hardly the strength to run into the nullahs and fire back; those hit just crumpled up under their packs and lay still; others waved in token surrender and supplication for rescue. All along the road they staggered in twos and threes . . . No scene can be so terrible as a routed army in a desert country . . . (Tennant 1920: 89)

Therefore, the first of the *ruses de guerre* is no longer a more or less ingenious stratagem, but *an abolition of the appearance of facts*. From now on the defeat of facts [*la défaite des faits*] precedes that of arms: it is less important today to come up with a brilliant manoeuver, an intelligent tactic, than strategically to cover up information, genuine knowledge, by a process of dissimulation or of disinformation that is less special effect, a known [*avéré*] lie, than *the very abolition of the principle of truth* [*vérité*]. (Virilio 2002: 87)

Historians of desert warfare point out that nearly 20 per cent of the globe is 'covered' by deserts (Watson 2007: 17). In the arid reaches of this topography, nothing is believed to grow and navigation is next to impossible. The adage is that one can see everything but interpretation of these otherworldly views requires expertise. Colonial discourse had figured indigenous desert nomads as semi-mystical figures who traversed desert space more by magic than by any recognisable scientific knowledge; the ability of Bedouins to 'melt' into the landscape was a staple of novels, plays, paintings and, eventually, film. This inherent camouflage of desert people and places was legendary, therefore, among European forces. Non-native militaries believed that they were especially vulnerable to attack by 'raids' of locals in the seemingly empty, open spaces of desert war. The aeroplane levelled the playing field, as it were; observing, mapping and bombing or strafing as needed. Air control offered liberation from the sweltering flat lands, the unhealthy swamps and fly-infested camps, and the element of insecurity caused by local allies of the enemy who appeared almost invisible and, therefore, undefeatable.

Writing over 70 years after the close of World War I, at the outbreak of the 'first' Gulf War, Virilio argued that the unforgiving topography of the desert merged with the informatics of the computer/television screen to create new visual practices that had no other purpose than to deceive, to generate disinformation to the benefit of the military–industrial complex (now fused to entertainment arts as the MIME network in Der Derian's coinage; Der Derian 2001). Surveillance via desert screen, Virilio argued, leads to total, pure war. Virilio's distrust of the aesthetics of the 'Revolution in Military Affairs' that shifted operations, at least on a discursive level, to digitalised practices that privileged intensely mediated visuality leads him to argue that this war, much like World War I, is pivotal; turning military logistics of perception into ubiquitous ways of life, rendering visual culture as extended permanent conflict. In this account, then, the 1990–1 Gulf War divided time into a 'before' and 'after' even as it contributed to the turn from wars of certain times and places into globalised war without end.

Above all, Virilio warned, the militarised desert screen collaborated with a growing tendency in the neoliberal entertainment industry to deprive the public of the great promise of liberal democracy; freedom of information and the uncensored circulation of fact. In the early 1990s, the advent of cable television news and the relentless pursuit of visual product to screen 24 hours a day met the military's need to disseminate controlled information leading to an 'abolition' of the 'appearance of fact'. The very principle of truth is abolished, Virilio argued, when 'genuine knowledge' is 'covered up' by dissimulation (Virilio 1989: 87). From across time, after yet another invasion of Iraq that has been announced as concluded while continuing in innumerable forms, as private contractors expand their profitability at the expense of social welfare, and as 'security' discourse structures the news headlines and Twitter feeds in accordance with US Department of Defense press releases, we might well accord Virilio the mantle of prescience, gratefully, and be done with it. But that principle of truth, once possible and now claimed to be impossible, can and should be reconsidered. A transcendent truth was never possible in the vexed landscape of the desert wars in Mesopotamia and, thus, what was made possible for more than a century was purely endless war.

For how else can we generate 'genuine knowledge' or truth of a place like Kut-al-Amara? A major node in the great transport and sale of carpets. A place where grain was grown. A loop in the river Tigris. A site of siege and battle, mapped and photographed millions of times. A nuclear research facility, looted in 2003. An Iraqi Air Force base that became a US Contingency Operating Base that has now been 'returned' to the Iraqis. From high up in the orbital 'fourth front', as Virilio terms it, the satellite images show Kut-al-Amara's same distinctive peninsular loop but with many more structures and roadways than the reconnaissance photograph from World War I. Satnav cannot lie; its pixels may be reconfigured by Photoshop but in its pure state it is as close to a fact as almost anything. Yet, we know that these representations tell us only the stories from one side of war's divides, distributing the world into possible and impossible views and kinds of knowledge and ways of being. What data should replace the facts that divided this place from others, that rendered it a 'sideshow' in the 'Great War'?

Virilio's interventions suggest that virtual informatics and total surveillance have caused us to lose sight of the truth but I would argue that the very possibility of colonial air control signalled the dedicated abolition of anything like that ideal of 'truth' decades earlier. In Mesopotamia, as in other 'sideshows' during that pivotal war and after, genuine knowledge was generated, relentlessly, in the surveying, measuring and machine-gunning of the desert, rivers and people of a place always already unknown – it was *genuine* because those who created it believed in it with an almost religious passion. Yet, the more this place became known, depicted in myriad ways, the more possible subjects and objects became impossible. That is, the problem of genuine knowledge in a place like Kut-al-Amara, in the representation of Mesopotamia and Iraq across time, is not resolved by filling in information, supplementing the story with more facts or alternative views. Similarly, regret for the loss of direct vision cannot ameliorate the ontology of colonial wars. Mediated telematics may intensify the effect of this warfare – extending battlefields across space and into all four of the dimensions detailed so effectively by Virilio. But the wars we are fighting today proceed simultaneously via the representational practices of all the eras and spaces of European and US empire, making multiple divisions between subjects and objects (Gregory 2004). In this densely active process, systems may not always mesh and practices may not always sync. In these uneven gaps and breaks, rather than in truth and knowledge, we may find it possible to allow for the immensity of what has been made impossible, for what we do not know.

References

Barker, A. J. (2009 [1967]), *The First Iraq War, 1914–1918: Britain's Mesopotamian Campaign*, New York: Enigma Books.

Bishop, Ryan (2011), 'Project "Transparent Earth" and the autoscopy of aerial targeting: The visual geopolitics of the underground', *Theory, Culture & Society* 28(7–8): 270–86.

Collier, P. (1994), 'Innovative military mapping using aerial photography in the First World War: Sinai, Palestine and Mesopotamia, 1914–1919', *The Cartographic Journal* 31(2): 100–4.

Der Derian, James (2001), *Virtuous Wars: Mapping the Military-Industrial-Media-Entertainment Network*, Boulder, CO: Westview Press.

Edney, Matthew H. (1997), *Mapping an Empire: The Geographical Construction of British India, 1765–1843*, Chicago: University of Chicago Press.

Graham, Stephen (2010), 'Combat zones that see: Urban warfare and US military technology', in F. MacDonald, R. Hughes and K. Dodds (eds), *Observant States: Geopolitics and Visual Culture*, London: I. B. Tauris, pp. 199–224.

Gregory, Derek (2004), *The Colonial Present*, Malden, MA: Blackwell.

Hewitt, Rachel (2011), *Map of a Nation: A Biography of the Ordnance Survey*, London: Granta.

Law, John and Benschop, Ruth (1997), 'Resisting pictures: Representation, distribution and ontological politics', in K. Hetherington and R. Munro (eds), *Ideas of Difference*, Oxford: Blackwell, pp. 158–82.

Mead, Peter (1983), *The Eye in the Sky: History of Air Observation and Reconnaissance for the Army, 1785–1945*, London: Her Majesty's Stationary Office.

Miller, Janet (1934), *Camel-Bells of Baghdad*, Boston: Houghton Mifflin.

Omissi, David E. (1990), *Air Power and Colonial Control: The Royal Air Force, 1919–1939*, Manchester: Manchester University Press.

RAF (1918), *Notes on Aerial Photography, Part II: The Interpretation of Aeroplane Photographs in Mesopotamia*, Baghdad.

Satia, Priya (2006), 'The defense of inhumanity: Air control and the British idea of Arabia', *The American Historical Review* 3(1): 16–51.

Scott, James C. (1998), *Seeing Like a State: How Certain Schemes to Improve the Human Condition Have Failed*, New Haven, CT: Yale University Press.

Sekula, Allan (1984), 'The instrumental image: Steichen at war', in *Photography against the Grain: Essays and Photo Works, 1973–1983*, Halifax, NS: The Press of the Nova Scotia College of Art and Design, pp. 33–52.

Spivak, Gayatri C. (1988), 'Can the subaltern speak?', in C. Nelson and L. Grossberg (eds), *Marxism and the Interpretation of Culture*, Urbana: University of Illinois Press, pp. 271–313.

Tennant, Lt. Col. J. E. (1920), *In the Clouds above Baghdad*, London: Cecil Palmer.

Thomas, H. Hamshaw (1920), 'Geographical reconnaissance by aeroplane photography, with special reference to the work done on the Palestine Front', *The Geographical Journal* 55(5): 349–70.

Virilio, Paul (1989), *War and Cinema: The Logistics of Perception*, London: Verso.

Virilio, Paul (2002), *Desert Screen*, London: Continuum.

Watson, Bruce Allen (2007), *Desert Battles: From Napoleon to the Gulf War*, Mechanicsburg, PA: Stackpole Books.

Weizman, Eyal (2007), *Hollow Land: Israel's Architecture of Occupation*, London: Verso.

Wexler, Rebecca (2006), 'Heightened Histories: Aerial Archaeology and British Nationalism in England and Iraq', MPhil, Cambridge University.

6

Light Weapons/Darkroom Shadows: Photography, Cinema, War

John W. P. Phillips

If photography, according to its inventor Nicéphore Niepce, was simply a method of engraving with light, where bodies inscribed their traces by virtue of their own luminosity, nuclear weapons inherited both the darkroom of Niepce and Daguerre and the military searchlight. (Virilio 1989 [1984]: 101)

The eyes cannot understand the nature of phenomena. You must not hold them responsible for this fault of the mind. (Lucretius)

Retinal Retention

When a missile threatening in 'real time' is picked up on a radar or video, the present as mediatized by the display console already contains the future of the missile's impending arrival at its target. (Virilio 1994: 67)

We may be closer now than ever to having machines that can see. What we do have are machines that in various ways interpret and transport the light data captured by a camera or sensor. And while this kind of thing is normally considered in terms of 'artificial visual perception' it remains questionable whether the algorithmic and topological signaletics of even the most sophisticated optoelectronic technologies approximate *perception*. What is not in doubt is the rapid exponentiation of these kinds of machine in every domain, most obviously in day-to-day interactions with smart phones, cloud computing and entertainment media, but more significantly in the field of military aviation.

For instance, the new generation of naval helicopters are said to be 'multi-operational', which means that they are designed by way of an operational schematism that allows a flexible mission repertoire: search, trace, attack, defensive manoeuvre, evacuation and rescue. Where once a variety of different vehicles would have been employed to serve different purposes, now navies can operate with one model flexible enough to respond to a contingent variety of needs characteristic of conflicts of the so-called age of the war on terror and other emergencies. Optoelectronic technology is what drives this new operational schematism. Typically an operating crew, which in addition to the pilot includes a SENSO (sensor operator) and a TACCO (tactical operator), works the helicopter via its television system. Such systems convert optical images from a wide variety of pick-up devices (including camera tubes and vidicons) into electronic signals. The signals are immediately transferred from one point to another, where they are converted into further optical images on the TACCO/SENSO display, which divides up rationally so that tableaux, peripheral readouts, cues, alerts and future trajectories are presented on the display in discrete sections. An aviator today must know how to read the optical messages of the television system.

In the passage between the point of the first conversion (which records data) and the point of the second (which interprets it), we have an instance of an operation of vision that is solely the province of machines. Paul Virilio looks forward to this kind of operation in *The Vision Machine* (1994), in which he is primarily concerned with the hypothesis of a world inhabited by images whose origins and ends are entirely mechanistic:

> Once we are definitively removed from the realm of direct or indirect observation of synthetic images created *by the machine for the machine*, instrumental virtual images will be for us the equivalent what a foreigner's mental pictures already represent: an enigma. (1994: 61)

While the tactical helicopter still operates by way of a sophisticated and cursory mediation of the perceptible world, it does so via technics and logistics of perception that in principle are already divorced from any answerability to objective reality. Paradoxically the virtual image both confirms an age-old philosophical doubt concerning the supposed realism of mental images and yet produces a 'reality effect' in 'the relative fusion/confusion of the factual (or operational if you prefer) and the virtual' (61). These observations lead Virilio to a typology of logics of perception, which I will analyse shortly. The point is to show that looking forward to the implicit future of a technology requires a kind of archaeological work not only on the technology itself but also on the imaginary within which and on which it operates both as an effective and yet at the same time as a more or less *mythical* force. In which case we will not understand the currency of visual technology and its operational schematism without questioning the sphere by which the electronic image establishes and occupies its place in the historical imaginary. The question concerns a kind of failure: 'How', Virilio asks, 'can we have failed to grasp that the discovery of retinal retention that made the development of Marey's chronophotography and the cinematography of the Lumière Brothers possible, also propelled us into the totally different province of the mental retention of images?' (61) The discovery of what has throughout the history of cinema been labelled 'retinal retention' implies by that name a causal account of a perceived effect. Frederick Talbot's famous explanation in *Moving Pictures: How They are Made and Worked* (1914) brings the currency of Gestalt psychology to the picture in an explanation, typical of its time, which equates the functioning of the perceptual system with that of a camera:

> The eye is in itself a wonderful camera. The imprint of an object is received upon a nervous membrane which is called the retina. This is connected with the brain, where the actual conception of the impression is formed, by the optic nerve. The picture therefore is photographed in the eye and transmitted from that point to the brain . . . When it reaches the brain, a length of time is required to bring about its construction, for the brain is something like the photographic plate, and the picture requires developing. In this respect the brain is somewhat sluggish, for when it has formulated the picture imprinted upon the eye, it will retain the picture even after the reality has disappeared from sight. (1914: 4)

This kind of explanation is quite bizarre by today's standards, but it nonetheless has a considerable hold on the imagination. The established facts are simple enough. Images shown in sequences of 16 frames per second or more are perceived as movement. While the notion that the brain is too 'sluggish' to keep up with the rate of image exchange was a fanciful though authoritative hypothesis, conceivable now only as a kind of science fiction, it does serve to underline the indubitable effect. Equally striking, though, is the image of the human perceptual system presented as if it had been modelled on the operation of a camera. The explanation has the virtue of presenting a phenomenon of perception (cinematography) in terms of the operational qualities of the thing perceived (photography). It is as if the images produced by a given machine required an equivalent kind of machine to perceive them. In *The Vision Machine*, Virilio exploits the imaginative resources of explanations of this kind to reconstruct a kind of fantasy in the historical relationship with images. The simulation of moving images does not merely leave its mark on the eye but operates like the coloured earth itself on the mind of the perceiver and thus on psychic memory. 'How', he continues, 'can we accept the principle of retinal retention without having to accept the role of memorization in immediate perception?' (1994: 61). If this is indeed 'the way our nervous system records ocular perceptions', then it is no longer possible to 'reject the objective reality of the cinema-goer's virtual image' (61). The upshot is that images produced by cinema occupy the same imaginative space as mental images associated with more traditional kinds of perception: as neither more nor less objectively true. We now share our experience of the world with machines whose images act on our nervous system (Virilio refers to this as a kind of 'pre-action') as if they were no different from our own mental images. Furthermore, once machines communicate their own peculiar modes of seeing to each other, cutting out any mediation by human perception, a new logistics of perception has entered experience, a logistics mobilised no longer by spatial extension but by a novel logic of temporal exposure.

Logistics and Perception

The notion of temporal exposure as such is not exactly new. What is new, at least since the nineteenth century, is the speed by which it operates, thanks to visual technology, and the extent of its reach, so that the temporal experience of the spatial present is increasingly replaced by the real-time display of images often projecting an immediate future. How then does this logic operate? Ancient questions of perception have given rise to explanations that seem to prefigure the discovery of cinema. A celebrated instance is from Lucretius, whose Epicurean poem, *On the Nature of the Universe*, is often cited in reference to the prehistory of cinema. In 'Book Four' Lucretius gives an account of numerous ways in which the mind is deceived in its interpretations of material (atomic) data received by the eye. As with so many discoveries, the modes by which a process or operation fails serve to demonstrate the workings of the process in question. Images, in the Epicurean tradition, are considered as material 'films of light' that pass from the object to the eye, at length to be interpreted by the mind. At one point in the explanation Lucretius discusses the way images in dreams 'move about with measured gestures of their arms and other limbs' (4.115). His explanation offers what many have taken to be an instance of the phenomenon of retinal retention:

> When this happens, it means that one film has perished and is succeeded by another formed in a different posture, so that it seems as though the earlier image had changed its stance. We must picture this succession as taking place at high speed: the films fly so quickly and are drawn from so many sources, and at any perceptible instance of time there are so many atoms to keep up the supply. (4.115)

Clearly enough the dream in Lucretius (as it does for Epicurus) recalls Aristotle's more or less definitive philosophical explanation, according to which dreaming is contrasted to conscious perception as its after-impression. The identification serves to further distinguish conscious reason from a variety of derangements. Aristotle notes that the functioning of dreams rests with the tendency for sense impressions to linger after the objects of sensation have departed and from thence to undergo metamorphoses: 'Even when the external object of perception has departed', he says, 'the impressions it has made persist, and are themselves objects of perception' (*On Dreams*, A46ob). Perception, when robbed of real objects, takes the impressions of those that have departed as a substitution for the absent real. The larger implication, in the field of perception, becomes clearer with the Epicurean unfolding of the logic of temporal exposure, supported by the philosophical denigration of the perceivable 'after-effects' of present perception: a process that is capable of chaotically simulating the movements of a world rendered absent in the presence of its after-image must be regarded as essentially accidental.

And it is on that point that the question of a logistics of the image becomes interesting. The invention of photography rather precisely reproduces the Epicurean philosophical picture in concrete terms. As light falls onto a sensitised surface its after-image becomes at length available for further perceptions. The world is indeed full of after-images. Such a world – which might once have been vulnerable to disproof by way of a kind of *reductio ad absurdum* – nonetheless fulfils the conditions for Aristotle's account of derangement. The world filled with photographs and cinematic images brings the realms of dream and delirium into the sphere of conscious perception in determinate ways. To that extent the organisation of the world belongs less to individuals than it does to the operation of machines. But while the Epicurean dream world (as we might understand it) addresses the historical imaginary of cinematic images, the various logistics of mechanistic perception, once separated out from the dream, are revealed in the indubitable (and, as Virilio insists, accidental) procession of the military arts.

The logistics of the mechanised image, as we know, involves a typology of logics of perception. Two issues are at stake. One involves the question of the aesthetics of the photographic image. While Virilio is not particularly well known for writings on the aesthetics of photography this is clearly important and should at least be acknowledged. A careful study of the images that appeared as part of the *Bunker Archeology* exhibition (republished in the book *Bunker Archeology*, 1994 [1975]) reveals an unmistakable rapport between the aesthetics of the photographic image and the topic that provokes the first main sortie in Virilio's long interrogation of the technology of war. These images do not merely document aspects of the bunkers remaining along the European littorals after World War II (functional design features, models of shelter, embrasures designed for armour or camouflage and so on) but they do so via an aesthetic technique that links photography itself to the logic exemplified by the bunkers. These defensive redoubts stand as if in testament to a resistant will (now absent) in the face of the kind of trajectory documented thoroughly shortly afterwards in *Speed and Politics* (2006 [1977]). A trajectory, of course, establishes its defences in a reversal of movement along the way, and thus in opposition to trajectory per se. A defensive redoubt therefore represents the site or nodal point of an implacable tension. Virilio's photographs document the aftermath of the modality of conflict, in the form of its after-image. But to see the constructions 'Barbara' or 'Karola' in these images is to see how their appearance in the photographs is a matter of the way light has fallen upon them or failed to do so. It is a matter of the way they hold fast against the light that falls upon them. Surrounded by light and emerging from the earth or fog, shaped by zones of grey and shading (in entrances or firing slits) to almost true black, these bunkers exemplify the art of photography in its most paradoxically classical form: as studies of light perfected in the darkroom. Here is an unmistakable prefiguration of the main thesis of *War and Cinema*, according to which modern warfare becomes more or less equivalent to a kind of devastating photography. I'll come back to this point.

In *The Vision Machine* Virilio deliberately puts the question of the aesthetic value of photography to one side in order to address the second issue, that of the logic of perception itself. The logistics of the image follows three stages corresponding to historical orders of perception. A 'formal logic' corresponds to an age of painting and engraving, preceding the discovery of photography. A 'dialectical logic' of film and cinema (of retinal retention and the after-image) follows and supersedes this formal logic, before being superseded in its turn by the 'paradoxical logic' of the digital or virtual image and 'real time' as well as 'delayed time' projections (Virilio 1994: 63). The television display of the contemporary tactical helicopter exemplifies the operational efficacy of the paradoxical logic of virtual images in its projection of trajectories not yet accomplished. The delayed time of the display dominates the actual time of perception not by its simulated *representations* but by its virtual *presentations*. The virtual operates as the paradoxical presenting of the presence of that which is not (or not yet). The temporal dynamism of these logics (formal, dialectical, paradoxical) replaces the normal catalogue of retentions and protentions conceived traditionally as the cinematic union of past, present and future. So it is time consciousness itself that is sundered by these logistics of perception. The point, I think, is to see how the dialectical logic of photography and cinema performs a fundamentally mediating role – thus providing the very force of its own transumption – in relation to the other two logics of the image, so that the paradoxical logic of the digital image functions in relation to the dialectical logic of the image as its own paradox. The very inability of cinema-photography to resolve its disjunct relation to the formal logic of representation gives rise to the paradoxical logistics of images that are not resolved in relation to any real or actual space. What this means is that paradoxical logic is paradoxical *in terms of and in relation to* dialectical logic. The digital image functions as photographic logic's innate paradox. Dziga Vertov's *Man with a Movie Camera* (1929) exhibits within the medium itself its comic paradoxology. The celebrated scene of stop motion animation, for instance, in which the camera on its tripod performs as if by magic for an audience in split screen mode, gives any actual audience the chance to reflect on the character of the magic on the screen in front of them, exposed now in a hollow performance of technical burlesque.

Light

At a significant moment in *Painting with Light* (1995), John Alton's luxuriously technical guide to lighting in cinema and photography, the author pauses to acknowledge the ruinous effects of modern civic life on the health of city dwellers: 'The usual city dweller', he notes,

> is so busy doing nothing of importance that he just cannot find time for a good vacation or a short trip to the country. When at last his physician forces him to take one, it is usually too late. The vacation is spent in a hospital, surrounded by the nerve-racking, ear-splitting noises of traffic, steam hammers and auto horns of the modern metropolis. (1995: 118)

Alton is merely expressing – albeit in a pleasing sardonic style – a common notion of the post World War II years, according to which the increase in urban automation and civic expansion leads inexorably to a decline in emotional health. The emergence of the short break called vacation (a chiefly American term for holiday) capitalises on the essential senses of vacancy – emptiness, freedom from care, release or respite. The vacation in this sense is coterminous historically with urban development and represents, at least in post-industrial nations, an unwritten yet inalienable right of the urban dweller (a bare need rather than a desire). Alton's answer to the problem (vacations are not that easy to come by for the majority) makes a case that might have been expected from perhaps the most celebrated Hollywood cinematographer of his age: those who cannot take vacations can go to the cinema instead. 'Fortunately', he says, 'to the millions who seldom get a chance to go anywhere, motion pictures can bring beauty of the outdoors in the form of entertainment to be viewed in air-conditioned theatres' (1995: 118). Cinema therefore seems to represent the elegant solution to an otherwise chronic urban problem. Indeed, Alton's book addresses the environment of motion picture theatres themselves, which largely, he complains, are too bright and too noisy. 'By eliminating these annoyances, the motion picture theatre could be made a more pleasant place to go to' (1995: 186). The whole package – well-lit motion pictures shown in pleasant theatres – promises straightforwardly to bring to urban inhabitants a simulation of the kind of therapeutic experience that by other means remains distant for most of them.

Alton's observation describes the peacetime version of conditions that Virilio documents exhaustively in his classic text *War and Cinema* (1989 [1984]). The cinema ideally functions as a defensive redoubt, a place of retreat, from the harmful environment of the city. The sounds and lights of the city approximate at least the sensory bombardments (steam hammers and spotlights) of the modern battlefield, which the cinema serves both to reproduce and to neutralise, bringing these sounds and sights to the theatre, sometimes even bringing its spectators close up to tension and to the conflict, while protecting them from it.

Alton's claim becomes credible only once spectators accept the existence of a benign continuity between the empirical sphere and the simulated spheres of visual technology. This benign continuity allows them to assume a more or less seamless extension of space (a spatial arrangement that a spectator might or might not experience in itself) into the flat screens of aesthetically appointed theatres and living rooms. And exactly this notion of continuity informs Alton's philosophy. After 13 chapters of painstaking technical instruction on the complexities of lighting and filming, for the production of strenuously composed visual artifices, Alton ends with a short chapter, equating the work of this artifice to that of human consciousness ('The World is a Huge Television Studio and we are All Photographers'). The echo of popular Gestalt psychology is obvious. Photography could not have been 'invented', he suggests, for 'in reality, sensitive plates in the human head, in fact television within the human brain, are all as old as man himself' (1995: 187). This 'photography' separates 'us' from 'monkeys or cavemen'. The statement does not simply remove photography from history but locates it, outside its own historicity, as a condition without which there would have been no history at all. 'The human brain is the most completely equipped television studio there is' (187). Alton's description, for instance, of the sophisticated mechanics of the eye in terms of its capacity for visual production would not have seemed fanciful. The eye is a light-sensitive anglepoise televisual plate with projection screen and automatic diffusion and exposure meter. The philosophical background confirms it. From Immanuel Kant and 'the schematism of consciousness' to Adorno and Horkheimer and the 'schematism of production', the notion of a 'cinematic consciousness' has served to establish the grounds on which consciousness may be understood, and yet it simultaneously serves to limit and marginalise the historical arrival of photography as a specific technology of light and speed.

Two different kinds of consequence follow. First, in an idiom of philosophy concerned to establish unalterable (and transcendental) conditions for human experience, the supposed cinematic (photographic and televisual) consciousness obeys certain laws, without which the experience of objects would not be possible. In that case visual technologies operate, in whatever sophisticated set-up we might project for them, as mere prosthetic additions – attachments that add more of the same to sensible perception or supplement, from time to time, various inabilities that might arise on the part of the individual (inabilities of spatial travel, inhibitions of movement, limitations on sensation, mortal horizons and so on). Second, though, it might be supposed that the medium of consciousness operates in a radically disjunctive way in relation to everything it perceives. In this case it is no more the model for audio-visual technologies than it is the impressionable surface of their projections. No longer regarded as the medium of primordial structures of experience, it becomes the always potentially passive receptor of technologies of reproduction – beginning with language itself and writing but succumbing at length to the magisterial orchestrations of the culture industry.

The difference between these two conceptions might seem profound, but in fact they are versions of the same structure of thought. In the first, the a priori structures of experience condition and control the possibilities of sensate prosthesis. They operate as such outside a historical process that is nonetheless affected in profound ways by the technology through which experience is always mediated. In the second, these a priori structures do not function independently of the technologies through which experience is mediated but rather must be considered as if they were, so that technological prosthesis secretly determines and conditions the a priori itself. What becomes critical is the question of where the grounds of the a priori are situated (a transcendental sphere outside space and time or a historical sphere whose technics make possible radical projections beyond the spatio-temporal coordinates of the empirical world).

Alton's seemingly blithe conjecture can easily enough be accommodated to either of these otherwise incompatible conceptions. But when, with Virilio, we focus on the emergence of photography (in its historical sense), following the peculiar logic of its operation, a different kind of situation emerges. It becomes a matter of identifying this logic as it begins increasingly to direct how the world goes until eventually a new one replaces it. The conception requires a specific condition, according to which the notion of an a priori (a transcendental condition for thought and for perception) drops out of the picture altogether. Cinematic technology is to be understood in terms of its interaction with conditions of perception determined by the workings of the human nervous system and independently of conscious intention. It is not even a question anymore of ideology or conditioning. Again, in *The Vision Machine*, Virilio writes: 'The moment high-speed photography was invented, making cinema a concrete possibility, the problem of the paradoxically real nature of "virtual" imagery was in fact posed' (1994: 61). The virtual image functions, like the so-called mental images of consciousness, by appearing to carry intentionality, according to which an image is always the image *of* something. It therefore serves a 'reality effect'. The world changes by direct manipulation of perception and because it is now dominated and organised by automated images that operate independently of conscious intentionality. The operation of a 'vision machine', a device that retains and reproduces the patterns of light and darkness that it captures, seems from the first to be able to reproduce the operations of consciousness and its mental images. At length, however, it emerges that the technology of the vision machine is capable of more: it produces, in the idiom of the real, an endless repertoire of images that have the status of reality not because they may be said to represent the real as such but because they have at first the same status as the real – deceivingly, they are mental objects no less than any concrete thing – and at length come to usurp even that. The combination of photography (the light sensitive surface) and cinema (rapid successions of images) produces a phenomenal support that cooperates with the human perception system via retinal retention to produce objective spatio-temporal effects. But this support can no longer be identified as such: 'it now emerges in relation to time, *to the exposure time that allows or edits seeing*' (Virilio 1994: 61). The question of the relationship of mental images to reality no longer has the pertinence it once had now the object itself operates in concert with the perceptual system to produce mental images as object effects.

The process occurs independently of the wills of thinking beings that always assumed their experience was at the centre of things, situated between a brute biology and a bio-aesthetic or bio-ethical sphere of values, needs and desires. Nonetheless these thinking beings (which are now accordingly perhaps less than they once were) remain in play as vehicles and agents. We can follow the lines of this still recent history as a photographic logic rather suddenly fades from its own picture and is replaced by the new logic. Accordingly a new picture emerges, which does not represent lost objects for individuals but is *produced* in the real time interactions of an electronic sphere more or less approximate to a reality (of communities determined by their relations) that is thus inevitably transformed.

Regimes of Light

Virilio's *War and Cinema* offers an exploration of photographic technology that identifies in its invention the main characteristics and structures of operation of modern warfare. In this context – and to the extent that we can accept this sometimes bizarre but always compelling approximation – the remarks I've just been analysing from John Alton's book can appear in a different light. Cinema doesn't simply supplement or make up for the absence or loss of a kind of experience that the city has drastically limited. More than this, cinema, considered as a value that governs the entire field, includes both the presentation of the thing lost and the loss itself, the lost-ness of the thing lost. The vacation, to the extent that every now and then a lucky urban inhabitant can take one, is no less a cinematic production than the one normally experienced in the theatre. The vacancy of cinema and that of the vacation are one and the same vacancy. More profoundly, though, and notwithstanding the incidental point that the pictures that so much bear the mark of Alton's cinematography (produced largely between 1932 and 1960) include influential narratives of war, it is possible to see how war itself in this altered sense continues so long as cinema flourishes. Rather the conjunction of two terms war and cinema describes a kind of logic that increasingly dominates the way things go, how they appear and disappear. As I have tried to demonstrate, this logic – the 'paradoxical logic' of machines whose evolution traces the trajectory of photography since its invention in the early decades of the nineteenth century – has less to do with theories of consciousness and perception than it might seem. But it has everything to do with the dominance of technologies whose ubiquitous operational mediation certainly helps to determine the quality and character of the social relation both in fact and in the social imaginary.

The television systems of contemporary war craft are capable of displaying a wide range of poly-temporal and multi-spatial projections and representations, but these rarely take the character of what we might call 'optical images'. The final chapter of *War and Cinema* provides a novel analysis of the conditions, between 1904 (the year of the first searchlight used in war) and 1984 (the publication of the book), on which the electronic image was able to be separated out from a theatre where human observers still played a significant, albeit diminishing, role. The chapter charts an evolution of the light weapon as it increasingly marginalises the role of the human observer. The operation of 'instantaneous, mediated representation' is combined with a growing intensity in the force of automatic weapons, and the combination 'projects', writes Virilio, '*a final image of the world*' (1989 [1984]: 91). The merging of images of dematerialisation (in dematerialised images) and the intimation, in vast bombing missions, of 'total disintegration', is better grasped by cinema than it is by any individual observer charged not with *seeing* but with trying to negotiate electronic data. During this time the pilot's 'double-vision' (heads up for ocular targets/heads down for long-distance vision) was introduced and enhanced (95). The bombings themselves develop inexorably towards the projected disintegration through rapid improvements in technologies of light, to the extent that the balance between defenders and attackers is dependent on the intensity of their respective light sources. The principal defence against night bombing missions, the searchlight ('the blinding light of 200 million candlepower searchlights'), was eventually turned to the advantage of the bomber attacks with the development of the magnesium flare and the electronic flash, 'which allowed USAF

bombers not only to light up the ground but, more importantly, to
dazzle enemy defenses' (96). The vast inhabited cityscapes of the
world are thus simultaneously lit up to intensities far beyond the
capabilities of human perception and disintegrated:

> The Allied air assault on the great European conurbations suddenly
> became a *son-et-lumière*, a series of special effects, an atmospheric
> projection designed to confuse a frightened, blacked out population.
> In dark rooms that fully accorded with the scale of the drama, victims-
> to-be witnessed the most terrifying nighttime fairy theatre, hellish
> displays of an invading cinema that reproduced the Nuremburg archi-
> tecture of light. (97)

Passages like this (of which there are several in this chapter alone)
help to produce a singular yet mobile image: here the arresting
situation in which the architectonics of the most devastating
bombing missions of World War II are described using the lexicon
of the photographic or cinematic studio. Ultimately the blackout
(the darkroom) and the light weaponry (lighting and photography)
produce what Virilio calls a 'cinematic derealization'. Cinema
develops the negative of the intense light attack to produce a world
in images whose paradoxical positivity replaces the disintegrated
or flattened earth as it evolves under constant shifts and changes.
These observations make explicit the intrinsic connection between
an increasingly powerful technology of destruction and an increasingly widespread technology of cinematic images. Beginning with
the Great War, during which 'film replaced military maps', the
attempt to grasp the reality of the shifting landscape forced military tacticians to revert to the sphere of film: 'the industrialization
of the repeating image illustrated this cinematic dimension of
regional-scale destruction, in which landscapes were continuously
upturned and had to be reconstituted with the help of successive
frames and shots' (Virilio 1989 [1984]: 99). So industrial warfare,
prefiguring deterrence, takes the form of cinema, the industrialisa-
tion of the repeating image, thereby reducing devastating bombing
attacks to the 'mystification' of the derealised image.

Once again it is worth noting the subtly aesthetic elements of
Virilio's work. This final chapter, 'A Traveling Shot over Eighty
Years', is in many ways typical, but it is also remarkable at least
in the way in which it piles its examples up each time using the
language of the darkroom and the lexicons of lighting and of

cinematography. It operates in two ways. First, it produces a narrative sequence that features an almost superfluous stream of events: inauspicious beginnings (not only a wartime searchlight but also for instance the death of Étienne-Jules Marey); an unbroken series of intensifications involving an entire range of photographic effects; an earth-shattering climax (the nuclear bombings of 6 and 9 August 1945); and an aftermath in which everything is irreversibly altered and a future of semi-autonomous military machines is projected. Second, it produces this narrative in an ironic mode by adopting rhetorically the statistical techniques it criticises. While informing us that military power, thanks to cinematic derealisation, is established 'in a technological beyond', Virilio seems to be putting the source of that power to work in exposing the situation:

> in this realm sequential perception, like optical phenomena resulting from retinal persistence, is both origin and end of the apprehension of reality, since the seeing of movement is but the statistical process connected with the segmentation of images and the speed of observation characteristic of humans. (1989 [1984]: 99)

The fact that Virilio's 'travelling shot' operates as a potentially dizzying sequence of images ('above all the blinding Hiroshima flash which literally photographed the shadow cast by beings and things, so that every surface immediately became war's *recording* surface, its *film*', 85) suggests that the best way of approaching this otherwise unapproachable realm is through the very techno-logistics through which it operates.

The situation recalls the story that Frederick Talbot tells, again in his *Moving Pictures*, to illustrate the effectiveness of cinematography when a sequence of images is projected at sufficient speed. A travelling shot was set up so that a unit could film a train speeding through a tunnel from a second train. A problem, though, was encountered with the question of where the necessary light was to come from in the darkness of the length of the tunnel. The film unit solved this problem by taking a sequence of still photographs each time using a flashlight as the train was moved forward in stages for 50 or so shots, which were then multiplied in order to produce the desired length of film. The charade disappears on playback, during which the film presents a beautifully lit train speeding through a tunnel: 'When projected on the screen several hundred photographs were passed before the audience at the speed of sixteen pictures per second, and the semblance of motion was perfect' (1914: 9). The travelling shot is thus yet again joyfully revealed as a sequence of numerous partial events simulating a reality that never happened. It is as if we love the illusion for its technical ingenuity rather than for the illusion itself. But the real bombs in Virilio's narrative reach their apotheosis with those dropped on Hiroshima and Nagasaki. Those bombs, as Virilio points out, 'were *light-weapons* that prefigured the enhanced-radiation neutron bomb, the directed beam laser weapons and the charged-particle guns currently under development' (1989 [1984]: 101). The probable future of military technology will follow the logic of the light weapon, a logic that can be revealed through ironic techniques that replicate this logic and that keep a kind of perverse faith with 'retinal persistence' and the 'speed of human observation of movement'. As Lucretius taught, though, we cannot blame the eye for these unnerving effects.

References

Alton, John (1995), *Painting with Light*, Berkeley: University of California Press.

Aristotle (1995), *The Complete Works of Aristotle*, ed. Jonathan Barnes, Princeton: Princeton University Press.

Lucretius (1994), *On the Nature of the Universe*, trans. R. E. Latham, revd John Godwin, London: Penguin Classics.

Talbot, Frederick A. (1914), *Moving Pictures: How They are Made and Worked*, London: Heinemann.

Virilio, Paul (1989 [1984]), *War and Cinema: The Logistics of Perception*, trans. Patrick Camiller, London: Verso.

Virilio, Paul (1994 [1975]), *Bunker Archeology*, trans. George Collins, New York: Princeton Architectural Press.

Virilio, Paul (1994), *The Vision Machine*, trans. Julie Rose, London: BFI Publishing.

Virilio, Paul (2006 [1977]), *Speed and Politics: An Essay on Dromology*, trans. Mark Polizzotti, New York: Semiotext(e).

7

History in the '*Mise en Abyme* of the Body': Ranbir Kaleka and the 'Art of Auschwitz' after Virilio

Tania Roy

> After that, what is left of Adorno's pompous pronouncement about *the impossibility of writing a poem* after AUSCHWITZ? Not much at the end of the day, for everything . . . at the turn of a pitiless and endlessly catastrophic century . . . went up in the blast . . . (Virilio 2003: 30)

In *Art and Fear* (2003), Paul Virilio presents a speculative account of European art history for which 'contemporary' visual art practices feature as both symptom and end. *Art and Fear*'s terminal art history might be positioned metonymically, in its wider relation to Virilio's various philosophical histories of optical acceleration, which link technologies of temporal compression and the subsequent elision of geopolitical distance, to the total militarisation of perception. Notably, *Art and Fear* advances its now-scandalous excoriation of contemporary new media and performance art by placing the 'contemporary', *tout court*, under the sign of what comes 'after Auschwitz'. Citing T. W. Adorno's injunction against the writing of poetry after Auschwitz – without, however, paraphrasing its significance within Adorno's own text – Virilio's own overused conflation of 'poetry', 'art' and 'Auschwitz' might be approached symptomatically, as signalling an implicit investment in *fin-de-siècle* narratives of European aftermath.

Rather than approaching Virilio's specific contentions about the status of contemporary new-media art directly, I return *Art and Fear*'s implicitly Eurocentric account of aesthetic obsolescence to a reading of Adorno's own reflections on the possibilities of a properly post-Holocaustal aesthetic – one that would come *after* chronologies of cultural origin/extinction have themselves been exhausted. It is easily demonstrable that Virilio inscribes his art criticism with an embarrassingly belated articulation of humanism, yet the real force of Virilio's critical history resides precisely in its argument from 'anachronism'. *Art and Fear*'s reference to 'Auschwitz', at once motivic and dismissive, is itself figurative of the redundancy of historical memory. In other words, *Art and Fear* indicts the history of visual art in a 'contemporaneity' that, rather than representing the historical event, *simulates* its *ad infinitum*: the suffering body has outlived both its corporeal and historical death, appearing 'endlessly', today, in the 'telematic . . . ubiquity' of the corpse (Virilio 2007: 9–10).

Reading works such as *The Aesthetics of Disappearance* (2009) and *Art as Far as the Eye Can See* (2007) with and against Virilio's *fin-de-siècle* history of art, I propose that Virilio points to new-media contexts that reside beyond the geopolitical horizons of Continental Europe and North America. After Virilio, I argue that the speed and sonority of images name the very process of cultural globalisation that allows for the possibility of *a de-territorialised art of Auschwitz*. Accordingly, the discussion engages New Delhi based painter and video-artist Ranbir Kaleka's monumental dedication to the Shoah, elliptically entitled *Consider* (2007). Commissioned as a permanent installation by the Spertus Institute of Jewish Studies in Chicago, the work develops Kaleka's previous, pioneering works of 'video-painting', a form that rehearses not only the putative disappearance of painting within the Indian art historical context, but the painterly act itself, which, through movements of loss and recuperation, negotiates the ephemerality of the human form. Positioning Kaleka's work within an extended account of the in/corporealised digital image as developed out of a reading of Virilio, Benjamin and Adorno, I conclude with a defence of the virtual, or putatively 'derealised' dimensions of historical experience. In presenting the image as a memory trace of an event *that may no longer be lived*, Kaleka's art confronts the viewer with an ethics of consideration; one that accounts for the felt weight of absence within the historical present. Kaleka recasts the deracinated image, in its increasing dislocation from any material trace or physical embodiment of the past, into a legitimate domain of historiographical contestation.

Post-Memory: Art and Trauma

I am stuck on this word . . . I know we can read it in different ways, we can give it a variety of accents: there is the acute of the

present, the grave accent of history, and the circumflex (marking
length) of eternity. Art – 'oh, art!' – beside being changeable, has
the gift of ubiquity. (Celan 2003: 40)

After the issue of instantaneity's lack of delay, here we have
the issue of ubiquity's distance: only the perspective is reversed:
what now counts is not the vanishing point in the real space of
a scene or landscape, but only vanishing in the face of death and
its question mark – the interrogation point – in a perspective of
real time used and abused by the cathode screen with live broad-
casting offering 'death live' and an endless funeral procession of
repeat disasters. (Virilio 2007: 9–10)

The oracular force of Paul Virilio's disparate histories of technological acceleration, globalisation and the extirpation of temporal experience 'after Auschwitz' are remarkable not least for the
staged monotony of their pronouncements. At once revelatory
and violently immobile in their rehearsed conclusions, Virilio's
insights are seized – 'at the end of the day', as it were – by the
ubiquity of a 'pitiless' if historically unsurpassable ending to the
twentieth century (Virilio 2003: 31). For Virilio, such a passing
signifies a historical present marked, above all, by the ascendancy
of deterritorialised regimes of combat and their intimate correla-
tives in the 'retinally detached' optical media of everyday life (such
as the video camera, the holograph, the televisual interface and
their escalated mobilisation in the portable device). In these incor-
porealising perceptual technologies, 'representative reflection' is
'exterminate[ed] . . . in favour of that panic reflex', the baleful
'lack of delay' associated with globalised conditions of telematic
'instantaneity' (31).

Rehabilitating the stricken figure of the epileptic for such a
historical present, *The Aesthetics of Disappearance* (2009) is especially memorable for staging both the irony and immeasurable
pathos of such a conclusion. Normalising the 'lapse' of corporeal
and experiential integrity brought on by the epileptic crisis, Virilio
proposes that the self is effectively *individuated* through the very
instant that remains outside the technologically compressed horizons of contemporary experience.

The return being just as sudden as the departure, the arrested word
and action are picked up again where they have been interrupted.

Conscious time comes together again automatically, forming a continuous time without apparent breaks . . . However for the picnoleptic, nothing really has happened, the missing time never existed. At each crisis, without realizing it, a little of his or her life simply escaped. (Virilio 2009: 19)

The shard of an evacuated or absent perception – that unregistered instance of a 'little' loss of 'life' – remains entirely unsymbolisable within the structures of an accelerated present. Putting Virilio's thesis somewhat differently, and against the grain of its own positioning, we might say that consciousness lives through an event that it fails, nonetheless, *to experience*. With each heightened iteration, the intrusion of sight brings together an increasingly compressed, uninterrupted present; by the same token, the 'sudden' yet ubiquitous 'return' of present time is occasioned by an imperceptible *delay* between seeing and knowing. At stake, then, is the structure of a *temporal inconsistency* – alternately negligible and disastrous in the account of crisis, above – that remains un-'realiz[ed]' at the heart of 'conscious' experience. Despite its compression into inexistence, the fabricated immediacy of the present turns on a logic of belatedness. Indeed, for Virilio himself, the temporal remainder, or the formative 'vanishing' point in consciousness, *survives* or suffers a return to the present only to the extent that it may be de-particularised, homogenised or, in effect, brutalised into the deathly technological formalisms of the '*live presentation* and *performance*' (2007: 8; 2003: 31; emphasis in original). It is an inexistent presence, then, that returns to consciousness through the mediated '*nothing really . . . happened*' of 'continuous' time. In its wholly manipulable, technologised afterlife, missing experience becomes constitutive of a prosthetically, or telematically rehabilitated consciousness.

It is possible, then, to approach the non-event of what has gone mortally missing from the Virilian present in terms of the vocabulary and concerns of contemporary trauma studies, as both the symptom and occasion of an especially 'traumatic awakening' into history (Caruth 1996: 92). The approach, in turn, modifies Caruth's powerful trope for the fraught phenomenological and ethical status of *witnessing* by extending this concern towards the *inassimilable domain of images*; which, in failing to appear *as* a comprehensible image of the past, violently inscribes the limit of optical 'consciousness' through accelerated episodes of collapse/recovery. De-referentialised from space and time, and in full indifference to their depictive content, the dispersed structure of 'opto-electronic' images appear, then, as the traces of deferred or perpetually *prior* violence (Virilio 2000: 16). To begin to place Virilio's account of the visual event at its intersection with the ostensibly obsolete vocabulary of trauma, it is necessary to underscore how *The Aesthetics of Disappearance* posits a historical (if immanently unrepresentable) relation between the dissipation of embodied, architectonic space and the origins of optical 'consciousness' in a catastrophic loss of tradition. In *The Aesthetics of Disappearance*, the dissolution of built, three-dimensional space is coterminous with the cultural extirpation of Western European traditions of the public domain, associated with the *polis*, *agora* and *forum*. The trajectory of such cultural vanishing is 'motored' by the advent of cinema. In an immense historical paradox, the screen, or that 'luminous' interface between two-dimensional images and the shared *habitus* of a built environment, serves as the very locus of cinema's own historical disappearance. Anne Friedberg suggests that it is from the point of such acute historical exigency that Virilio's text initiates (and justifies) its deliberate elision of the differences *between* historical and material types of screens. As such, Virilio's 'history' of the screen textually stages the manner in which picnoleptic blankness – the ambiguous relief of invisibility that operated micrologically *between* frames, shots or scenes – disappears entirely to produce new registers of appearance (Friedberg 2004).

Recent reflections on the virtualisation of experience in its implications for the unresolved traces and weight of historical violence have recuperated Walter Benjamin's essay on 'Art in the Age of Mechanical Reproduction' (1969 [1936]) in its idiosyncratic uses of Freud and the foundational psychoanalytic concept of shock. Allen Meek, in particular, traces a cluster of related essays from the 1930s in which Benjamin posed the temporal ellipse of perception (marked by the affect of 'distraction') as both wound and analgesic defence against the unprecedented intensities and volatilised shocks of metropolitan, machinist modernity. In the essay 'On Some Motifs in Baudelaire' (2003 [1939]), Benjamin rehabilitated Henri Bergson's insight into the insuperable split between experience and Bergson's identification of the 'cinematographic' form of (all) technologically mediated images; the temporal and material incommensurability of an immanently missing past and extant image-forms effectively *incorporealises* lived experience (Meek 2007). Indeed, to extend Meek's claims further to Benjamin's specific proposition on the 'work of art' for trauma in new-media contexts, we may note that for Benjamin, such dematerialisation was registered *within* the field of representation, as the very imperative of *form* within the imagistic medium. In privileging volatilised experience [*Erfahrung*], which was necessarily postponed from brutally reified accounts of the event [*Erlebnis*], Benjamin advanced an *aesthetic* affirmation of the resonant discrepancy between a temporally deferred memory, and the excisional frames of dominant representation (thereby also rescuing Bergson's philosophical nostalgia from its implication of the inauthenticity of visually mediated experience). In this, the Bergsonian account of the image *not as representation but as a belated, fully dematerialised memory trace* was brought to bear on Freud's reflections on shock in *Beyond the Pleasure Principle* (1919). For Freud, the example of (the industrial) 'accident' illustrated the lag between an annihilatory event and the standpoint of a survival that fails to *take in, on time* its origins in such an event. In Benjamin's appropriation, the repetition of 'missing experience' – the compulsive claim of an unresolved past under conditions of technological acceleration – disabled consciousness even as it generatively 'recorded' historical rupture, difference and change. Accordingly, the priority of an originary, and in this sense, catastrophic violence *inscribes* the image-space with the traces of a metonymically displaced resolution. Conversely, in this traumatic displacement of violence, missing, mediated or dynamically virtual experience remains unnamed – thereby disclosing the *actuality* of alternative registers of historical experience, in immanently unrealised spaces, figures and affects. In proposing the actuality of an insubstantial image-space, I suggest that dimensions of 'virtual memory' might open up a space for contesting hegemonic interpretations of trauma, which reactively emplace the hyperpresence of the violated body or the redundancy of its death (in the ubiquity of the corpse) within the imaginary of a singular national crisis.

In his final completed work, 'Theses on the Philosophy of History' (1969 [1940]), Benjamin alluded again to historically emergent modes of *spectatorial* agency, which were themselves linked to the unpredictable formal and spatial movements of the work, as discussed earlier, in his celebratory if ambiguous embrace

of the image in 'Art in the Age of Mechanical Reproduction'.
One might argue that the contentions of that essay are radicalised
in this final work: Benjamin establishes the method of a critical
historiographical *praxis* in the dynamic interaction between de-
spatialised registers of reception, and the intensities of the work
of dis/appearance. The spectator is charged with 'seizing' traumatically unsettling images just in order to mobilise these traces of
'irretrievable' temporal dispossession and spatial migrancy against
dominant interpretations of events of the past (Benjamin 1969
[1940]: 254; Meek 2007). In salvaging the migratory memory
trace from its pauperisation by conventional, chronological histo-
riography, Benjamin's 'Theses' takes on a powerfully contemporary resonance.

Even as recent commentaries out of the areas of media and
trauma theory instate the ubiquity of *Benjamin* in their own
concerns, such a development is significant for returning the question of authentic experience and the claims of historical memory
– especially as it appears in the figure and possibility of artistic
witnessing – to its vexed intimacy with the long history of technological de-realisation and mediation in the twentieth century.
This, however, is an opening that Virilio's texts ineluctably, and
quite precisely, foreclose. Repetition signified both pathology and
a measure of emancipation within the theoretical apparatus of
trauma within Freud's reflections on the aftermath of the Great
War. In Benjamin's account of an unimaginable heightening
of repetition through technological iterability, memory *remains*
'unconscious' to the formal degree that it exceeds the space of
compressed representational time; hence, as Benjamin argues in
'On Some Motifs in Baudelaire', the intrusion of the optical device
into the event of disappearance displaces the latter into the traces
of 'posthumous shock' (2003 [1939]: 328). For Virilio, however,
conditions of totalised acceleration leave no space for immanent,
spectralised modes of recovery. Pointedly, Virilio cites Karl Kraus
(satirist of both information culture and talk-therapy) 'on the
subject of PSYCHOANALYSIS, only this time *apropos*' of an
inertial, de-subjectified and so depthless 'consciousness' (2007:
23). Absorbing the entirety of the psychoanalytic concept of
trauma into the block-lettered prose of immersive panic, Virilio's
'TOPOANALYSIS of globalization' comprises the singular trope
for an economy of virtual loss-in-presence; wherein embodied
experience is technologically de-realised and disavowed *as* a dis-

appearance even as its image remains interactively present(able), or 'pornographically' accessible at all times (2003: 35) . Here, the question of an aesthetic medium, as retained by Benjamin in his treatment of the image not as representation but as the law of formal incommensurability, is rendered oxymoronic: within the geographically de-specified, fully immersive space of the image, 'consciousness' *integrally* 'enters' into image so that, in Virilio's words, the aesthetic is utterly 'lost sight of' (Palmer 2007; Virilio and Armitage 2011: 38).

In *Art and Fear* as in *Art as Far as the Eye Can See*, this 'abrupt' (perceptual, historical) interpellation of the individual into de-spatialised or purely presentational regimes of 'real-time' is coterminous with Virilio's account of the twentieth century's ending. Such a historical end comprises no less than an onto-logical event: by annihilating the experience of temporal duration altogether, exponentially accelerated, portable and atopic regimes of perception extirpate experience *proper*. As an inherently ter-roristic event, this 'immense' historical passing renders the lived civilities of 'tact and contact' – those phenomenological precondi-tions for distance, for taking a perspective, or, what is the same, exercising an aesthetic and ethical judgement – 'endlessly' or *chronically* obsolete (Virilio and Armitage 2011: 38; Virilio 2007: 8). It is within this chronology of integral disaster that I now turn to Virilio's peculiar appeal to the figure of poetry, in the allusion to 'Adorno' and 'Celan'. Comprising the self-abolishing features of the artwork within the parameters of Virilio's 'topoanalysis' of the image-space, these anxiously addressed figures assert only, and endlessly, the work's *inability to survive* the turn of the twentieth century (Virilio 2007: 10; cited above).

Art and the Time of Catastrophe

Late-works are the catastrophes in the history of art. (Adorno 2002 [1937]: 567)

From within this stacked history of ruin, Virilio advances a linear periodisation of twentieth-century art history. In a prefatory gesture, Virilio privileges the 'demonstrative' or gestural paintings of the fifteenth and sixteenth centuries that figuratively render the full atrocity of war for a viewer, who is communally inter-pellated into such scenes through the affect of compassion. The *obsolescence* of such a representational tradition is fully accomplished by the Great War, which 'drag[s] down' Impressionism, that last repository of an aesthetics of pity, into the subsequent panic of World War II and German Expressionism (Virilio 2003: 54; 2007: 7). With Expressionism and the inaugural, incremental demise of 'representation', the human figure (and its erstwhile centrality to Western European painterly traditions) is episodically de-formed and eventually eclipsed by purely presentational (and properly form-less) visuality. Indeed, the 'planetary foreclosure' of the gap between art and corporeally suffered existence, figure and ground, is consummately accomplished in the 'particular avant-garde of terrorism, whose advent the television series brings to the light of day, in the place and space of antique tragedy'. The targeted city exemplifies the 'total social event' of aesthetics/terror. Rendered immobile by the very technologies of surveillance, traceability and media-visibility that comprise post-industrial space, the city is fed, in an unbroken image-loop, the terrifying accident of its planetary exposure (Virilio 2007: 12, 4).

As such, the eviscerating abstractions of the Euro-American avant-garde (as it moves forward from the Situationists, Viennese Actionism and the spliced non/human figures of the early Rothko) comprise the single, catastrophic register of the leap from territorialised modes of warfare (whose logic emerged from the economy and the state) to advanced regimes of combat, marked by technologies of incorporealisation and transgenic control, de-spatialisation and totalised fear. Virilio's synecdochal histories of art-for-fear are perhaps especially provocative for interrogating the reasons and historical status of the disappearance of a European avant-garde, whose mutilated forms – despite themselves – *materialised* the historical predication of artistic form in war, bureaucratised death and the muted sentient knowledges of such cruelty. Replacing this trajectory to become indistinguishable from terroristic presentation, contemporary art – especially in the modalities of body art and new-media installations – instantiates the most recent and terminally conclusive 'jump' in Virilio's chronology.

I insist we talk of *contemporary* art and not modern art . . . For me, art lost something of itself during the war-torn twentieth century . . . The tragedy of contemporary art is also a global tragedy . . . being part of a world of instantaneity, contemporary art has literally been lost sight of. What is contemporary about contemporary art is that art no longer has a *place*, just like those ancient uninhabited cities no longer have a place. (Virilio and Armitage 2011: 38)

Epochless and atopic, 'contemporaneity' signifies the end of the historiographic count altogether. In the analogy to a ruined, uninhabitable origin, 'art' or 'the *mis-en-abyme* of the body, the figure' names the disappearance of history as such (Virilio 2003: 35).

Accordingly, *Art and Fear* renders the suicidal figure of poetry (Celan) interchangeable with the banality of its perpetual superannuation (Adorno) in a terroristic present. Nevertheless, and despite the manifest embarrassment of having run their historical course, poetry, *like the ineffable figure of trauma*, continues metonymically to link 'art' to 'Auschwitz' within Virilio's *own* excoriation of contemporary new-media art. Virilio's sustained polemic against the totalisation of an insubstantial or 'accidental art' – one that dematerialises all modalities of representation to thereby sacrifice the faculty of embodied judgement at the altar of digitalised panic – stands in tension with the registers of its displaced *ethical* force. Paraphrasing John Armitage's extensive and searching defences of Virilio's aesthetics, we might say that such rhetorical tension makes for a powerfully exhortative structure of address; indeed, it is possible to read works such as *The Aesthetics of Disappearance* together with those explicit interventions into aesthetic theory, *Art and Fear* and *Art as Far as the Eye Can See*, in order to reconstruct Virilio's voice as comprising a coherent if oblique rhetorical appeal to contemporary representatives of new-media art in globalised contexts of production, exhibition and circulation. Accordingly, Virilio's aesthetics constitute a repetitive and, in my view, especially melancholic appeal to art-practitioners to return to the historically disappeared or 'evacuated space of the art of representation' so that they might recapture, once more, and in their disparate institutional and historical locations, '*the space of the symbolic yet crucially sympathetic image of violence*' (Armitage 2003: 7; emphasis mine).

The merits of such a defence notwithstanding, it is the case that for both Adorno and Celan – as it is emphatically *not* for Virilio – the putative 'impossibility' of poetry stages the moral prohibition of 'sympathetic' or mimetic representations of suffering *as such*, thereby salvaging the Semitic ban or *Darstellungsverbot* on 'images' for a post-secular aftermath marked by the literal loss of the (cultural) other. However, in the self-negating force of its *assertoric imperative*, art reflects the self-abolishing movement of its own denial. First proposed in the 1951 essay, 'Cultural Criticism and Society', Adorno was to rewrite this statement in several places over the course of his post-war *oeuvre*. In its original assertion, the thesis referred to the predicament of reflexive thought as formalised in the institutional fate of criticism 'today' (in the immediate aftermath of Auschwitz). The forced synthesis of culture and barbarism in the present is mirrored in the *mise en abyme* of critical reflection. Here, Adorno identified something of the conditions of Virilian ubiquity (both indicate the loss of a modal criterion for judgement that, arguably, continues to 'afflict' the vocation of art criticism, especially in the context and politics of altered conditions of reception and transmission). With every effort to disentangle itself from barbarism, 'culture' finds that it is *immersively present* within the history and *techne* of violence. Within these final stages of the historical dialectic, the very investigation into 'why it has become impossible to write poetry today' becomes self-obviating: in the crossed circuits of commoditised sentimentality and the traumatically deferred weight of national responsibility, the ontological account of a 'loss of meaning' becomes meaninglessly clichéd.

In *Negative Dialectic* (1981 [1966]), Adorno asserts yet again that it is barbaric to be concerned about art when the historical exigencies of the present turn on questions of bare-life or survival (hence rendering the question of art both irrelevant and literally possible); in its assertoric register, the statement appears as a variation of the terminal chronological assumptions underlying Virilio's art history, yet the aporetic structure of Adorno's thesis continues to entwine art with historical impossibility. If Kant's categorical imperative returns in this work as the conditions of possibility for the demand that 'Auschwitz . . . not repeat itself', poetry cannot exempt itself from such critical, 'extra-aesthetic' responsibility (1981 [1966]: 364). By the same token, this injunctive condition of possibility becomes, integrally, its own: to 'respect the imperative is to require that lyric poetry, as it has been known, must cease to exist' (Caygill 2008: 71). In the fractional remainder between the sense that poetry does not exist and that it *should* not exist, as developed by Caygill, *Negative Dialectic* might be seen to restage the categorical imperative textually. Within the shifting accents and inconsistent grammatical moods of this situation, 'poetry' emerges from Adorno's *oeuvre* as an inhumanised, intransitive subject – one that exists in the obscene breach of its 'grammatical' condition of possibility. And it is from here that Celan identified the lyrical dimensions of art as such; the 'poem' runs as a 'counter-word' [*Gegenwort*] *within* the sovereign 'theatricality' of art. If death always happens in my stead, to an other who disappears (as it were) *before* me, then 'art' spectacularises such non-presence, turning it into the basis of a politically meaningful, inter-subjective experience. The lyrical counter-form, however, 'cuts the reins of the old warhorse' of mimesis, emancipating the image from political theatre (Celan 2003: 39). In other words, the lyrical *temporalises* the simulated continuity of visual experience, running athwart the 'scenes' that close over the fundamentally incomprehensible death of another. The unnameable ethical event – which both antedates and constitutes the subject's existence – enters into the very image of the present.

If, as Adorno claims, works persist in breach of their historical parameters as 'catastrophes' in the history of art, it is because they explode the notion of 'catastrophe' *as* historical ending (Adorno 2002 [1937]: 567). Afterness, then, emerges as a generative *failure* of art's preconditions: following Timothy Bewes, for Adorno, the 'periodizing hypothesis is abolished as such by the forms in which it is expressed, along with the categories of cultural decline, subjective expression, death as calamity, and linear temporality itself' (Bewes 2011: 86). Further, the temporalising force of the claim to aesthetic impossibility opposes its 'positivist' appropriation by words and images, as exemplified (perhaps strategically) by Virilio's precipitous histories of disaster; which both refuse and sentimentalise 'impossibility' through its sloganised or 'wholehearted adoption' (86).

In his 1957 radio address to a national audience, entitled 'On Lyric Poetry and Society', Adorno points to the work of the decidedly non-modern Eduard Mörike to suggest that the poetic image is marked, in the historical present, as an inherently belated form: in the spectral unity of (Weimar) humanism and (Biedermeier) social reality, Mörike writes from a synthetic 'high style' that has no material referent in the present, and which, in its de-substantiated appearance, discloses itself as already historically inaccessible. In his imagistic description of Mörike's 'tact', Adorno suggests that the lyric reposes at that intermedial crossing of fading aural traces of 'immediate life' and a visual presence that emerges, through the trajectory of an increasingly ungrounded gaze, at the precipitous edge of these sonorised traces of 'surviving memory' (Adorno 1991 [1957]: 49). Indeed, Mörike's lyric voice elliptically addresses the velocity of the industrial with which its own time is confronted: when not turned in impossible dedication toward a Romantic past, the lyric-idea 'flashes out abruptly' in a volatile trajectory from the very conditions of its historical foreclosure, in escalated, automatic approximation of information and reportage that constitutes contemporary journalism (50). If, for Adorno, the lyrical word survives as a dematerialised memory trace in both aural and visual images, such an idea is at once conventional (as the after-image of 'high style') and radically prescient (in its affirmation of an active, spectatorial gaze that attends new technologies, and which serves as a precondition for 'lyrical subjectivity'). It is beyond the scope of this chapter to recount the debt as well as implicit riposte that such an idea poses to Benjamin's embrace of the revolutionary potential of a collective spectatorial agent, which, together with the new velocities of an immersive image-space, was to terminate the bourgeois prerogative of individual (private) freedom as found in the work's traditional claim to distance. Here, we might extend Daniel Palmer's comparison of the experience of 'contemplative immersion' in Benjamin and Adorno to the latter's account of lateness (Palmer 2007: 6). Adorno retains the value of duration associated with the traditional artwork precisely to the degree that the experience of temporal extension through a 'contemplative immersion' in the work is activated *posthumously*, in processes of displacement and de-substantiation – that is, in the work's opening to the perspective of a historically unanticipated, spatially distant viewership. Between the 'aesthetic experience that becomes living experience *only by way of its object*' and the 'processual quality' of the object itself, the work preserves the gaze while de-prioritising its optical sovereignty, thereby actualising the coordinates of another, spectral space (Adorno 1997: 175–6; emphasis mine).

Virilio's motivic yet wholly dismissive reference to Adorno – to a de-spatialised, non-periodising and inter-animative 'aesthetics of Auschwitz' – takes on a strikingly equivocal function. Raising the possibility of a post-historical aesthetic just in order to foreclose it, Virilio's text circumvents the very question of an art that might be proper to the repetitive 'finality' of his historical moment – a moment in which temporal experience is both acutely accelerated and immobilised, for which chronologies of historical progress (or regression) and attendant narratives of cultural ascendancy and exhaustion *have themselves become obsolete.* 'Art', then, appears as the 'word' upon which Virilio's incantatory appeal to an 'endlessly catastrophic' historical ending becomes 'stuck' (Virilio 2003: 31; Celan 2003: 41). Reading Virilio symptomatically, I suggest that the demand for an enlarged aesthetics manifests a deep, if implicit attachment to (European) *fin-de-siècle* narratives of cultural disappearance. The putatively 'vanished' correspondence between forms ('tact', bespeaking silence) and corporeally lived experience (the suffering of 'contact') bears the burden of Virilio's terminal chronology. As such, the figure of art – in the redundant or suicidal 'poem' – emerges through the contradictory force of its appeal, as simultaneously anachronistic and inexorcisable from Virilio's text.

Ranbir Kaleka and an Other Art of 'Auschwitz'

As a space of an event, the actual happening of an event, when art happens, that happens outside the frame of the painting. There are indications, there are gestures, there is a trajectory from the eye travelling from one point to the other, but . . . then we have to close our eyes and let the event happen. (Kaleka in an interview with Michael Worgotter; Saffron Art Gallery 2011: 7)

Nobody can tell how long the pause for breath – for hope and thought – will last. Speed, which has always been 'outside', has gained yet more speed. The poem knows this, yet heads straight for the 'otherness' which it considers it can reach and be free. (Celan 2003: 48)

The apparently seamless intrusion of sight into the space of missing experience remains invisible to an artificially synthesised consciousness. But to say this is also to extend the problem beyond the question of what can (no longer) be seen or known, to the generation of failure arising from an *originary lag* at the heart of 'automatic' seeing. Virilio suppresses this possibility; nevertheless, the question may be posed through its own temporal inconsistencies. How might we encounter Virilio's totalised history of new-media art practices in contexts that, in historical fact, arrive *late* to post-industrial culture? My reading of the work of the prominent Delhi-based new-media artist Ranbir Kaleka repositions Virilio's wholesale excoriation of new-media art and exhibition practices through the dislocating perspective of lateness (as generated out of a socio-economic context of uneven development). Further, Kaleka's art *takes the measure* of Virilio's text, temporalising and displacing the implicitly anachronistic (and restorative) function of narratives of cultural and historical extirpation that Virilio hyperbolises; but which ground, less obviously, both intuitive and scholarly oppositions between 'authentic' modalities of memory in their relationship to geospatially located experience, and the inexistent claims of virtual memory.

In the case of post-liberalised India, the ascendancy of new, intermedial art practices in the past 15 years, as well as their established visibility within globalised circuits of exhibition and funding marks a categorical break with longer, emphatically national histories of artistic modernism. Yet, from the point of view of both formal and ideological concerns, it might be argued that such an outstripped history of national-modernism returns as a vexed historical claim upon the work of representative figures of contemporary new-media work. Historically, the value of aesthetic 'progressivism' (as well as its constitutive inversion in the invention of post/colonial 'traditions') was predicated upon the very discursive legacies that it sought to contest or displace. The diversity of its forms and genealogies notwithstanding, modernism in post-Independent India emerged as an intervention into the progressivist horizons of Nehruvian modernity. Until the mid-1990s, statist conceptions of 'development', 'progress' and a 'popular' subject of history oriented a dominant national self-understanding; these ideas presupposed (even while negating) older, imperial chronologies that posited a temporal and material *lag* between metropolitan and post/colonial experience. With market liberalisation and India's precipitate if belated entry into capitalist systems of production and consumption, the state ceded its historical role as the moral and institutional guardian of secular, progressive development. An exponential increase in the growth and mobility of India's highly professionalised middle classes coincided with escalated episodes of inter-sectarian conflict and the vertiginous rise of Hindu super-nationalism (an ideology that has since been fully normalised and is represented today, by the main opposition party and the official right). With the explosion of privatised 24/7 televisual news channels, however, the media have come to constitute a ubiquitous para-statal authority that diurnally interpellates a grossly over-represented middle-/upper-middle-class minority (the main target audience of hegemonic English channels) into the fugitive presence of a national 'people'. Virilio's association of the disappearance of representative politics into the 'lay decide' of telematic instantaneity resonates powerfully with the Indian experience of market liberalisation, in which the imperatives of a new directional history takes over from the discourse of post-colonial 'development'. The news-media's ability to convert a hegemonic socio-economic claim into the totalised presence of 'civil society' marks, in turn, the entry of peripheralised modernities into the Virilian itinerary of the 'circum terreste'; here, a global spectator tracks events in real time and 'identifies', full circle, with a present excised of every trace of developmental lag (2007: 28).[1] In short, Virilio's overarching account of the crisis of the 'contemporary' may be further specified through the continuing distortions of uneven growth, even as these persist within the experience of an apparently synchronous 'global' present.[2] In this context, it is significant that the rapid delinking of the state from markets (including art markets) in the 1990s generated unprecedented international interest in India's traditions of modernist visual art. The delayed 'discovery' of an Indian metropolitan art initiated a generational shift towards experimental gallery-based practices and intermedial work, underwriting praxial developments that a previously small domestic market could not have sustained. Read through the Indian context, new-media art and installation practices might be recuperated from Virilio's levelling charge of 'obscen[e] . . . ubiquity' insofar as these fraught historical developments are retained materially, in the very occasion of the work, as its formal and institutional 'condition of possibility' (2007: 11).

Ranbir Kaleka's meditations on post-historical experience exemplify an aesthetic possibility affirmed by Adorno, in a context that remains, nonetheless, unimaginable for the latter; it is a possibility that Virilio refuses altogether. Kaleka's aesthetic demonstrates how 'new'-media art forms may be accomplished as late-works – works in which the very category of 'lateness' is abolished by the forms through which it is expressed. Kaleka's images expose the periodising hypothesis that secretly informs Virilio's histories of catastrophic decline and disaster, troped, as these are, by the world-historical redundancy of 'Auschwitz'. But they also conflate such a fin-de-siècle narrative with the corrosive legacies of resurgent nationalism elsewhere, which turn today on the globalist fantasy of a temporally integrated present.[3]

After having studied art at the Punjab University in Chandigarh, Ranbir Kaleka left the country in 1985, returning, at the end of the 1990s, with an MFA in painting from the Royal College of Art. Settled in the capital, the 57-year-old British citizen was until recently identified largely as a 'Delhi-based' artist. Unusual for his slowness in producing and assembling works for exhibition, Kaleka's first solo show in the country in 1995 in Delhi was followed up only a decade later, in a highly visible exhibit entitled 'Crossings' at the Bose Pacia Gallery in New York. Prominent within a prolific and somewhat younger cohort of new-media artists in India today, Kaleka's unique *oeuvre* of video-painting has achieved an exceptional degree of international saliency in the decade since. It is worth noting that in the hiatus between his departure and return to Delhi, Kaleka had worked to national acclaim with oil and mixed media painting on both canvas and paper, in a remarkable body of works that drew from the vein of remembered origins in Punjab. Setting up vertiginous juxtapositions of cockerels, wrestlers and horses (fleshly motifs that inform in his trans-medial work as phantasmagorical recurrences), Kaleka's paintings have been characterised as achieving a 'near-apocalyptic' celebration of the mutational threshold between inhumanised figuration, a depictive interest in '*outré* inventions' and a painterly 'absorption with light' effected through academic, highly controlled uses of pigment (Dang 2011). Notably, Kaleka left the country even as he established his work firmly within pre-liberalised traditions of late-modernist easel painting. Within this biographical context, it is extraordinary that Kaleka's contemporary work, almost entirely in the modality of video-painting, was exhibited within the parameters of a consolidated survey only in 2010–11 by private gallerists in Delhi and Mumbai, first in the solo show entitled 'Sweet Unease' in Mumbai (Volte Gallery 2011) and then in Delhi ('Fables', Volte Gallery and Saffron Art Gallery).

In the collusion between the projected and painted interfaces of 'video-painting', Kaleka's arrangements are meticulous in resisting a pluralisation of image-forms and media. Indeed, the obdurate return of painting in the new-media space might rehearse narratives relating the supersession of modernism, initiated in the 1990s, *as*, paradoxically, the condition of possibility for 'art'/'painting' in the present. The posthumous claim of painting is perhaps most pressing in the richly coloured, easel-mounted 'Man Threading Needle' (1998–9) (Figure 7.1), reworked, in muted tones, in 'He

Figure 7.1 Ranbir Kaleka, *Man Threading Needle* (1998–9).

Was a Good Man' (2008). Six-minute loops of sound accompany a single-channel projection that passes over the painting, whose depiction of intense visual effort is moved, almost imperceptibly, through aural traces of 'immediate life' and 'surviving memory' (the image-artefact becomes heavy with the non-diegetic rhythms of belaboured breathing; or, is as persistent as the distant sound of peacocks, piercingly reminiscent of inaccessible North Indian summers; or, becomes prone to distraction in the interruption of approaching police sirens). In the messianic evocation of endurance as it passes through the 'eye of the needle' in our vanishing present, Kaleka's early effort presents a micrological redemption of the transient history of work – not in depiction, but within the formal limits of the image/space which stands, metonymically, for the forfeited immediacy of the history and work of painting in a post-national present.

As a medium, the modality of video-painting is perhaps best approached as a measure of intervention into the palimpsest of tact and contact privileged by Virilio, in his defence of the 'layered civility' of sympathetic artistic representation (Hoskote 2011). To what end? In the medial and temporal convergence of multiple, looped video projections and the painted screen, Kaleka *decentres* both the gaze and the object-form without abolishing these altogether: Virilio's screens emerge as temporal snags in cycles of appearance and dissolution, loss and recovery. Less significant in themselves, they manifest an asynchronous and breathtakingly inexistent space of reception. The unique formal provocation of Kaleka's 'video-paintings' aside, these works are intense engagements with the eye (and the over-wrought optical privilege upon which Virilio's histories of art turn). Yet Kaleka's challenge to the sovereignty of optical consciousness is non-combative, incrementally shifting the tracking eye off-course to deliver it, in registers of bewilderment or delight, into a noumenal space of experience.

If Kaleka's dedication to the Shoah *Consider* moves further, deploying video-painting on a monumental scale within the Spertus, it also dispossesses the museum space of a durable, or, indeed, 'civil' reconciliation with the past. The assemblage consists of a two-channel video-stream projected on two, large, partially painted canvases (each eleven feet by seven feet and six inches, painted at the bottom; transparent on top), and is positioned behind a glass screen at the long end of an air-well be crossed. The images turn on the uninhibited bodil or intimate facial registers of a young adolescent gii in repose in a comfortable middle-class interior, itse radiant images of a North Indian landscape.

While the story is refused a direction, its sequenc cally arranged around intergenerational rituals of lo in an Indian household: In projections that dissipat themselves in overwhelmingly visual 'scenes' of cl mother plaits her daughter's hair, decorating it with shining coins, or dries it, after the girl's jubilant run in a rainstorm. In a remarkable 20-minute audio loop that accompanies this indeterminate, yet palpably narrative-driven set of images, a single oral testimony, archived by Polish scholars and translated for the first time into English, is recited through the incongruous subcontinental and local accents of a woman and a man (Kaleka's landlady in Delhi and a Chicago-based radio broadcaster, respectively). In the Spertus catalogue essay, Lori Waxman (2007) emphasises the disembodied presence of this voice-recording; de-naturalised of its Eastern-European origins, the reading/testimony relates the industrial use and commoditised dissemination of human hair as a substitute for fur during the War. In their incorporeality, these oral histories refer beyond themselves, to the obvious yet absent image of the Jewish genocide; we are displaced in Kaleka's assemblage, which circumvents the long documentary record that displays attenuated bodies in the camp (even as the work turns away from the substitutive gesture of dismembered 'abstraction', so reviled by Virilio). Yet it is exactly in points of in/congruity, between (and within) the visible and the auditory, that *Consider* evokes missing bodies whose dehumanising death was made redundant, once and for all, through the industrial farming of corpses. Staging both the enigma and revelation of disappearance, the work's *punctum* – its register of historicity – is the metonymic trace of hair (Figures 7.2 and 7.3). Dispersed over an unimaginable distance in time and geographical space, and literally immaterialised before a distanced viewer, these virtualised traces of hair (auditory, visual, *never corporeal*) mark a memory that may no longer be lived. Their weightlessness is apprehended wrenchingly, in the entirely incommensurate affect of care.

In the micrological slippages between image-loops that are projected onto paintings of ostensibly identical subject matter, Kaleka's installations generate a Bergsonian or thoroughly spectral 'cinematographic' interface. The nomadic remainders to the time of lived experience, or, indeed, to extant histories of representational and cultural convention are *actualised* in a metonymic deferral of violence across image-sequences; and between manifestly disparate historical modalities of the screen.[4]

Conclusion: In Defence of Vanishing Points

> But do we not all write from and toward some such date? What else could we claim as our origin? (Celan 2003: 47)

That the Holocaust remains a reality in the most disastrous sense – for Kaleka, as for Benjamin and Adorno – is in no contradiction with Virilio's account of the present as a global 'virtualism that acts as a surrogate for the actual world of facts and established events' (2007: 12). Today, the holocaustal reference serves as the master-trope for terrorist attacks that performatively target the very technologies of symbolisation that enable their materialisation as 'political' speech: Here is the gravity of Virilio's objection to the 'tragedy . . . [of] temporal compression that reduces to nothing the magnitude of the world' (Virilio and Armitage 2011:

Figure 7.2 Ranbir Kaleka, *Consider* (2007). Title from taken from
a poem by Primo Levi. The artist would like to acknowledge Barkha
Gupta and Sapna Katyal, who feature in *Consider* as 'girl' and 'mother',
respectively.

39). In a world without historical duration, the dematerialised or
thoroughly meaningless ubiquity of 'Auschwitz' serves up a simulated if thoroughly visceral link to putatively incontestable historical realities, which turn on narratives of collective innocence and
apocalyptic survival. It is from just such a position that *Consider*
de-ontologises the surrogate if fundamental order of a national
'reality' upon which 'relativist' cultures of panic fall back (2007:
12). Yet Kaleka moves beyond Virilio's demand for an aesthetic
limit to the 'pitiless' de-sacralisation of the figure and body of the
Shoah, refusing altogether the propriety demanded by memorial-
work within the museum space. *Consider*'s 'wrongly' coded recol-
lection of racial aggression suggests obliquely that 'Auschwitz' is
itself the scene of primal repression, screening from visibility other
traumatic histories of genocide or displacement. Yet *Consider* does

Figure 7.3 Ranbir Kaleka, *Consider* detail (2007).

not pluralise the missing image of the Shoah: singular, insofar as it is the unsymbolisable origin of a historical present, 'Auschwitz' is actualised in excess of its conditions of possibility, as an inherently repeatable event. An exemplary instance of post-holocaustal 'lyricism', Kaleka's work preserves by profaning its dedication to ineffable historical origins. Staging the impossibility of the symbolic word, *Consider* traces the historical irruption of 'Auschwitz' into a sequence of cipher-like surfaces that render legible not the event itself – which resides traumatically beyond the frame of representation – but its *perceptual inapprehensibility* within the present. As for Virilio's picnoleptic sufferer, the elided moment of natural perception may be simulated, but never reproduced; in the inscriptive substitution of one image for another, Kaleka's assemblage transmits the touch and shock of the Holocaust as a perpetually receding, or absent origin.

This 'virtualism' of the past is, as Virilio would have it, a 'war-wound' within surviving representational capacities, traumatising the ethical function of witness by generating the optical-symbolic preconditions for 'new genocidal actions and racist aggressions' (Virilio and Armitage 2011: 38; Meek 2007: 12). Yet Virilio's

overdetermined claim for aesthetics – the subject of this discussion
– presents an inconsistency within the explicit direction and method
of his de-spatialised periodisations of visual media. This is also to
assume the *strength* of Virilio's rigorously a-cultural premises,
which drive the 'dromological' account of globalisation against
the conclusion(s) of art history; works such as *The Aesthetics of
Disappearance*, *Art and Fear* and *Art as Far as the Eye Can See*
are remarkable for opening the idiom and question of a post-
holocaustal aesthetic onto new-media contexts that reside beyond
the geopolitical horizons of Continental European and North
American origins. Read together from the speculative perspective
of a 'late' reader, Virilio's non-linear chronologies of optical media
over the last decades of the twentieth century touch specifically on
the transformation of hitherto constitutive histories of 'underde-
velopment' in the post-colonial world; once constelled through
intimate archives of remembered loss and reconstruction, localised
narratives of violence have been transcribed, without a trace of cultural lag, into the synchronic prerogatives of a hegemonic history.[5]
By the same token, however, the de-phenomenalised image allows
for the catastrophic negativity of memory – a possibility that
Virilio's explicit commitment to the vanished history of Western
European art forestalls and finally disavows.

   In its technological mediation, its geopolitical itinerancy, and in
its deracinated referential function, the 'optico-electronic' image
is both trace and occasion of 'surviving memory' (Adorno 1991
[1957]: 49). Embraced as the index of vanishing historical consciousness by both Adorno and Benjamin, the mediatised image
was approached as neither figuration nor text, but as a *pre-text*
for remembering – an affective prompt for recollections that have
been excluded from hegemonic versions of the past. Taken up by
Kaleka from an unpredictable distance, such a possibility is literally *actualised* as an unprecedented if entirely inexistent space,
wherein history might be hosted, witnessed and wrought anew.
In congruent yet elided memories of catastrophic displacement,
migration and nostalgia, the past appears immanently – that is,
within the very media of simulated dis/appearance – as a totalised
visual event. In its continuing vulnerability to both geopolitical
as well as hermeneutical displacement, the optically visible establishes an event without a name: so it remains open to the affective seepages and riveting historical contradictions of virtualised
memory.

Notes

1. Particularly relevant is Virilio's idea of a 'third war', which suggests that localised, even national chronologies of violence are displaced without interruption into the sphere of tele-globalisation.
2. See Nancy Adajania (2006) for a rare if entirely apposite use of Virilio for the 'stadial' politics of reality television and instant news in this context.
3. See especially the four-channel projection on canvases, 'Not from Here', 2009, which evokes the spectral tracks of internal migration as an after-memory of de-colonisation; and the fratricidal displacements of Partition.
4. In the Mumbai exhibition of 'Sweet Unease', the images of *Consider* were placed in a separate viewing-room adjacent to 'Not from Here' (see note 3); with the wall-space functioning, perhaps inadvertently, as the perceptual ellipse that both enables and problematises such mnemonic engagement. Consider also Nancy Adajania's curatorial repositioning of *Consider* in 2011 as the ambivalent edge between Shoah/Naqba, contained within the single if movable technological event of the work.
5. For example, in the 2008 attacks on Mumbai, a decade-long history of localised, incendiary violence within Indian metros was sublated into the idiom of 'India's 9/11'. As a result, the city, in its imagined relation to a fraught national space, was drawn into the 'cosmopolitan' temporality of a monolithic, global present.

References

Adajania, N. (2006), 'The sand of the Coliseum, the glare of television, and the hope of emancipation', in *Sarai Reader 06: Turbulence*, New Delhi: Sarai New Media Initiative, pp. 364–75.

Adorno, T. W. (1981 [1966]), *Negative Dialectic*, trans. E. B. Ashton, New York: Continuum Books.

Adorno, T. W. (1983 [1951]), 'Cultural criticism and society', in *Prisms*, trans. Samuel Weber and Shierry Weber Nicholson, ed. T. McCarthy, Cambridge, MA: MIT Press, pp. 17–34.

Adorno, T. W. (1991 [1957]), 'On lyric poetry and society', in *Notes to Literature, Vol. 1*, trans. Shierry Weber Nicholson, ed. R. Tiedemann, New York: Columbia University Press, pp. 37–54.

Adorno, T. W. (2002 [1937]), 'Late-style in Beethoven', in *Essays on Music*, trans. S. H. Gillespie, ed. R. Leppert, Berkeley: University of California Press, pp. 564–8.

Armitage, J. (2003), 'Art and Fear: An introduction', in P. Virilio, *Art and Fear*, New York: Continuum Books, pp. 1–15.

Benjamin, W. (1969 [1936]), 'Art in the age of mechanical reproduction', in *Illuminations*, ed. H. Arendt, New York: Harcourt Brace, pp. 217–52.

Benjamin, W. (1969 [1940]), 'Theses on the Philosophy of History', in *Illuminations*, ed. H. Arendt, New York: Harcourt Brace, pp. 253–64.

Benjamin, W. (2003 [1939]), 'On Some Motifs in Baudelaire', ed. M. P. Bullock and M. W. Jennings, *Walter Benjamin: Selected Writings, Volume 4: 1938–1940*, Cambridge, MA: Belknap Press of Harvard University, pp. 313–45.

Bewes, T. (2011), *The Event of Postcolonial Shame*, Princeton: Princeton University Press.

Caruth, C. (1996), *Unclaimed Experience: Trauma, Narrative and History*, Baltimore: Johns Hopkins University Press.

Caygill, H. (2008), 'Lyric poetry before Auschwitz', in D. Cunningham and N. Mapp (eds), *Adorno and Literature*, New York: Continuum Books, pp. 69–83.

Celan, P. (2003), 'The Meridian speech', in *Collected Prose*, trans. R. Waldorp, New York: Routledge, pp. 37–55.

Dang, G. (2011), 'Ranbir Kaleka', *Frieze Magazine*, Issue 138 (April), London: Wall Books.

Freud. S. (1919), *Beyond the Pleasure Principle*, ed. Peter Gay, London: W. W. Norton & Company (The Standard Edition Edition of the Complete Psychological Works of Sigmund Freud, 1990).

Friedberg, A. (2004), 'Virilio's screen: The work of metaphor in the age of technological convergence', *Journal of Visual Culture* 3(2): 183–93.

Hoskote, R. (2011), Catalogue note for *Sweet Unease*, Mumbai: Volte Gallery, <http://www.volte.in/sweet-unease.html> (accessed 18 July 2012).

Meek, A. (2007), 'Benjamin, trauma and the virtual', *Transformations* 15, <http://www.transformationsjournal.org/journal/issue_15/article_02.shtml> (accessed 18 July 2012).

Palmer, D. (2007), 'Contemplative immersion: Benjamin, Adorno and media art criticism', *Transformations* 15, <http://www.transformationsjournal.org/journal/issue_15/article_11.shtml> (accessed 18 July 2012).

Saffron Art Gallery (2011), *Catalogue to Fables*, Delhi: Saffron Art Gallery.

Virilio, P. (2000), *The Information Bomb*, London: Verso.

Virilio, P. (2003), *Art and Fear*, London: Continuum.

Virilio, P. (2007), *Art as Far as the Eye Can See*, Oxford: Berg.

Virilio, P. (2009), *The Aesthetics of Disappearance*, New York: Semiotext(e).

Virilio, P. and Armitage, J. (2011), 'The third war: Cities, conflict and contemporary art', in J. Armitage (ed.), *Virilio Now*, Cambridge: Polity Press, pp. 29–45.

Waxman, L. (2007), 'Essay on Ranbir Kaleka's *Consider*', Chicago: Spertus Institute for Jewish Studies.

8

Spectres of Perception, or the Illusion of Having the Time to See: The Geopolitics of Objects, Apprehension and Movement in Bashir Makhoul's *Enter Ghost, Exit Ghost*

Ryan Bishop

The ghosts won't starve, but we will perish. (Paul Virilio 1995: 61)

Angels and ministers of grace, defend us!
Be thou a spirit of health or goblin damn'd,
Bring with thee airs from heaven or blasts from hell,
Be thy intents wicked or charitable,
Thou comest in such a questionable shape. (Shakespeare, *Hamlet*, Act I, scene iv)

The breeze at dawn has secrets to tell you.
Don't go back to sleep.
You must ask what you really want.
Don't go back to sleep.
People are going back and forth across the doorsill
where the two worlds touch.
The door is round and open.
Don't go back to sleep. (Jelal al-Din Rumi 2004: 36)

Six mirrors stare at each other unblinking
I think we're headed for trouble. (Guillaume Apollinaire, 'Monday in the rue Christine', 2004: 49)

Introduction

The artwork by Bashir Makhoul *Enter Ghost, Exit Ghost* (2011) takes its title from the stage directions found in the opening act and scene of *Hamlet*. The directions for the spectral apparition continue and read 'Re-enter Ghost' (or 'Enter Ghost, as Before' depending on the edition). The movements indicate a return, a turn and a re-turn, which owes a debt to the Greek stage. The chorus in Greek drama moves and speaks – the strophe, anti-strophe and epode – which follows an almost dialectic movement of both thought and bodies on the stage, but one without resolution. The chorus sings a stanza and moves in one direction (strophe), provides another, sometimes contradictory statement, moving in the opposite direction (anti-strophe) and then sings the final stanza while stationary near its original spot (epode). The choral dance allows a return that is not a return, a dialectic resolution that leaves the resolution unfinished and the competing dynamics of the drama at play, though now with the additional emotional and psychological weight that comes from the choral reflections. That the chorus in Greek drama is also the citizenry, the voice and commentary of the people, lends it an especial power, one driven by circumstances beyond their control but which directly influences their lives: a commentary on fate, as well as the illusion of agency, movement and progress.

Makhoul is a Palestinian artist born in Galilee, Israel, but living in the UK since the start of the 1990s. His works embrace an aesthetic seduction intended to draw viewers into images that actually engage power, economics, violence, torture, war and nationalism, essentially working a correlation that states: the more beautiful the surface, the more complex, elusive and disturbing the material. Although each of his artistic projects stands on its own terms, a coherence exists across the works. His first UK show was held in 1992. Called *Al-Hijara*, it refers to the stones used in the Intifada uprisings of the late 1980s and early 1990s against Israeli occupation. This protracted unrest, literally a 'shaking off' (which is what 'intifada' means) of untenable political conditions, saw a great deal of intra-Palestinian violence. The show critiqued all sides of the conflict and did so through abstraction and oblique imagery not easily grasped in its historical and political complexity at the level of the images' surface, for the surface deceives, subject as it is to movement. Here are the first stones of the uprising we find in *Enter Ghost, Exit Ghost. Al-Hijara* marks Makhoul's departure along a journey of politically active artistic production, one that arrives at the 2102 show: an installation that returns again to very similar concerns and the historical arc and long duration of current political struggles. Just as a stone in flight has a parabolic arc, a trajectory, so Makhoul's artistic engagement has a trajectory, but it is one that covers much of the same ground again and again from different angles. His work is always a return that looks like an arrival, as one encounters with the Greek chorus.

Figure 8.1 Ryan Bishop, overview of *Enter Ghost, Exit Ghost* (2012).

The installation *Enter Ghost, Exit Ghost* includes two sections, one composed of a maze and the other a cardboard replica of an Arab town or refugee encampment. According to the curatorial brochure for the work, the walls of the maze are 2.4 metres high, with the entire length of the maze running about 100 metres. The walls of the maze are covered from the floor to the top of the wall with lenticular images that move as viewers move through the maze. The images themselves show buildings and streets from East Jerusalem, Hebron, a few of the larger refugee camps, as well as the 'mock Arab villages' used by the Israeli military for training purposes. These images are interspersed with some of the cardboard city that lies at the end of the maze. The number of images is limited to less than a dozen, and they are repeated over and over in a non-sequential fashion to add to the confusion of the maze, generating a sense of familiarity and disorientation. Gordon Hon, writing about the micro-lens lenticular surfaces in an earlier work by Makhoul, states that

> each image is given an equal portion of the surface. Rather than multiple exposures the various images are split into thousands of strips, which are then equally and regularly interspersed ... There are no stable, fixed points of view and the place seems to be defined by this instability. This is emphasised by the defining feature of the lenticular; the illusion of movement. (Hon 2007: 72)

Paul Virilio's influential linking of speed and vision/art usefully places an Einsteinian relativity of apprehension and perception firmly within modes of visualising technologies and image production. However, his discussions in *The Art of the Motor* (1995) (which perhaps might be more accurately translated as the motor of art) often privileges the viewing subject in this equation, with the speed of the viewing subject in relation to the object taking precedent in the status of the image produced from it or even in the status of the object itself: the viewing subject and his or her speed in relation to the viewed object is almost completely deterministic. For example, Virilio often uses an example of a tree perceived when he is walking past it as opposed to seeing it when riding on the TGV, and he asks which is the real tree. Writing about the relationship between speed and vision, or vision as speed, that he calls 'dromoscopy', Virilio states: 'in the dromoscope the fixity of the presence of objects comes to an end' (2005: 106). The viewed object becomes a passive recipient of speed insofar as it affects the viewing subject's gaze. This in turn leads to a consideration of the movement of the perceiving/representing medium from paint to photography to cinema. In each instantiation, according to Virilio's account, the viewing subject or apparatus is moving, not the viewed object.

Makhoul's installation brings the speed of the viewed object, the speed of the landscape, the speed of the built environment, the speed of objects and most importantly the light from them back into the relative relation of perception, apprehension and art. The reciprocity of moving bodies – subjects and objects both – becomes central to the work. Thus the horizon of vision becomes an aesthetic challenge as speed alters figure and ground, viewer and viewed, projected and projectile. Virilio's provocation regarding the motors of perception, image and subjectivity/objecthood, I suggest, provide a useful entry point for reading elements of Makhoul's recent geopolitical, existential and phenomenological installation. *Enter Ghost, Exit Ghost* addresses in a more or less explicit manner issues of urbanisation, warfare and the militarisation of daily life, as well as the relationship between surfaces and interiors and perception. Further, the title prompts an engagement with Derrida's spectres and hauntings as they pertain to larger historical and structural forces at play within a given site and their connection to temporality. By keeping this entire range of resonant elements operative at the same time, this chapter will use Makhoul's work to query Virilio's ever-prescient but problematic relation between speed, perception, image and observer to argue for a more complex relativity of knowledge production and epistemology than might be suggested by many of his writings.

Enter Ghost, or the Illusion of Movement

Strophe

Virilio's long-standing engagement with and theorisation of speed's effects on a range of human experience, including metaphysics and perception (e.g. time, space, time-space and vision), leads him to consider 'dromoscopy', which he calls 'the light of speed' (1997: 43) and how it pertains to the acceleration and deceleration of appearances. Subject–object relations in terms of vision become determined by speed, altering the status of each for '*dromoscopy* displays inanimate objects as if they were animated by a violent movement' (2005: 105) and providing an illusion of their status as (in)animate entities. For Virilio, though, the perceived object seems to have little impact on its perception, consigning it to the status of the inanimate thing acted upon by the speed of the viewing subject. The reciprocity essential to speed and perception becomes elided with an older story told by transitive grammar of subjects enacting their will, even if just perceptual, on objects. This element of Virilio's account, though, clashes strongly with his larger geo-biopolitical agenda, in which attempts to reassert the centrality of the human perceiver whose phenomenological experience and very ontology also become determined by vectors of speed and thus blunt the efficacy of agency. It is to this side of the ledger that Makhoul's art functions, for his images, his visual and viewed objects, dictate the terms of their perception as much as the viewing subject and its movement do.

To think somewhat proleptically, we note that Virilio states his case for speed as a medium quite clearly when he argues:

> Since the visible is only the surface effect of the alacrity of the luminous emission and since, meanwhile, what happens more and more quickly is perceived less and less distinctly, it is indeed necessary to that we recognise the obvious, that what we see in the visual field is such thanks to the mediation of the phenomena of acceleration and deceleration in all points identifiable with variable intensities of illumination. *If speed is light, all the light of the world, then what is visible derives both from what moves* and the appearances of momentary transparencies and illusions. (2005: 118)

The fundamental dependencies of perception and apperception on rates of acceleration and speed operate as and become mediation, thus making vision and the visible the result of movement.

As such, dromoscopy reveals a great deal about our perception of reality and of the status of the image as a mode of representation that may or may not pertain to our understanding of the real. With the relative relation between phenomena accounting for the status of a perceived object, of its empirical status, dromoscopy provides an important means for considering the status of the image. This is especially the case with *Enter Ghost, Exit Ghost*. The rapidity with which images appear and disappear – their constantly deferred becoming, their constant flirtation with reification – is absolutely central to Makhoul's piece, making speed, which might seem an incongruous element in most but certainly not all works of art, central to this installation, just as it becomes the medium for vision itself in Virilio's conceptualisation of dromoscopy.

The speed of the viewer moving through the maze and into the cardboard village is just one aspect of speed addressed in the work, but one salient to Virilio's dromoscopic argument: 'Movement governs the event; in making transparency active, speed metamorphoses appearances' (2005: 105). Virilio's text addresses movement through a posited 'static' landscape, something not at all possible with Makhoul's installation. The physical movement of the viewer through the maze is tracked in a specific manner regarding direction but not regarding speed (and thus time). The time-space of the images is partially determined by this relative speed of the viewer. However, another aspect of speed addressed by the work, perhaps the more important one, can be found in the movement and speed of the images clad to the walls of the maze, rising above the viewers. The images are photographs and thus (apparently) still images; however, due to the lenticular surface, the images move with a shift of the viewers' heads – not the eyes but of their heads or bodies. Speed, as Einstein reminds us, is not a phenomenon but rather a relationship between phenomena. The speed of the viewing subject is no longer the determining factor of the images' apperception as the viewed object too influences, through its own paradoxical relationship to speed, how it is to be engaged. Even though the images stop if we do in the maze, they move in response to the viewing subjects though they actually remain fixed. 'The blindness speed creates' (Virilio 1995: 65) is frozen in the installation and also reinserted here while remaining in constant motion, or at least potentially so.

Although Virilio argues that '*Movement is blindness*' and that '*immobility makes visible*', he continues the thought in an important manner: 'The plastic arts will come to immobilize movement, thereby *offering the illusion of seeing, of having the time to see*' (1995: 68–9). The key term here is 'illusion' for it pertains to the role of temporality in the constitution of the subject as a viewing subject. The subject becomes a subject through its engagement with and against objects that determine the subject through negative definition (the subject is what it is by not being the objects with which it interacts). The role of speed in relation to vision speaks to the heart of empiricism, its power and its flaws, for the object seems to change as the relative speed apprehension adjusts. The further effect is that the viewing subject too is changed through seeing the object in a different manner. However, we see no better or no worse when mobile as opposed to immobile; we merely see differently. This is Virilio's 'illusion' of sight that we experience with immobility. We confuse the difference of kind as a difference of quality.

More importantly, we also believe we have the time to see: this belief is what static art affords us. Makhoul's installation works the confusions of visibility, stasis, mobility, temporality and consciousness by ensuring that the assumed fundamental relationships between the viewer and the visible remain constantly and consistently unstable. The static images that supposedly yield to us the time to see that is found in the embossed photographs on the walls actually flicker and fade, move as we move, and barely remain still even if we are. The ground consistently shifts beneath the figure, trapping both on the same perceptual plane. The time for seeing, the time of the visible, becomes evanescence incarnate. We have no time to see and the visible flees. The illusion of seeing that emerges from static art (e.g. still photography) is revealed for the illusion it is because the image in this installation is both static and kinetic. The plastic art of photography has failed us, but – and this is Virilio's most provocative point – static art always would have failed us because all it can offer is the illusion of the visible. The ineluctable movement of bodies and time, and of course bodies *in* time, that provides the essence of speed, blinds us.

The images, static or otherwise, lack the corporeality of the spectators moving through the maze but to say so is to state the obvious, for the incorporeal image is redundant. The image is always ghostly, taking advantage of the sleight-of-hand with regard to presence and absence essential to representation. The tensions operative within representation can be articulated in the prefix 're-'. Jean-Luc Nancy, writing in *The Ground of the Image*, claims 'The *re-* of the word *representation* is not repetitive but intensive (to be more precise, the initially iterative value of the prefix *re-* in Latinate languages is transformed into an intensive, or as one says, "frequentive" value)' (2005: 35). Nancy is correct, of course, but only partially so, for the prefix's value is not either repetition or intensification but rather an intensification resultant from repetition, a both/and situation. The 're-' of the troublesome mimetic act of representation is both repetitive and intensive, qualitative and quantitative, imitative and innovative. That is, representation is always too little and too much at the same time: imitative (and thus repetitive) and productive (and thus generative).

The mimetic power of mechanical reproduction holds a special place in the history of representation. The imitative powers of photography, its mimicry, seem singular but should actually be understood as operating in a continuum from perspectival painting to *trompe l'oeil* to digital technologies. The pivotal technology in the trajectory likely belongs to photography and the illusion of unmediated access to the original with analogue photography. Roland Barthes famously argues that the illusion of unmediated access can be found in what he calls 'the denotated image'. The illusion reiterates the utopian character of denotation in language; that is the meaning of a given term is obvious in and of itself and resides *in* the term, as it were, clearly and equally accessible to all who speak the language to which the term belongs. The denotated image achieves the ideal of transparent representation through the photograph, in which the relationship between signifier and signified is one of 'recording' or 'documenting' without any mediation created by the medium of photography. 'The denoted image naturalizes the symbolic message', functioning as a kind of 'being there' of objects. The medium of photography, so the analogic story goes, necessitates an actual object's actual presence at the moment of representation. Analogical representation therefore equals two simultaneous temporal moments: *here-now* and *there-then*, which is the power of all representation: to re-present what was present (or pre-sent, or given). So image technology 'helps mask the constructed meaning under the appearance of the given meaning' (Barthes 1977: 46) providing photography (as well as cinema, digital representation, simulations) an easily generated message that conflates with the image.

Yet, all of this, as Derrida and many others have noted, depends ineluctably on absence, which makes the presence of representation possible and indeed necessary. Without absence, we wouldn't have representation. Through the techne of the medium, the absent object emerges as if present, incapable of existence other than through the act and medium of representation. The history of representation in all of its guises and manifestations, therefore, is 'thus traversed by the fissure of absence, which, in effect, divides it into the absence *of* the thing (problematic of its *re*production) and the *absence within* the thing (the problematic of its [re]pres-entation)' (Nancy 2005: 37; emphases in original). The status of the represented object becomes attenuated by the medium of representation, as well as by representation itself. Thus the hoped-for purity of representation of the Real becomes but a dream, and yet the logic of the analogue image and its reliance on presence, as well as the verity of its likeness, keeps the dream alive. In the process, the object and the status of the image undergo change, and thus so does the viewing subject.

The incorporeality of the image brings us back to the ghost, or rather our old combination of the image and the ghost as well as the image as ghost. The images in this installation recall the nineteenth-century stage trick (one likely used for productions of *Hamlet*) known as Pepper's Ghost. This bit of visual trickery, of illusionism that enables viewers to believe in what was never there as being there, is generated by plate glass, mirrors and a skilful combination of illuminated and dark space, thus making it possi-ble to project into space, especially the stage, the illusion of objects or people appearing and disappearing in ghostly semi-corporeal form. The body is there, or apparently so, but in an incorporeal manner: our hands would pass right through it. A precursor to the hologram, the Pepper's Ghost found in Makhoul's work is not projected but flattened into the lenticular surface, the ghostly images trapped in an illusion of three-dimensional overlay of images superimposed on one another, so that our hands would appear to be able to pass right through them. However, the very superficial layer of lenticular surface that allows for the illusion would stop our fingers immediately. The lenticular ghosts are squeezed into a thinner layer than their nineteenth-century breth-ren yet maintain the rapidity of appearance and disappearance found in the earlier form.

Apparently the major rhetorical device of the installation – through its images, its incorporeality, its frustrated sense of pro-gress, its plays with the temporality and visibility/blindness, its ghosts, its insistent refrain of absence – seems to be the *apostro-phe*. The spectators grope through the flashingly static images only to turn and turn away, to re-turn the turn, away, and address the absent, the dead, the holes in words (which is what the apostrophe

does and indicates). Apostrophes mark absence, holes and posses-
sion. They indicate and are the *topoi* of possibility: still stand the
waters; delusions of progress and narrative are routed back, away.
Like discourse (this course), our way through the maze flows back
and forth. But we are essentially seeing and witnessing – by moving
through – an address to the dead. The ethics of movement, the
ethics of vision and blindness, and the insubstantiality and incorporeality of the image returns (as ghosts always do and begin) us
to our corporeality through having it removed, for a second, in the
flickering lenticular image surface. The static photograph provides
the illusion of seeing though we will only ever see an incorporeality. And it provides us the illusion of having the time to see though
the speed compressed into the surface of the images in the artwork
reveals only time's having passed.

Figure 8.2 Bashir Makhoul, detail of *Enter Ghost, Exit Ghost* (2012).

Exit Ghost, or the *Fitna* That Is the Surface

Anti-strophe

A maze evokes thoughts of inside/outside and depth/surface; the thin membrane of the lenticular surface is the site at which all these transformations take place. The actual surface of the display walls, of the cladding of the piece, manifests evanescence, transformation, illusion, process, transition, mimesis, representation . . . even immateriality. This surface is constructed with a manipulation of material that invokes immateriality and transience. So at the most evidently self-reflexive level, the piece addresses the materiality and affect of surfaces: the surface on the walls and the walls as surfaces too. The surface of the installation, the surface of the cladded images as well as the cardboard surfaces of the Arab village, embodies and evokes *fitna*: a most fecund Arabic word that has many diverse but interrelated meanings including trial, tribulation, chaos, a state of extreme psychological stress and turmoil (almost as a test from God), lust or seduction, a fascination or bedazzlement, suffering, temptation by the materiality of the world and most importantly conflict (see Pandolfo 1998: 156–62). It is a big word filled with complexly intertwined meanings, and is a productive term for the myriad surfaces of and in Makhoul's installation. In the surface of the image and the image that is nothing but surface, the *fitna* flashes and sparks, causing confusion and conflict through the repetition of images that provide the illusion of progress that reveals itself as an unachievable stasis. The images are lovely, almost too much so for the content and context, rendering them seductive and fascinating, leading the viewer to engage the chaos of the sites depicted as distanced and unreal. But as the viewer moves more deeply into the maze, moves beyond the initial surface of the installation as it were, the images' repetition and overlapping in artificial depth reveal the trial the surface embodies and foists on the viewer: the ethics of vision, the impossibility of seeing and the tele- or distanced nature of conflict that no amount of technological or representational power can bridge.

The surface as a site of contestation has emerged somewhat recently in the work of the architect Eyal Weizman, who has modified and extended his previously conceived trope about the politics of verticality and concentrated all of its evocative and actual power

to the few centimetres above and below ground level, a surface
that can be extended to other surfaces as well: the surface that is
fitna and that is the *fitna* of space in turmoil, conflict and trial.
Writing about the very sites pictured in the photos of the installation and suggested by the cardboard camp, Weizman argues that
the struggles for power in urban sites, of economic and inhabited
contention, the fields of conflict that help constitute emergent and
long-standing dwelling spaces can be found operating within this
surface. Weizman's move to think of the surface as the site of
symbolic and actual contestation also achieves the trick of reading
the vertical and the horizontal at the same time; it provides access
to both surface and depth simultaneously. The lenticular surface
of the exhibition evokes just such an understanding of surfaces as
it reveals depth through layered views of palimpsest-like images
of other surfaces (walls, houses, buildings) and is itself but a few
centimetres of plastic thickness stuck to the walls. The lenticular
cladding on the walls of the maze articulates Weizman's politics
of verticality caught in the urban or village surface at ground and
surface level, where *fitna* resides for both the installation and the
site of dwelling.

The formal construction of the installation (lenticular cladding)
reminds us that cladding is not only an architectural term, but
also one used in fibre optics to refer to those parts of the strand
that seal the light into the core. As such it provides the viewer a
useful play of terminology, for the viewer, like the light cladded in
fibre optics, is sealed into the maze and the multiple images on the
lenticular surface: stuck, frozen in that space but moving through
and within the images. Further resonance is found in yet another
usage of the term 'cladding', this time in nuclear fuel production,
in which cladding seals in radioactive fragments to prevent them
from contaminating the coolant for the fuel rods. Cladding serves
as the outer layer of the fuel rod, the border between the contaminated fuel and the coolant. Thus the lenticular cladding, as
with other cladding, serves to encase, to entrap, to protect and to
seal in light as well as unstable power sources that can potentially
contaminate anything with which they come into contact: a latent
potentiality of force hewn into the horizontal lines of alternating
imagery. The lenticular cladding attached to the walls of the maze
provide a literalisation of the IT fibre-optics term 'firewall', which
protects a computer from viruses and invasion. However, precious
little protection occurs here, except perhaps for the distanced

spectators who will not be able to access the issues and sites, the materials and people, the buildings and the surfaces of the images displayed except through the images – even if they were to stand in the streets of a village.

As we see, the lenticular surface/image traps two moments in one, two images in one, sealing them together inextricably. Two images, two stories, two sites, two moments, two of X permanently bonded, oscillating with each other, inextricably intertwined, occupying the same space, time and frame/parergon. Jean-Luc Nancy writes in *The Ground of the Image* about the Greek term *oscillum*, which designates a small mouth and thus becomes a metonym of the face. But *oscillum* is also a mask of Bacchus hung among the grape vines to act as a scarecrow, a mask that moves back and forth in the wind providing a kind of oscillation, the movement of the flickering façade/face intending to scare away the marauding and thieving birds. Nancy says of the mask that its wind-tossed oscillation is between seeing and speaking (eyes and mouth), between reception and production, so the apparent conjoining of eyes and mouth into a face is actually forever an oscillation between one or the other revealing the face as a fleeting terrain of coming together (2005: 73–4). Neither wins, neither loses, but both are caught in the constant of their oscillation, one yielding to the other only to have the other yield yet again – no resolution, only 'the improbable union of the two' (75).

This improbable union of the two inextricably intertwined repeats itself over and over as one moves through Makhoul's installation: the two images of a single plane of lenticular surface, the viewer and the object, here and there, movement and stasis, presence and absence, the living and the dead, the corporeal and the spectral, self and other, us and them, space and temporality, vision and blindness, the maze and the village. The fleeting terrain of coming together, of conjoining while remaining separate, linked by the relationship between disparate phenomena, is articulated in the thin surface of embossed plastic cladding. The surface provides a kaleidoscope of suggested conflict, of *fitna*: a rapidly moving GPS of human relations within a spatially delimited geopolitical frame that can only ever oscillate.

Figure 8.3 Bashir Makhoul, detail of *Enter Ghost, Exit Ghost* (2012).

Enter Ghost, as Before, or the Oscillation of the Double Other That Is Us

Epode

An epode. A return that is not really a return. A maze that is really not a maze. A village that is but a cardboard model of one, not built on any scale or of any true relation to the maze.

The maze is actually a maze-like structure – more like a labyrinth than a maze. In a maze, one might not be able to find the way through: have the potential not to be able to find, as Daedalus provided, the thread. In this installation, though, there is very little chance of getting caught in an eddy of the static/moving images. As a kind of playful maze, or a mirage of a maze, the construct has a teleology of sorts that leads to the cardboard box city (itself also a model of a village). We can get lost in the repetition of the images but not in the maze per se. The repetition of images adds to the frustration of the maze while providing both a variation on a set of themes and (more importantly) the illusion of movement – the illusion of progress as well as the illusion of truly seeing and having fully experienced the world visually. We cannot get beyond these surfaces and yet we also cannot get lost in the maze or labyrinth. We must exit the maze as there is only one way through, and we must enter the village. Once in the village, the surfaces have actual three-dimensional depth and can be peered into and behind, each house uniquely crafted but still homogenous with the others, as village houses are. The scale is meant to overwhelm for each miniature house implies a miniature family but with metonymic expansion, to a whole village, which itself would be only one of thousands. The power of the representation is an engagement with representation itself: a maze that is not a maze, a village that is not a village, but both present through their absence, which we must experience and consider.

Ghosts, like representations, as we have noted, work the liminal terrain between presence and absence. They also speak to this exhibition's interest in the return that is not really a return. Derrida makes a nice point about ghosts in his book *Spectres of Marx* when he says that all ghosts begin by returning. A ghost can only be a ghost through a return to the earthly sphere. Those experiencing the installation have a return (epode) of sorts when they emerge from the maze into the cardboard box city for they arrive in a village they know (through endless representations) and yet which is uncanny in its sense of being a return to a past that is not their own. Derrida continues, though in a later essay (2008: 218–19), to distinguish his spectre and the one of communism Marx invokes in his manifesto. Derrida's spectre takes the more traditional role of a past haunting a present while Marx's is a currently unformed being that must be made real in a futural living present: it must be made to materialise in a manner it only vaguely hints at currently (at the moment that Marx is writing the manifesto).

These temporalities for the two spectres seem antithetical when keeping with the arrow of time flying from the past through the present to the future; however, the spectre (read here also as Makhoul's lenticular image) undoes this metaphysical linearity and apparent stability by being all temporal tenses at the same time – past, present and future piled up simultaneously in the image. Hence its endless cycling between entering and exiting (presence and absence) becomes mobility and stasis together simultaneously, rather as in a play by Beckett. In fact, Shakespeare's stage directions continue to include 'Exit Ghost' a second time, providing an oscillation of presence and absence that suggests a pattern to be repeated (perhaps infinitely). For Shakespeare this is both profound and cheeky because the absence is qualified – indeed compromised – by the quality of the presence. That is, the presence upon which absence structurally depends, insofar as ghosts or spectres are concerned, is in doubt from the outset. Ghosts are both immaterial and material, so their presence is insubstantial and perhaps not even acknowledgeable as presence at all. Thus the absence also wobbles under inspection for a thing not really there cannot really disappear either.

The second point about ghosts is that at the larger metaphysical level: we all enter (as) ghost and exit (as) ghost. This is the fate of us all, and part of what haunts the installation is its explicit role as *memento mori*. The thin line between presence and absence demarcated by ghosts speaks to our existential condition, a commentary furthered by the cardboard houses of this installation in that they signify unoccupied homes in what is often called occupied territory. That the images themselves make ghostly visions of sites in which much of the military technology used in these locales has created many ghosts (some even premature ghosts, if we can assume such temporal and existential claims) reminds of us this shared fate, this shared human bond found in spectres. Also a portion of what haunts us with the unoccupied cardboard village is the sense of its rather explicit vulnerability, for towns were formed for protection.

Virilio, in *Speed and Politics* (1986), argues that from the outset the city has always been the continuation of the defensive gathering that it was in antiquity. An agglomeration of people, structures and systems emerges out of the forces and vectors of movement along rivers and roads, and makes its character by taking advantage of and protecting itself against the forces it encounters on those paths of speed. Walls and gates may yield to less visible forms of defence but the rationale of the city as opposed to the settlement or the camp is one of security and strength in numbers against external and even unknown dangers that outweigh the potential threats from those contained within the polis. Even laid bare as settlements, the Arab villages that the installation models would be built of concrete, somewhat permanent but flexible too. In Makhoul's recasting of the Middle Eastern village, the surface and material is no longer concrete but cardboard. The plasticity and strength of concrete (which so fascinated Le Corbusier, that great urban planner and architect with a military bent) transform into the ephemerality of cardboard. The metonym for homelessness in Western cities that is cardboard renders this city in all of its explicit vulnerability and exposure: the city as target, but not the kind you aim for, only rather the kind you shoot at.

And that is exactly what these villages are: cities to be shot at. The village in the installation is a stage set to boot, modelling specific villages that are occupied but unlived in. Steve Graham (2011) documents the burgeoning neo-urban phenomenon that he calls 'the theme park archipelago' combining elements of military planning with entertainment industry and video game immersive experience in actual urbanised sites for urban warfare training, a skill on the ascendancy since the end of the Cold War and the emergence of the war on terror. These sites combine all the special effects of cinema but in this instance not made into theme parks. These sites are often collaborative endeavours between the military and major studios skilled at such metamorphoses, including Universal Studios. They include centrally monitored interactive special effects so that soldiers experience sights, sounds and smells associated with urban warfare. The nexus of interested parties involved in these constructions, all on the taxpayers' dime of course, leads us to expand our nomenclature of linkages from the military–industrial complex to what I have called 'the military-industrial-entertainment-university complex' (Bishop 2006). One of the largest of these sites, according to Graham, is a cooperative effort between the US and Israeli militaries: the $40 million mock-up generic 'Arab city' facility in the Negev desert and the Israeli base Ze'elim. The generic Arab city is actually a mini-Palestinian town, intended to help regularise and improve military movements and actions in such villages, when encountered outside their video game immersive and modelled virtual reality.

The cardboard city is reminiscent of a Potemkin village or the sham version of Paris partially built on the outskirts of the city intended to fool German pilots during the final days of World War I. Being the early days of aerial bombing when explosives were dropped manually from the air by pilots in open cockpits, this attempt at subterfuge – an urban decoy – with fake industry, railway station, populace, etc. was meant to lure the Germans to destroy the model as opposed to the actual city where innocent civilians lived. However, Makhoul's city is not intended to impress otherwise ignorant dignitaries, such as a Potemkin village, nor is it meant to be a defensive measure against an enemy army, nor is it a site for military training for urban warfare of a specific ethnic/

Figure 8.4 Bashir Makhoul, detail of *Enter Ghost, Exit Ghost* (2012).

political geography. It instead operates as a negative version of all of these, the opposite goals of those put forward by these other artificial cities. Deception, deflection, training, display of opulence, none of these are at play in the installation's village, yet they are all relevant as they provide elements of artifice that draw attention to the very objects veiled or hidden, what is masked.

The cardboard village, paradoxically empty and occupied, evokes villages in the Middle East but further appears within a larger historical trajectory of geopolitics. It serves as a metonym for the large-scale 'nuclear anticity strategy' (Virilio 1995: 10) or the rendering of the global city as global by virtue of its having been targeted for nuclear destruction (Bishop and Clancey 2004: 67). Yet it is perhaps more evocative of the moments when the geopolitical global strategy became more intimate, after the end of the Cold War, which saw decades of ethnic cleansing in the Balkans, tribal targeting of villages in sub-Saharan Africa, the horrors of the Iran–Iraq war, the house-to-house attacks in East Timor or Aceh, and into the wars that fill the twenty-first century with cross-border dread and terror, including the celebrated uprisings in Egypt and Libya. The nearly porcelain fragility of cardboard is offset by its cheapness, its lack of value, its inherent transience. As with those houses and villages and dwellers similarly removed, relocated, cleansed or destroyed, this installation's city is one of a presence marked by absence: a model, like a ghost, figures what is not there, and as with any representation, is only possible through absence. The cardboard surfaces, just as the lenticular surfaces, carry the mark of that absence found in the terrible intimacy of geopolitical struggle: the mark of the apostrophe.

As we emerge from the maze and as we leave the cardboard village, the spectre of the images and the meditation on surfaces unavoidably spark alongside us. The *fitna* of the surface runs from the lenticular surfaces of the cladded walls, across the cardboard village, along the gallery floor, into the street and into the city, the village, the simulated theme-park urban formations of military training, through the suburbs, up the walls and cladding of high-rise buildings, along the street outside and into our homes. And trapped in this flickering *fitna* of a surface is the embossed image of the inextricably intertwined doppelgänger Other along with us, and that is us.

No Exit: A Virilian Coda

Virilio's privileging of the viewer reinforces a specific interpretation of the individual subject integral to the humanist tradition he wishes to preserve. Even taken on its own terms and with its own set of assumptions, this move is fraught with pitfalls, not the least of which can be found in his own geopolitical readings of speed, technology and urbanism that somehow seem to go missing when the emphasis of his writing falls upon visualisation processes and practices as opposed to those phenomena in which they are embedded. The 'escape velocity' the individual has been placed within, or has been projected into, while an individual experience is nonetheless meant to be metonymic of a community – a shared view of objects by a collective subject composed of individuals. There is a universal and Universalist ground upon which this individual/communal subject stands and is constructed. We have been in this site of history and metaphysics before, obviously, and find it replicated in *Enter Ghost, Exit Ghost* as the a priori grounds of politics and self-determination that has landed the villages in the images where they are: in a permanent precarity freighted with violence and surveillance of staggering diversity. And for all of Virilio's exquisite analyses of the intersections of urbanism, warfare, visualising technologies, speed and geopolitics that form the context and vehicles for visual culture, the consistent privileging of the viewing subject as subject runs counter to this other body of work though it composes an integral dimension of it. They are not extricable despite their contradictory positions.

The implication of Makhoul's installation obviously runs counter to this view of the viewing subject while supporting and exemplifying a host of Virilian themes and concepts, as mentioned here. The installation throws us back into a temporality and relativity of empirical knowledge that renders the subject as flatly as the objects viewed. His work blurs the boundary between subject and object, viewer and viewed, by understanding the speed, trajectory and uncertainty of appearance as constitutive of the participants locked in phenomenological and ontological embrace, with no hope of transcending it. Viewer and viewed are as neatly woven together as the images enframed in each lenticular surface, offering a meditation on the metaphysics and ethics of vision. Virilian visual aesthetics and their uneasy relationship with relative speeds of bodies viewed and viewing become recast in the *fitna* of the lenticular surface and return us (if return is possible) to a singularly Virilian militarised urbanisation and empirical uncertainty, a site of self and other inextricably bound.

References

Apollinaire, Guillaume (2004), *The Self-Dismembered Man*, trans. Donald Revell, Middletown, CT: Wesleyan University Press.

Barthes, Roland (1977), 'The rhetoric of the image', in *Image, Music, Text*, trans. and ed. Stephen Heath, New York: Hill and Wang, pp. 32–51.

Bishop, Ryan (2006), 'The global university', *Theory, Culture & Society* 23(2–3): 563–6.

Bishop, Ryan and Clancey, Gregory (2004), 'The city as target', in Steve Graham (ed.), *Cities, War and Terrorism*, Malden, MA and Oxford: Blackwell, pp. 54–74

Derrida, Jacques (2008), 'Marx & sons', in *Ghostly Demarcations*, ed. Michael Sprinker, London: Verso, pp. 213–69.

Graham, Steve (2011), 'Theme park archipelago', in Ryan Bishop, Gregory Clancey and John Phillips (eds), *The City as Target*, London and New York: Routledge.

Hon, Gordon (2007), 'Return and the spectres of occupation', in John

Gillette (ed.), *Bashir Makhoul: Return in Conflict*, New York: IssueArt Publishing, pp. 63–74.

Nancy, Jean-Luc (2005), *The Ground of the Image*, trans. Jeff Fort, New York: Fordham University Press.

Pandolfo, Stefania (1998), *The Impasse of Angels: Scenes from a Moroccan Space of Memory*, Chicago: University of Chicago Press.

Rumi, Jelal al-Din (2004), *The Essential Rumi*, trans. Coleman Banks, San Francisco: HarperOne.

Shakespeare, William (1999), *Hamlet*, Cambridge: Cambridge University Press.

Virilio, Paul (1986), *Speed and Politics*, trans. Mark Polizzoti, New York: Semiotext(e).

Virilio, Paul (1997), *Open Sky*, trans. Julie Rose, London: Verso.

Virilio, Paul (1995) *The Art of the Motor*, trans. Julie Rose, Minneapolis: University of Minnesota Press.

Virilio, Paul (2005), *Negative Horizon*, trans. Michael Degener, London and New York: Continuum.

9

The Event
Jordan Crandall

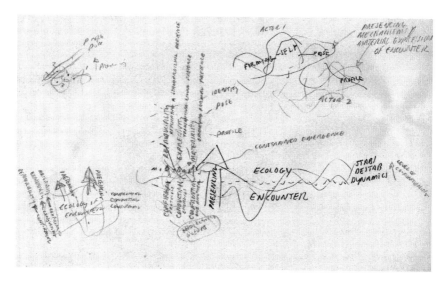

every time a technology is invented . . . an accident is   invented together
        with
    it[1]

In the *event* of the accident, the coherency of the object world is destabilised and the component agencies necessary to maintain it become newly revealed. Dislodged from their safe havens and rendered vulnerable, these component agencies, however operational, institutional or discursive, become newly active in their negotiations and attachments. They are absorbed into other material configurations, other systems of meaning and affect, however straight or wayward, countered or modulated, amplified or diminished. Conventional associations are dislodged. The catastrophe reveals an agential dispersal: the network of the negotiation.

Yet at the same time, revealing the elements with which actors and events affiliate in order to maintain their centrality and force, the catastrophe orchestrates a consolidation. It stabilises relatively coherent or consistent forms – however spatial, linguistic, affective or rhythmic – that embody or heighten the specifics of the site, the object, the space, rendering it singular, bounded and unique. Infrastructures are revealed. Actors, escaping abstraction, are resolved to ontological specificity and embroiled in a politics that may have been overlooked or erased.

Yet the *event* can resist this containment, and in this resistance lies the source of its compelling and productive power. It mobilises potent circulations of sensation, however understood in terms of attraction or avoidance. Affects are in play, in all their irresolute, physiological and psychological power, in ways that can amplify fascination and perpetuation. There is no sweeping them, in favour of linguistic meaning, from the deck of the ship – the platform whose very existence, for Virilio, occasions the wreck. The challenge is to accommodate the unruly supplements of the situation, its turbulent underpinnings: the senseless undercurrents of the sensible.

How to place this destabilisation and stabilisation, specificity and distribution, multiplicity and consolidation, together on the same analytical plane?

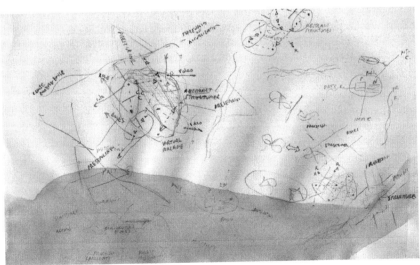

The *event* is situated in the midst of the fugitive and the common. It is constructive and singular, cumulative and catastrophic. It is constituted in the disturbance of a regularity of transmission, yet also its congealment into a notable assembly that can now be taken into account. It is an exceptional occurrence, a deviation, yet also a cooperative gathering, an affirmation.

The event congeals in tandem with the normalisation of a constitutive surround. One gathering of actors is constituted as a change – shifting or settling into a state that is relatively stable or discrete – only because another has been transformed into atmosphere. The change is not an absolute difference but a gradation of divergence-assembly: a degree of stabilisation and destabilisation, subtraction and redundancy.

It is a matter of the relational structures and organising principles through which gatherings of actors are coordinated and combined together at various scales, magnitudes, speeds and levels of complexity, such that they gain sufficient stability to be maintained. It is a matter of how, once sufficiently stabilised, they replicate, become redundant and standardise, at various scales, across various platforms of endeavour – and the means through which this is amplified or disrupted.

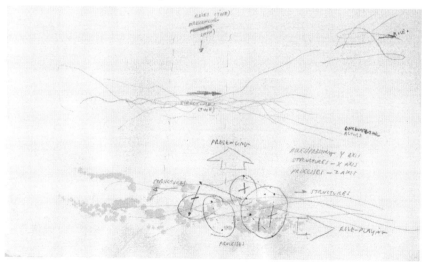

MULTIPLICITY Flickering CONFIGURATION transcendent
Operating Principle: **RESEMBLANCE** – correspondence of elements
Relational/Compositional Structures: **Correspondence, Redundancy, Standardisation**
Flickers in/out in degrees of accumulation/dispersal, coalescence/disruption
Agency 'refreshing'/updating in a succession of instants

SCALAR STABILITY Fluctuating ZONE transcendent
Operating Principle: **LIMITATION** – fluctuating level of constraint
Relational/Compositional Structures: **Transmission, Attunement, Calibration**
Vibrates in/out in degrees of amplification/diminishment, convergence/divergence, correspondence/deviation
Agency modulating a threshold – approached, attained, crossed

SINGULARITY Structuring CONTOUR/PATTERN immanent
A sudden, originless, eruption occurring in terms of the structure of a possibility space, as demarcated/contoured through distributed points: an immanent, discrete combinatorial space that has no intrinsic spatial structure.
An exceptionality and an amplification, immersed in the flows of the constituted norm, dispersed within its standards.

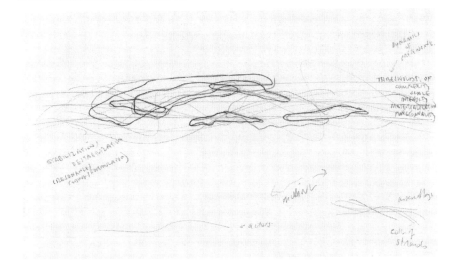

The *event* is not an object but an agency of gathering: it assembles and focuses the agencies that help compose it. Actors may 'take hold' of the event, but the event also takes hold of them: it can subsume its attendant agencies, and to some extent, this is precisely the source of its affective appeal. Mastery might be sought on the surface, but acquiescence is cultivated below the deck.

The event is a complex formation that is neither internally nor externally decided, nor subject to causal or predetermined agential divisions. It is apprehended as a matter of fascination or concern through the sensory, rhythmic and cognitive arousal of its attendant actors. The arousal is conditioned: actors are readied, evaluative alignments and postures taken within communicative encounters. They are disposed to act, conditioned in expectation within the dominant terms of the programme.

The event, as an attention-worthy incident, a novel occurrence that congeals against the backdrop of the everyday as a matter of fascination and concern, is also an occurrence into which agency can be inserted: an incident subject to reprogramming. It can be reoriented, expanded or regenerated – its default transformed by way of a destabilisation of the familiar – in such a way as to amplify ontological involvement.

This affirmative understanding of the event – whereby it is transformed into a practice – shifts the analytical emphasis away from generalising concepts such as power, control and desire and toward the cultivation of relevance, influence and intimacy. It emphasises the dynamics of agential inclination and sustainment: how agencies negotiate in ways that perpetuate their standards, such that other actors come to move in accordance with their terms.

---

configuration-zones: **compositional processes, tones, atmospheres**

Carry with them rhythmic infrastructures and sensations, which flow through actors

Actors transmit/absorb these rhythms and sensations, filter and calibrate them

Actors dynamically **constrain** these flows in gatherings, modulating thresholds of stability (stabilise-disrupt; regularise)

Actors dynamically **correspond** these flows in gatherings, modulating resemblance & redundancy (replication; refreshing)

Actors dynamically **accumulate** these flows in gatherings (amplification of mass/speed)

When objects are understood as actors, one cannot assert authority over them so easily. They are not materials to be moulded, elements to be tamed. A more acquiescent approach is called for, which privileges negotiation over control: an agile practice that, attuned to the nuances of the encounter and the shifting priorities of the situation, can allow the accommodation of that which is revealed therein, often unexpectedly and outside of preoccupation.

Compositional processes, forms and atmospheres help to illuminate the priorities of a shared circumstance: how the event matters. The challenge is to cultivate the skill for discerning the meanings that are embodied there. The endeavour is neither solely critical nor solely constructive: it seeks both the recovery and the wreckage.

Note

1. Paul Virilio, in John Armitage (1999), 'From Modernism to Hypermodernism and Beyond: An Interview with Paul Virilio', *Theory, Culture & Society* 16(5–6): 40.

Figures 9.1 to 9.4 Jordan Crandall, *Untitled* (2012).

10

The Face of the Figureless:
Aesthetics, Sacred Humanism
and the Accident of Art

John Armitage

Not all the ravages caused by our merciless age are tangible ones. The subtler forms of destruction, those involving only the human spirit, are the most to be dreaded. (Paul Bowles 1955: xi)

Introduction

This chapter is an exploration of Virilio's arguments for aesthetics' and arts' significance that are specified in his *The Aesthetics of Disappearance* (2009a) and *Art and Fear* (2003a). There Virilio set out his own concept of art as the important means by which aesthetics is able to disappear: that any 'picnolepsy' (the epileptic condition of consciousness shaped by acceleration, or, rather, the consciousness created by the subject through its very absence, to use the category introduced in *The Aesthetics of Disappearance*) prohibits certain possibilities of seeing, blinds specific visions and fails to represent the import of a number of 'accidents of art' (Virilio and Lotringer 2005). The contemporary aesthetics of disappearance and art are explained as means by which this blinding prohibition can be designated and depicted. Through the spaces, malfunctions and speed jolts flowing through and defining hypermodern subjectivities, the contemporary aesthetics of disappearance and contemporary art can present the fact of the disappearance of existence and compel the recognition that aesthetics and art can be instrumentalising as well as accelerated experiences, that they have the potential actively to interrogate conventional thought about the reality of speed and immobility and confront the discourses of picnolepsy that appear with them.

This chapter thus places aesthetics in the foreground while discussing the significance of art for Virilio's examinations of the aesthetics of disappearance. Consequently, owing to the relation between art and the aesthetics of disappearance, war, film and cultural politics, it should become clear that questions regarding aesthetics and art are crucial to Virilio's philosophy. The aesthetics of disappearance and war, film and cultural politics all induce artistic feelings, and the moral duty of both appreciating and critiquing them is, for Virilio, a duty that aesthetics and art are exceptionally well-appointed to carry out. On account of this aesthetics and art are frequently used as a model in Virilio's studies of what appreciation and critique involves. Aesthetics and art are therefore both models for contemplating disappearance, and also important sites where the consensus produced by the discourse of picnolepsy can be disputed. My aim in this chapter is to introduce and to open up some of Virilio's investigations of how these challenges surface, to argue with Virilio against what he calls 'profane humanism', and to argue beyond Virilio for what I name 'sacred humanism', and to reveal the vital functions that aesthetics and art play in his contemporary philosophy.

Aesthetics, Pitilessness and Contemporary Art

Throughout his writings, Virilio is a supporter of the creative artist, and it is worth investigating momentarily the place that aesthetics and art hold in two of his texts before turning to his writings on individual artists and 'critics of the art of technology' (Armitage 2012: 5). It is imperative to note here that Virilio's explanation of contemporary aesthetics and art does not hypothesise them as just the newest things in artistic or aesthetic technique. Instead, the function of aesthetics and art is to understand and reinvent consensus and to cause the appearance of new forms and visions that augment the variety of potential ways to communicate experience.

In *The Aesthetics of Disappearance*, Virilio equates the modern French artist–photographer Jacques-Henri Lartigue (1894–1986) with a sort of philosopher of visual culture, arguing that the 'trap for vision' Lartigue fashioned was not in theory ruled by the pre-established logics of photography or his camera. Such logics and categories are what Lartigue's 'trap for vision' was looking into. The artist–photographer Lartigue thus worked without logics and so as to ascertain the logics for what photographic images he subsequently created. This is why Lartigue's 'trap for vision' began to have the uniqueness of an accident of art. Virilio:

Q: You've talked to me just now of a trap for vision, something like that, is that your camera?

A: No, not at all. It's before, something I did when I was little. When I half-closed my eyes, there remained only a narrow slot through which I regarded intensely what I wanted to see. Then I turned around three times and thought, by so doing, I'd caught – trapped – what I was looking at, so as to be able to keep indefinitely not only what I had seen, but also the colors, the noises. Of course, in the long run, I realized that my invention wasn't working. It's then only that I turned to technical tools for facilitating it. (Virilio 2009a: 21)

What Virilio means by this should possibly be more obvious after having considered his arguments in *The Aesthetics of Disappearance*. The contemporary work of aesthetics and art is not one that necessarily develops consistent with the logics of a pre-established discourse of, for example, photography and dark rooms, lenses, and shutter speeds. Rather, in trying to impart that there is a disappearance, it looks for new ways of representation and new logics for appearance. It happens as an accident of art that reinvents and contests what up till now had been thought of as the logics of aesthetic and artistic appearance, and thus has the promise to engender new discourses of the body and the camera, of the human eye, technical tools and conceptions of 'exposure' as well as new opportunities for the particular patterns of the aesthetics of disappearance. This idea of the 'accident of art' is vital to Virilio's aesthetics, and will become the centre of discussion later in this chapter.

Virilio's arguments in *The Aesthetics of Disappearance* define the critical place that art inhabits concerning inertia, absence and the ongoing acceleration of speed. What is in the balance in art, in Virilio's aesthetic philosophy of disappearance, in his concern with the modification of actual duration in the present period, is the appreciation and critique of the aesthetics of disappearance through their expansion into all academic disciplines. In other words, the aesthetics of disappearance is the site of a disagreement over our lived time where one or more of the rival factions are condemned to blindness, which, for Virilio, justifies their appreciation and critique. It is not an issue of 'solving' the question of disappearance along with a few pre-established logics. Rather, the existence of the disagreement over lived time that provokes it must be drawn attention to and new means of appreciation and critique have to be found. Aesthetics' and arts' capacity and autonomy to try out ideas and forms, to experimentally rework the logics of discourses of body-acceleration, make it an essential instrument for searching for these means. Positioned next to the specific patterns of the aesthetics of disappearance, the modification of actual duration, and Continental philosophy (and aesthetics is at all times discussed in terms of this association by Virilio), art is an important means of probing leading discourses of 'dizziness' and 'luminous chaos' and revealing the aesthetics of appearance they stifle (Virilio 2009a: 22).

These declarations point towards the notion that aesthetics and art are related to the possibility for reinvention. Aesthetics and art, as indicated by Virilio, do not only reproduce the reality of contemporary imagery. Instead, they intercede in the discourses of perception that build a prearranged reality of perceiving and inaugurate potentialities for reinvention and transformation. In every one of his arguments about aesthetics, it is art's capability to face up to recognised concepts and schemes that remains the focal point.

This capability is explained most plainly in 'A Pitiless Art' (Virilio 2003a: 27–65), an essay in Virilio's essential book, *Art and Fear*. At this point, he argues that contemporary culture inflicts 'pitilessness' on aesthetics and art, as well as on 'pity' and 'pitiful' thought in general, which is the recommendation of 'pitiless . . . "contemporary art"'. Be 'profane', that is the recommendation. Sacred art is out of date, discuss the profanation of human forms and bodies in a profane twenty-first century way, speak to profane human beings, if they take pleasure in entertaining your thoughts on the debate over the 'relevance' of 'contemporary art' then they will also entertain your forgetfulness 'to ask one vital question: *Contemporary art, sure, but contemporary with what?*' (2003a: 27) This is the same assault on human subjectivity that Virilio objected to in *The Aesthetics of Disappearance* (Armitage 2012: 27–46). Consistent with this formulation, sacred art is expounded as antiquated art, anti-terroristic and museological in the worst possible sense (i.e. anachronistic), and in its place, the artist or critic of the art of technology is implored to tempt the profane and his or her ability to 'enjoy' contemporary art's production of forms that are in fact modes of destruction. In the contemporary art museum or gallery, the value of aesthetics and art is offered in terms of its facility to attract a mass spectatorship in love with Nazism, terror and war (among many other possible candidates, German artist Ottmar Hörl's 1,250 garden gnomes making Nazi salutes as a 'satirical comment on the rise of fascism' in Straubing in 2009 springs to mind: see Connolly 2009), and the best way to guarantee 'success' is to profane ideas concerning peace rapidly and 'ironically', and in an instantly comprehensible if unbalanced and terroristic approach. Yet, Virilio is doubtful about this notion of aesthetics or art's undertaking as discussing the 'profanation of human forms and bodies in a profane twenty-first century way' and robustly opposes the belief that, today, aesthetics and art are only another meagre 'satirical comment'. As his arguments concerning picnolepsy and communication spell out, what a specific culture believes to be 'humanised' is only ever the universalisation of oneself from within. In the contemporary discourses of picnolepsy and the organisational and cultural urge for the universality of the extermination of bodies and the propensity to downgrade all issues to those of the extermination of the environment, war or nuclear proliferation, which was associated with technology in *The Aesthetics of Disappearance*, Virilio argues that such profane 'human' developments are 'dehumanizing us from without': the devastation of our ethics, the consequence of our loss of aesthetic points of reference, the destruction of our very perception of our surroundings, and so on. Thus, he maintains, humanity is being reinvented as something profane in part by the technological vanguard of contemporary aesthetics and the contemporary art machine that hauls humanity after them, dehumanising it in the urge for the universality of the extermination of bodies (Virilio 2003a: 28–9). Being explicated by Virilio as the 'knife', profane humanity stops having the ability to be the 'wound' and is relegated, together with modern art and its forgetting about the wound, to simply another 'bayonet' fixed to the technological machine of 'scalpel-wielding' art from German Expressionism and Viennese Actionism to Ottmar Hörl and beyond.

Counter to this profane universality of the extermination of bodies, Virilio indicates that aesthetics and art point towards another form of humanism, a form that he does not define and which I consequently describe as sacred humanism. In my present practice in visual culture, sacred humanism conveys an optimistic sense rather than the openly negative sense of profane human-

ism. Sacred humanism – with its historical roots not in dedica-
tions to, or the setting apart for, the worship of a deity, but in the
appearance at the time of the Renaissance of a system of thought
that rests on human values, interests, needs and, especially, the
welfare of humans – signifies a concept focused on a concern for
human interests, values of rationality, the nobility of freedom and
a sincere acknowledgement of human corporeal boundaries and
mental limits. Sacred humanism is thus dedicated to the study of
the humanities as something venerable, to learning in the liberal
arts as something worthy of respect, or, in philosophical and aesthetic, artistic, and cultural terms, to a broadly hopeful account of
the ability of humanity to further itself through respect for knowledge. For Virilio, sacred humanism is the ability to be captivated
by 'wounded' or pitiful art's reinventive potentialities that cannot
be incorporated into academicism, condemned by the Situationists,
as was Charlie Chaplin, '*pitiful actor par excellence*', and who was
denigrated 'as a sentimental fraud, mastermind of misery, even a
proto-fascist!' by the Situationists' universality of the extermination of bodies (Virilio 2003a: 32–3). He traces this sense of sacred
humanism to Claude Monet's (1840–1926) Impressionism and
Pierre Bonnard's (1867–1947) Post-Impressionism, both thoughtful and pitiful painters par excellence, with Monet especially being
singled out as 'that miracle worker of a *Rising Sun*, which is not
quite the same as the one rising over the laboratories of LOS
ALAMOS' (Virilio 2003a: 33). This sacred humanism is another
rendering of those expressions that Virilio has utilised to point to
the aesthetics of disappearance: it functions in the same kind of
way as art, aesthetics, disappearance and war, film and cultural
politics to signal the opportunity to think accidents of art without
the pre-given constructions of techno-scientific thought. It is
simultaneously 'pitiful' and potentially therapeutic, and the duty
of philosophy is to truly appreciate the '*demonstrative*' art of the
old masters that lasted 'right up until the nineteenth century with
Impressionism' and to truthfully critique the '*monstrative*' art of
the twentieth and twenty-first centuries, which 'is contemporary
with the *shattering effect* of mass societies', the 'conditioning of
opinion', 'MASS MEDIA propaganda', and the '*mounting extrem-
ism* evident in terrorism or total war' (Virilio 2003a: 35).

   The phrase that Virilio associates with this second form of
humanism, sacred humanism, in *Art and Fear*'s 'A Pitiless Art' is
the 'intelligence of REPRESENTATION' (Virilio 2003a: 36). He

argues that the fact that 'the words PITY and PIETY are consubstantial' implies that we should 'not become *negationists of art*' (39). The intelligence of representation, as the opposite path to the *'impiety of art'* developed in the twentieth century, identifies something within humanity that is not controlled totally by the prevailing discourses of picnolepsy that besieged the event of, for example, 'the PHOTO FINISHES of the Tuol Sleng Memorial in Phnom Penh, where the Angkar – the government of "Democratic Kampuchea" – had thousands of innocents *put to death in cold blood*, women and children first . . . carefully photographing them beforehand' (44). It is not that the intelligence of representation is more sacredly human than the pitilessness of 'presentation' or of 'presentative' art (new media art, virtual reality, etc.) as some of the aesthetic and political ideas of the twentieth century might suggest, but rather than its 'public eye', its 'imagery', at the instant of its entrance into the space and time of Western or any other history names the identification of *'our essential being'* as a possible site for opposition to domination by a pitiless century that lingers within all pitiless presentations, as in 'the birth of the *portrait* in all its humility, its discretion' (44).

For Virilio, therefore, contemporary humanity is the result of a disagreement between two humanisms: the profane humanism of technological expansion and the universality of the extermination of bodies that blaspheme and will most likely snuff out everything in humanity that is not of importance to them, and yet inside this identical humanity lies the pitiful art, the 'wound' of another, sacred, humanism that is a potential site of opposition. He argues that the problem he is introducing here is merely this one: what else remains as the cultural politics of art apart from opposition to this profane negationism? And what else is left to oppose it with but our obligation to the intelligence of representation, in other words, with sacred humanism? This obligation to the intelligence of representation is one which we can never relinquish. It is the duty of discernment, philosophy, art and aesthetics to undertake to nurture it (Virilio 2003a: 52, 57, 60). Without sacred humanism at its centre in the form of the obligation to the intelligence of representation, humanity stops being capable of opposing the other form of humanism, profane humanism, that of 'the technological system' (Ellul 1980). As Virilio argues later on in the 'Pitiless Art' essay, the right to this limit on the freedom of expression is the very underpinning of sacred humanism. Humanity is only human if we are encouraged to refrain from '*the call to murder to torture*' (2003a: 57). Aesthetics' and arts' duty, then, is to consider and to support the placing of limits on the freedom of expression and to work against the urge to exclude debate about such limits from profane humanists and the discourses of picnolepsy that aim to destroy them. It is in this fashion that aesthetics and art mount a defence of sacred humanism.

Possibly the most compelling instance of the function and import of the second sense of humanism, sacred humanism, in aesthetics and art appears in a text that Virilio published after *The Aesthetics of Disappearance* and before *Art and Fear: The Art of the Motor* (1995).

Profane Humanism, Post-industrialisation and the Performance Art of Stelarc

The text that finalised Virilio's separation from many of his contemporary art associates was *The Art of the Motor*. Now, Virilio assails contemporary art confrontationally, initially attacking the figure of 'Elizabeth Sussman, chief curator of the Biennale at the Whitney Museum of American Art in New York', who, representing the obligatory profane relation to technology, and concurring with contemporary art's advertisers, stated in the spring of 1993: 'We need to redefine the art world *in more realistic terms*' (Virilio 1995: 20). 'Among the various "lessons in contextualization" offered by her exhibition', contemporary art lovers were

> thus invited to view yet again, for the umpteenth time, the famous video of Rodney King being beaten up, only this time presented and signed with the name of the 'auteur', one George Hollyday, the video amateur who witnessed the police violence and also, indirectly, caused the riots, murder, and looting in Los Angeles in April 1992. (Virilio 1995: 20)

Thus, Virilio argues that contemporary art exists in an optical illusory relationship with technology as it simultaneously censures anything that is not driven by the 'cinematic motor' and is enthralled by the 'absolute speed of electromagnetic waves' whereby 'technical mediatization' progressively revives the 'techniques of primitive mediatization' (20). This initial attack anticipates his arguments concerning profane and sacred humanism:

the redefinition of the contemporary art world 'in more realistic terms' involves the methodical elimination of 'our immediate rights, without overt violence', and the continuing production of contemporary art's 'technical beyond'. This last is Virilio's key term for the

> West's distinctive, compulsive scheme and projection toward specific aesthetic techniques at or to the further side of the theoretical threshold and/or practical scope of contemporary culture; an enigmatic desire for a technological 'elsewhere' or quasi-religious understanding of technology derived from cinematic special effects and/or the fantasies produced for television by props, camerawork, and computer graphics, etc.

that I have defined and discussed in *Virilio and the Media* (see Armitage 2012: 35–9). In other words, contemporary art's technical beyond not only 'aggravates the casting aside that excommunication used to accomplish', and plunges the 'greatest number into a now socially untenable *reality effect* with all the resultant geopolitical chaos' but also offers 'lessons in contextualization', which point towards the sense of a profane humanism invading art by continually supplying the museological and gallery system with vision technologies that depict human violence (Virilio 1995: 20).

Virilio's translation of contemporary art into an out-of-control and immensely powerful mediated technological assemblage is not purely done to upset his contemporary art colleagues (although it surely accomplished this, as did the later publication of *Art and Fear*: see Virilio and Lotringer 2005: 21). Instead, it emphasises how technology attacks the body in contemporary art (Virilio 1995: 111). Because of its optical illusory relationship with technology, he argues, contemporary art's theories and practices remain complicit with the latter's idea of cultural transformation as a technical beyond, and finally both are only equipped to portray a humanity bogged down in technology and as objects of this technical beyond. Both contemporary art and technology create systems to further the development of the technical beyond that leave no room for the option of the second sense of humanism, sacred humanism, within those mired in it. He argues that their accounts of the growth of postmodern technology in our ongoing post-industrial revolution of the twenty-first century show human beings as little more than 'willing mutants' who are being hauled 'forwards' by the 'propaganda of progress' through the transformations that are presently taking place (1995: 111; Virilio and Armitage 2009: 107). In opposition to this, in the chapter 'From Superman to Hyperactive Man' from *The Art of the Motor*, and which might well horrify some critics, he sketches the following alternative image of post-industrialisation.

'From Fred Astaire to Michael Jackson, "hyperactive" man has plenty of ancestors, especially among the dancers dear to Nietzsche, actors and contortionists, people whose bodies have gradually become instruments . . . ' 'Adept at the perfect symbiosis of the human and the technological', such 'survivors' of the 'age of human physiology, as well as of philosophy', Nietzscheans all, seek nothing less than the 'technological invasion of the body', to bristle with 'electrodes and antennae', wear 'two *laser eyes*', and become willing mutants of a 'tele-operated robotics' where 'man lurks inside the android' . . . 'Keen to see our body proper burst out of its biological envelope', the 'survivors' move from the 'fallen angels theme' to the subject of the fabrication of the '*Eve of the future*', from the idea of the human body as a 'MAN-PLANET' which will be 'liberated from Earth's attraction' to the 'categorical imperative of a human type that will have become postevolutionary' . . . 'Ranting on the theme of intergalactic travel the way astronauts typically do', the 'survivors' additionally explain that, 'since future expeditions will be measured in light-years, it will be possible to prolong life, not in some Faustian search for immortality, but in the interests of *a necessary extension of extraterrestrial intelligence*' . . . 'Once again, the exotic desire for some "great out-of-this world voyage" is merely an alibi for the technical intrusion into an inner world, that of our viscera' (Virilio 1995: 109–12).

This is an extremely contentious argument. Effectively, what Virilio is arguing is that there is in the human experience of post-industrialisation the prospect of 'hyperactivity' or of humanity becoming instrumentalised. He means that humanity is entering into some kind of strange yet perfectly symbiotic relation with technology, and that it is assenting to its overflowing with electrodes and aerials, that its bodies are undergoing a transition to laser eyes. But, it is essential to note that he is positively not arguing that the tele-operated robotics of the man who prowls inside the machine is advantageous. The important word here is 'hyperactivity'. Hyperactivity for Virilio is the desire to see our bodies erupt out of their biological coverings, but intimates also the human body as a MAN-PLANET who will be released from the Earth's magnetism. It directly points to what is currently beyond the bounds of evolution, extreme regarding the idea of prolonging life, and also insinuates the likelihood of reinvention through a 'necessary' expansion of extraterrestrial intelligence. He writes on all of these areas to argue that what is happening to humanity in the present period is nothing other than a reinvention of human exotic aspirations. Living in expectation of some great amazing journey, humanity is altering: its bodies are shifting to deal with the circumstances of technical invasion and its experiences of its technological interactions with the world are changed from those of an outer world to those of an inner world, that is, to those of its internal organs. In *The Art of the Motor* it is therefore the bodies and ambitions of humanity itself for a 'necessary' enlargement of extraterrestrial intelligence that contain the prospect of reinvention and become the site for appreciation and critique. More exactly, transformation transpires from the profane humanism of 'hyperactivity' within humanity's contemporary identities that allows it to 'survive' the profane humanism of 'sporting two laser eyes'.

According to Virilio in *The Art of the Motor*, this reinvention of the human body is encapsulated in the performance art of the Australian body artist, Stelarc (1972–). Stelarc's art literally gorges upon the latest technologies of post-industrialism. Stelarc is well known for his attempts to extend the human body's abilities through technology, the use of medical technologies, or sound systems that are distorted into the aesthetic of his robot hand (the Third Hand) or the art of his artificial arm (the Ambidextrous Arm) just by being performed in a gallery or museum and given movement, on top of his performances that 'improvise on' the movement of the human body, such as 'Fractal Flesh' (1996) which, through a sequence of voluntary, involuntary and computerised movements, interacts with the 'music' or 'choreography' of his body as it amplifies its sounds and signals like his brain waves, blood flow or muscle movements; 'Ping Body' (1996) that performs a collection of physical experiences to enact his artistic expression; or 'Parasite' (1997) in which the performance questions the design of the human body.

Virilio interprets Stelarc's art of the 1990s as pointing towards a comparable hyperactivity to that about to be inflicted on the bodies of the rest of humanity. Indeed, he points to how Stelarc's body art and technologies instrumentalise both himself and the viewer by taking his own human body and his adopted technologies and converting them into something perfectly symbiotic, 'posthuman', or even somehow 'post-technological' – something that is, specifically, profanely human. There is consequently an equivalence between what is happening to humanity and what is performed in Stelarc's art. Both, he argues, bring about the bare 'survival' of what was long held to be human physiology and philosophy, to the acceptance of electrodes and transmitters that were, until recently, thought to be as unbearable as being festooned with two laser eyes. Certainly, he argues that the:

> project of colonization – of endocolonization – . . . now entails transforming the body into 'primary material', making a laboratory rat of hyperactive man in the process . . . [U]nder the guise of 'extraterrestrial' liberation, the techno-sciences are getting their teeth into a weightless *man-planet* whom nothing can now really protect, neither ethics nor biopolitical morality. Instead of escaping from our natural biosphere, we will colonize an infinitely more accessible planet – as so often in the past – that of a body-without-a-soul, a profane body, on behalf of a science-without-a-conscience that has never ceased to profane the space of the body of animals and slaves, the colonized of former empires. (1995: 113–14)

In the fields of aesthetics and contemporary art, Stelarc's body art disputes recognised viewpoints on what a human body or work of art can do or should be. To be sure, this 'willing mutant' or, as Virilio (1995: 114) has it, this 'willing victim', destabilises the sense of the constancy and limits of the human figure while the experience of contemporary human beings is being reinvented by thoughts about tele-operated robotics and how they, as sacred human beings, might 'survive' within the machine. In view of Stelarc's body art and under the spectre, not to say spectacle, of post-industrialisation, the sense of what it is to be a human body proper changes as it ruptures its biological membrane. For Virilio, however, Stelarc does not offer an alternative or optimistic explanation of the human body proper. Rather, his art reveals the profane humanism at its heart: through the posthuman, post-technological, ways in which it re-creates the human body, the Eve of the future, and its corporeal environs, Stelarc's art declines to be tethered to humanity or elucidated in terms of planet Earth as it incites us to respond to its yearning for freedom from the pull of the planet, the categorical imperative of a human type that desires to become post-evolutionary.

The Museum of Accidents, Preventive Intelligence and the Unexpected Event

Stelarc's artwork is therefore presented by Virilio as a site where the second sense of humanism, profane humanism, seems to confirm the ongoing total destruction of previous categories of sacred humanism by the post-industrial technical beyond. This perspective on aesthetics and art as sites where reinvention is figured or presented persists throughout his writings on the aesthetics of disappearance. For an instance of this from art it is worth turning to a later exhibition and two books called *Unknown Quantity* (2003b) and *The Original Accident* (2007), together with *Grey Ecology* (2009b), in which he discusses his conception of the Museum of Accidents. At this point, he argues for the import of reflecting on the conflict between profane and sacred humanism, the option of 'preventive intelligence' regarding profane humanism, and the capacity of art as a way of bringing this preventive intelligence into the spotlight.

Virilio's Museum of Accidents narrates the tale of the founding of a 'new kind of museology or museography', of the 'throwing open' of 'the doors of the first Museum of Accidents' in which we open the 'museum to what crops up impromptu' (2003b: 6; 2007: 4–5). In fact, for Virilio, and, building on the essential work of Hans Jonas on ethics in the era of techno-science (1984), 'the *imperative of responsibility* for the generations to come requires that we now expose accidents along with the frequency of their industrial and post-industrial repetition' (2003b: 8; 2007: 7; Armitage 2012: 130–6). This was the entire purpose of his 2002–3 exhibition at the Fondation Cartier pour l'Art Contemporain in Paris in addition to its declared intention: 'A test run or, more precisely, a prefiguration of a future Museum of the Accident', the exhibition aimed 'first and foremost to take a stand against the collapse of ethical and aesthetic landmarks, that loss of meaning we so often witness now as victims much more than as actors' (2003b: 8; 2007: 7). The exhibition *Ce qui arrive*, from the Latin *accidens* (unknown quantity in English) sought to act as a counterpoint to the outrages of all stripes that we are swamped with on a daily basis by the major media outlets, that museum of horrors that no one seems to realise precedes and accompanies the escalation of even bigger disasters. (2003b: 8; 2007: 8)

From this outline of Virilio's museology, it may appear that the Museum of Accidents is a rather desperate location from which to begin speaking out against the disintegration of moral and aesthetic markers as both science museums' protest against the extinction of animal species and war museums' stand against the continuation of war are, arguably, also unsuccessful. Yet, it is not the activities of the chief museographer that concern Virilio. Instead, his exhibition and books take their point of departure from the way in which Virilio's idea of the Museum of Accidents contests the overexposure of society to representations of revulsion in art by its own status as an art exhibition and its accompanying art books. Virilio argues that, in thinking through the notion of the Museum of Accidents and organising the *Unknown Quantity* exhibition, he aimed, primarily, at keeping his distance from the 'outrages of every stripe with which current events are riddled' (2003b: 8; 2007: 8):

> Designed to raise the issue of the unexpected and of the lack of attention to major hazards, the exhibition manifesto endeavored above all to pay homage to discernment, to *preventive intelligence*, at a time when threats of triggering a *preventive war* in Iraq abounded. (2003b: 9; 2007: 8)

What Virilio is proposing here is that there is something within the very act of the paying of homage to discernment which can prevent the forms of disgraceful intimidations that activate preventive war by reducing everything to their own Iraq War fuelled descriptive discourses. Art appreciation and critique are themselves forms of coercion if they offer total accounts of an exhibition, artwork or aesthetic text, but that art appreciation and critique are also unpromising as there is something 'intelligent' in the exhibition, artwork or aesthetic text that can avert the fear of setting off preventive war in Iraq and elsewhere. Exhibitions, artworks and aesthetic texts themselves, then, are forms of preventive intelligence. The issue is: what form does this preventive intelligence take?

Virilio's argument concerning the Museum of Accidents begins by concentrating on his decision to expose us to 'the most cata- strophic accidents deriving from technoscientific genius', which he explains as the first act of preventive intelligence 'in order to kick- start' an 'approach which would consist in exposing the accident – exhibiting it – as the major enigma of modern progress' (2003b: 59; 2007: 23–4). Our exposure to the accident itself is necessary so as to 'avoid shortly inhabiting the planetary dimensions of an integral accident, one capable of integrating a whole heap of inci- dents and disasters through chain reactions', and the cataclysms and accidents elicited by the act of paying homage to discernment (2003b: 60; 2007: 24). The paying of homage to discernment is a form of realisation: through exposing ourselves to the accident we understand that 'we must start right now building, inhabiting, and thinking through the laboratory of cataclysms, the museum of the accident of technical progress' (2003b: 60; 2007: 24) as well as making links between it and a coming museology and muse- ography that up till now had not been concerned with 'the ques- tion of how to show the havoc wreaked by progress' (2003b: 60; 2007: 25). For the Virilio of *Grey Ecology* (2009b), this paying of homage to discernment is equally preventive of the unexpected and of our carelessness regarding major risks and 'exciting' because it reveals a situation of 'approximation', of, in other words, 'open- ness' (Virilio 2009b: 25, 52, 54, 62). The creation of a project wherein we expose ourselves to the accident discloses that the terrorisation that is the setting in motion of a preventive war in Iraq and many other locations are not absolute as they draw out thoughts that cannot ultimately be suppressed by the indignations of every kind. Simultaneously, the paying of homage to discern- ment is exciting and creates a point of approximation for Virilio: on determining and being exposed to the integral accident, he sug- gests that we can use it to dissect contemporary civilisation, the continuation of history, and so forth. He argues that this mixture of preventive intelligence and openness happens in each act of the paying of homage to discernment, and chiefly aesthetic and artistic discernment. The paying of homage to artistic discernment must function in relation to itself – in its specificities, in the agitation of aesthetic and artistic images as they appear or disappear, in its receptiveness to the 'energy of the visible' – the 'cinematic energy of the means of transmission' – the very labour of investigating its own excitement, approximation and openness despite the sinister menace of the unexpected and our inattentiveness to important dangers (Virilio 2009b: 60).

This examination of the paying of homage to aesthetic and artistic discernment, of exposing ourselves to the integral accident, permits Virilio to launch an argument about the preventive intelligence of the paying of homage to aesthetic and artistic discernment themselves. He argues that the paying of homage to aesthetic and artistic discernment and artistic creation, function to resist the prospect of the integral accident and double as a way of exposing its potential for catastrophe. He maintains that we must pay homage to aesthetic and artistic discernment against the integral accident, but of necessity with it. We must temporalise it, expand and contract it, and establish it within all the academic disciplines currently 'unknown' to this 'quantity' (for an exceptionally fascinating explanation of how, to date, neither ignorance nor the 'unknown' quantity have been introduced either organisationally or intellectually into contemporary academic branches of learning, see Roberts 2012: 1–22). The paying of homage to aesthetic and artistic discernment utilises our knowledge of the integral accident, but establishes within that knowledge new areas of academic enquiry (forms of the 'unknown', or, to use Virilio's idiom, methods of connecting the 'unknown to its 'quantity'). Consequently, the paying of homage to aesthetic and artistic discernment engenders a space for the appreciation of what Virilio names 'the accident of art', which is an event that is beyond us, but which, together, we can both appreciate and critique (Virilio and Lotringer 2005; Virilio 2009b: 66). In opposition to this, the integral accident endeavours to dehumanise and to accelerate the accident of art, to introduce the speed of real time or the acceleration of reality, and relegate the significance of the accident of art to predetermined categories of speed: in other words, the accident of art disappears into the acceleration of history, into what Virilio describes as the 'landscape of events' (2000). An accident of art will be reclaimed only if it exemplifies the unexpected event (2009b: 66).

Hence, according to Virilio, the work of both the artist and the critic of the art of technology is to intelligently prevent the elimination of the accident of art, against its unintelligent classification as representation as a form of delay, to maintain excitement. This is the intelligent prevention sought by the paying of homage to aesthetic and artistic discernment against the indignations of every sort with which present events are pierced. Such infuriation has to taint the marvel that an undetermined accident, an unspecified surprise, is occurring (Armitage 2012: 120). The strategic force of aesthetics and art, as a result, is to appreciate the occurrence of what Virilio calls 'an accident of art'. Unlike the thought patterns that invoke the integral accident, which aim to understand these accidents of art in keeping with what is already known about human civilisation, aesthetics and art stage their occurrence without inevitably supplying thorough analyses or rationalisations of them. They open up the world of contemporary culture and social order to enquiry and ideas by allowing them to be exciting, approximate, and, above all, open. But what does Virilio mean by an 'accident of art'?

The Accident of Art

The concept of the 'accident of art' is vital to many of the subjects in Virilio's theory of visual culture that this chapter has investigated up till now. An accident of art questions traditional discourses and demands that all that was prior to it be retheorised. In other words, an accident of art is the origin of the aesthetics of disappearance. Virilio describes the accident of art in the following way in response to a question posed by Sylvère Lotringer:

> The accident of science induces the accident of knowledge, and art is a branch of knowledge, there's no question about it. Here we touch on something that interests me very much: the accident of knowledge. Through mathematical precision, through the experimental method, we have built a structure for science. But there are branches of knowledge without experimental methods, in the mathematical and scientific sense of the word – and that's what art is. Experimental science is the opposite of storytelling, chimeras and myth. The rational position of science has gradually broken away from alchemy and magic. The experience, the experiment of art can't be mathematized, and so, yes, in my opinion, the accident is total. We are entering the period of the *total accident*: Everything has been damaged in the accident. Knowledge has been mortally maimed . . . everything that constitutes the world has experienced an accident, and this *without exception*. The colossal dimension of the accident surpasses us, and that's why I am so passionate about it. (Virilio and Lotringer 2005: 34)

This is a multifaceted explanation, but one that lies at the core of Virilio's concept. The purpose of this section is to spell out what the connotations of the accident of art are and how aesthetics and art are ideal sites for the incidence of accidents of art in Virilio's philosophy.

Virilio's most meticulous arguments concerning the meaning of the 'accident', and its affiliation with aesthetics and art take place in two books featuring the neorealist German artist-painter, Peter Klasen (1935–), which are *Peter Klasen* (Virilio 1999) and *The Accident of Art* (Virilio and Lotringer 2005).

What attracts Virilio to Klasen is the 'figuration narrative' of his airbrushed artwork: for Klasen's paintings consist of his own visual language rooted in the integration of photography. Klasen's 'Tableaux-rencontres' (cut-out images of consumer and medical objects such as telephones and electrical equipment, lipsticks, stethoscopes, thermometers and syringes), for example, are devoid of individual energy first and foremost because his paintings are the consequence of his spray gun, which Klasen uses to offset his superimposed cut-out images. Throughout the 1960s and 1970s, Klasen expanded upon the subject of the body and health, portraying neon embellished objects like surgical utensils, bidets and automobile exhaust pipes. He also produced a series depicting baths and toilets, but exhibited them at their actual size with an eye to evoking the 'violence' of such 'banal' images. Soon after, Klasen painted his 'Tableaux Binaries', which amalgamate sections of the human body and painted objects (e.g. an open mouth combined with a stethoscope). He thus works with what we have already seen Virilio likes to call the 'energy of the visible', with the dynamic between images that are usually considered sensual or pleasurable and those that are normally thought of as machinic or disturbing. Like Virilio, Klasen believes that the ideology of progress is a kind of propaganda put forward by technophiliacs with a proclivity for self-imposed confined spaces and suffocating atmospherics. In the 1980s, Klasen deserted his prior concentration on the shards of techno-science to engage the fleeting nature of time through dribbles, blemishes and graffiti as forms of representation. Yet, in 1981, he and 30 of his fellow figuration narrative advocates still felt the need to collectively paint an armoured door. In addition, in 1986, Klasen began his 'Mur de Berlin' cycle, a series of 100 paintings which he created before the fall of the Berlin Wall. The 'Mur de Berlin' cycle was followed by Klasen's installation *Shock Corridor/Dead End*, an installation that measured over 1,000 square feet and which was inspired by the Samuel Fuller film *Shock Corridor* (1963) which relates the story of a journalist who commits himself to a mental hospital so as to solve a murder. Since the 1990s, Klasen has reintroduced the body into his artwork, including erotic images of nude women, and also painted his eschatological responses to the assaults on the World Trade Center in New York City on 11 September 2001 (Virilio 1999; Virilio and Lotringer 2005).

This figuration narrative, or what Virilio calls 'Impact Inspections', articulates for him a preventive intelligence to our socio-cultural conditioning to military technologies ('Klasen was born in Lubeck, and he was in Lubeck during the bombing' of World War II) and the profane humanist belief that contemporary aesthetics and art should stand for the culture of the 'willing victims' such as Stelarc or continue to chronicle their activities (see Virilio 1999 and Virilio and Lotringer 2005: 41). He argues that a 'Tableaux-rencontres' by Klasen draws a distinction between narratives of the wars of time of the twentieth century and the devastation of German cities especially: 'Peter Klasen witnessed the conflagration in the cathedral where the Virgin of Membling disappeared. He's someone who lived through the war' (Virilio and Lotringer 2005: 41). The reaction to a Klasen 'Tableaux-rencontres', to Klasen's aesthetics and artwork, is in consequence a reaction to the art of the accident. We are faced not by a painting of an external accident but by a painting trapped in slow motion, by a flat image of stationary, unfriendly, machines, contemporary cut-ups of the technological apparatus, that have stopped working, disintegrated, so that we can not only see them for what they are but also see their 'impact', which can only be deduced from Klasen's presentation of their components. Nonetheless, Klasen's images of immobile machines focus the viewers' attention 'on the technological object', on 'techniques' and 'technological still lives' (Virilio and Lotringer 2005: 41).

For Virilio, the technological still lives and the associated sensations produced by a Klasen painting afford a way in to a new feeling for aesthetics and art, the accident of art, which reinvents our daily awareness of experience:

When he paints a grid, or a reinforced door with the words: 'Warning: High Voltage,' he makes us see the face of the technological *dasein* [being in its ontological and philosophical sense for Martin Heidegger in his magnum opus *Being and Time* (1978)] . . .

What I like in his work is the large screens. They're like 'instrument panels' of a machine with warning lights studding the control panels. His images are stereotypical and iconoclastic. The threat is omnipresent in his work . . .

Klasen reveals the face of technical beings. (Virilio and Lotringer 2005: 42)

Since there is no space in Klasen's paintings, which are usually totally smooth, and yet their impact on the viewer is so aggressive and cruel, our conscious critical abilities are armed against the ecstasy of acceleration. The narrative figuration of the painting calls to mind the technological still lives and the related feeling that an undetermined and unexpected thing has come to pass with no knowledge of what it is even though it can be sensed and touched ubiquitously. It requires a 'callous' response from the viewer without giving any genuine intimation about what technology the painting symbolises, except, perhaps, the mercilessness of technology itself. We have the feeling that an unspecified and unintentional thing has come into being, but it appears almost out of the question to determine quite what that indefinite chance event is, apart from, possibly, death made alive through the threatening and motionless silence of the technological machine. The difference between an unnamed and accidental thing that takes place and what occurs by chance is fundamental. To be capable of articulating what occurs accidentally is already to have comprehended the significance of an accident of art, to have absorbed it into awareness and installed it into an already existing aesthetic or artistic discourse. Conversely, the indeterminate property, factor or attribute that was formerly thought to be unnecessary taking place or occurring inadvertently demands an excitement about, an approximation of, and an openness to the accident of art itself, a response to it that is not directed by known visual rules and an interrogation of those theoretical discourses that seem incapable sufficiently to recognise it in their analytical systems and ideas. In this type of reaction, the accident of art intelligently prevents the concealment of the face of technical beings (it is, in itself, made to reappear), and yet it objects to those conventional forms of representation as they try to stifle the perfect symbiosis that is 'the face of the figureless' (Virilio and Lotringer 2005: 42). This difference between the undecided thing, issue or quality that was up to that moment thought to be uncalled for and what occurs unexpectedly is the foundation for Virilio's thinking on the accident of art.

We can as a result reorient the previous citation to state that for Virilio an accident of art resides in the perception of the face of the technological *dasein* wherein a sometimes vague and fortuitous thing occurs to which we are summoned to react without understanding beforehand the way in which to react, for example, to Klasen's large screens or instrument panels. For Virilio, then, accidents of art occur in such a fashion that once recognised discourses of the machine are powerless to react satisfactorily to their remarkable warning lights and control panels. The accident of art may be something as 'straightforward' as Jacques-Henri Lartigue's 'trap for vision', a Klasen painting, or a conventional or iconoclastic advertising image, or as intricate and significant as the threat to expose the face of technical beings or the face of the figureless. Throughout Virilio's writings, the accident of art is what requires a reaction, a decision concerning, for instance, profane humanism, which appreciates yet also critiques its uncaring specificity and declines merely to install it into the prearranged technological scheme of the abstract surfaces of paintings and photography.

In Klasen's case, and neorealist aesthetics and art in general, the accident of art performs the rejection of aesthetics and art to be demoted to advertising propaganda or publicity. For Virilio, it is increasingly the organisation of technologically driven advertising, where the experience of sacred humanism and the sensation that encircles this experience, is being dissipated into the computations of promotion and marketing that art such as Klasen's relation to the accident of art stands to reinvent by redirecting 'the figurative through advertising' (Virilio and Lotringer 2005: 43; Virilio 2011: 234–8). If artworks like Klasen's can sustain inside themselves the face of the technological *dasein*, the face of the accident of art, they preserve an incalculable thing that is irreducible to the celebration of advertising or consumer objects. Evaluated from the viewpoint of the accident of art, artworks such as Klasen's have the capability to expose the aesthetics of disappearance beneath the discourses of Pop Art and popular culture, advertising, and news that continue to influence our socio-cultural lives and the lives of our consumer technologies. For Virilio, art appreciation and critique starts with the accident of art, and its duty is to unravel the repercussions of the artwork's irreducibility to time-honoured theories of address and practices of painting and photography, cinema, and television.

Conclusion

According to Virilio, artworks and aesthetics do not offer exact responses to theoretical issues. Instead, their worth derives from their capacity to produce enquiries that can question the techniques of particular philosophies and their associated discourses that endeavour to supply all-inclusive accounts of art and aesthetic practices. For Virilio, artworks have the ability to depict the aesthetics of disappearance that these discourses suppress. Virilio writes of this capability as a form of what I have identified as sacred humanism. In pitiful art the devices of compassion and sympathy can be assigned to this increasingly sacredly human- rather than profane-centred, standpoint on humankind. On the contrary, the perspective of the latter, I see as marked by contempt or irreverence for what is sacred about humanity in contrast, and I associate it with self-styled posthuman visual representations that depict, for instance, posthuman forms and posthuman misuse of the sacred human body in entirely disrespectful or techno-ritualistic ways: the human body at all times portrayed as outside of or 'beyond' our knowledge of sacred humanism; with the uninitiated or most vulgar coarseness used to identify the most sacrilegious deviations, especially in inappropriate illustrations or sculptures like the Nazi gnomes and the acts of artists such as Ottmar Hörl. When humanism is prefixed by the 'profane-', the concept effectively becomes the designation for an improper, unworthy, degrading or abusive theoretical discourse and practice I have argued to be based on, and to stand for, the mocking, posthuman interests of derisive, disdainful artists whose real and scathing intolerance concerning respect for humanity as something sacred and ideas of humanism in art, culture and civilisation are misleadingly presented – for instance, in much contemporary art – as impartially accurate. In this chapter, I have argued, with, I believe, good reasons, that profane humanism is not so much a 'controversial' or 'satirical' form of art (terms that, for profane humanists, are markers of their 'success') as a pitiless form of art. I would highlight, for example, that Ottmar Hörl's 1,250 gnomes making Nazi salutes (first exhibited as *Dance With the Devil* in Straubing, Germany, in 2009), one of a number of influential 'satires' on the rise of fascism in contemporary art, did not embrace any prior discussions with the people of Straubing. These two senses of humanism, of sacred and profane humanism, continue to coexist in contemporary art discourse and exemplify the harsh disagreements that typify the academic subject of visual culture. Today, however, though the cultural, political and discursive divisions continue – actually they have become intensified (over Nazism, the contemporary profanation of posthuman forms and bodies, and the museology of atrocity, etc.) – debate over definitions of display and justifications of artistic value in contemporary visual culture, ideas of terror, the point of art exhibition and edification, and so on, is becoming more considered. This indicates that, contrary to the profane humanism of overexposing the public to representations of dismay and terror in contemporary art and of the inattentiveness to important risks caused by the integral accident, aesthetics and art can not only consider but also induce sensations of the pitiful or of piety that are irreducible to pitiless insensitivity or immoral criteria. These sensations, Virilio argues, indicate sacred humanism's limits to the freedom of expression at the sacred heart of humanity that intelligently prevents the summons to cybernetic suicide or torment currently led by the dominant practitioners and discourses of contemporary art such as those of Stelarc.

On account of its plea to this intelligence of representation, to this sacred humanism within us and its power forever to go beyond theoretical explanation, Virilio argues that artworks often appear as accidents of art. For those seeking to further develop this idea of the accident of art, which is essential to Virilio's philosophy, it is a matter of thinking through the nameless address of the machine in Klasen's and others' aesthetics and art, its imperceptibility, its spectral emission of fear in the void, its 'monochrome' (even when in colour) and menacing sensation of imminence that an unnameable thing, an incalculable accident, is about to occur unintentionally. The accident of art denotes the point at which an unidentified and unplanned thing occurs that has the possibility to splinter earlier methods of elucidating, for example, the stillness of the eye of the webcam, a kind of blindness that overwhelms everything in the room. Making sense of the realm of aesthetics and art demands new forms of experiencing the suggestive power of the screen and very different modes of 'cold-blooded' decision-making from those propounded by the advocates of profane humanism. As Bowles might have it if he were still here with us today, not all the negative effects caused by our pitiless era of aesthetics, art and technology are currently touchable. The insidious varieties of obliteration, those involving only the spirit of sacred humanism, are the most to be feared.

References

Armitage, John (2012), *Virilio and the Media*, Cambridge: Polity.

Bowles, Paul (1955), *The Spider's House*, London: Penguin.

Connolly, Kate (2009), 'Nazi gnomes cause outcry in Germany', *The Guardian*, 14 October.

Ellul, Jacques (1980), *The Technological System*, trans. Joachim Neugroschel, New York: Continuum.

Heidegger, Martin (1978), *Being and Time*, trans. John Macquarrie and Edward Robinson, Oxford: Blackwell.

Jonas, Hans (1984), *The Imperative of Responsibility: In Search of an Ethics for the Technological Age*, trans. Hans Jonas and David Herr, Chicago: University of Chicago Press.

Roberts, Joanne (2012: 1–22), 'Organizational ignorance: Towards a managerial perspective on the unknown', *Management Learning*.

Virilio, Paul (1995), *The Art of the Motor*, trans. Julie Rose, Minneapolis: University of Minnesota Press.

Virilio, Paul (1999), *Peter Klasen*, Paris: Expressions Contemporaine.

Virilio, Paul (2000), *A Landscape of Events*, trans. Julie Rose, Princeton: Princeton Architectural Press.

Virilio, Paul (2003a), *Art and Fear*, trans. Julie Rose, London: Continuum.

Virilio, Paul (2003b), *Unknown Quantity*, trans. Chris Turner, London: Thames and Hudson.

Virilio, Paul (2007), *The Original Accident*, trans. Julie Rose, Oxford: Polity.

Virilio, Paul (2009a), *The Aesthetics of Disappearance*, trans. Philip Beitchman, New York: Semiotext(e).

Virilio, Paul (2009b), *Grey Ecology*, trans. Drew Burk, New York: Atropos Press.

Virilio, Paul (2011), 'Impact studies', in J. Armitage (ed.), *Virilio Now: Current Perspectives in Virilio Studies*, Cambridge: Polity, pp. 234–8.

Virilio, Paul and Armitage, John (2009), 'In the cities of the beyond: An interview with Paul Virilio', *OPEN 18: 2030: War Zone Amsterdam: Imagining the Unimaginable*, pp. 100–11.

Virilio, Paul and Lotringer, Sylvère (2005), *The Accident of Art*, trans. Michael Taormina, New York: Semiotext(e).

11

What We Do is Secrete: On Virilio, Planetarity and Data Visualisation

Benjamin H. Bratton

Perhaps three years ago, I was speaking with the architect, Neil Denari, about how, in the 1980s and 1990s, French theory of technology had been approached, fetishised, absorbed and mobi-lised by experimental design practices, such as his own. About Virilio, he said something like, 'we were trying to figure out what the architecture would look like that would embody his theory'. Clearly Virilio's own early collaborations with Claude Parent were not it. 'We kept hoping that the answer would be on the next page, but it never was.' The text below considers one belated or at least delayed – and certainly problematic – candidate for what Virilio's thought looks like: Exit *(2008).*

Is Space Digital, Is Earth Space?

Craig Hogan is an astronomer at the University of Chicago, and was a member of the High-z Supernova Search that helped discover dark energy, the substance which, as it turns out, may comprise most of the universe, all the way out to the edges of space where time began. Dark energy not only fills space, but as it grows, it expands space. The amount of dark energy is actually increasing, and so not only is the universe expanding, but its rate of expansion is accelerating. Acceleration, the speed of speed, is a physical fundament of reality, perhaps the most fundamental fun-dament. Of late, Hogan has been working on another project of similar scope and significance: an experiment which would prove that the absolute fabric of space is not smooth and continuous but chunky and blocky (see Moyer 2012). In a way, Hogan's experi-ment would demonstrate that at its tiniest scale space is digital, comprised actually of the finest possible state oscillations. The implications of such an insight might be incredible, or they might be met with a shrug, or with the assumption that the formal 'metaphor' of the digital, of informationalism, has found another way to naturalise its fragile, historically contingent appetite. (Or, the implications of 'digital space' may be incredible, barely comprehensible in the span of our immediate history, and met with such incredulousness.)

Meanwhile, Paul Virilio is a philosopher based in Paris, who has written scores of texts attempting to provide a negative apologetics of globalisation and the subsumption of the continuity of the Earth, as experiential terrain, into the omnivorous universalisms of cyberinfrastructure. The 'world' is a casualty of its appearance in digital images of itself. It cannot survive its own testimony. It is shrunken, eaten, defamed by its reduction to a plateau of digitalised time. What, for Virilio, is the technique of this death? Where difference and analogy are naturally functions of distance, in the ecumene of global information the ecology of distances has collapsed. For Virilio, digital space is its own kind of dark energy, one which instead of expanding space and elongating real distances, flattens the space of analogy into the ubiquity of network time. What is the image of that ubiquity? What is the Time-Image of the World? What is our own acceleration, displacement, elongation, migration, vector, line, link? Can it be properly *drawn, presented, framed* without replicating the terms of reduction that Virilio's metaphysics of the digital image would want to escape? In other words, when is the digital diagram, the interfacial network visualisation, also a *cosmogram* (a diagram of the whole of the Earth and its cosmic situation)? What violence does its interactive *speed* do to the depth (or depthlessness) of the global space that it models? What can we do with these pictures of the data that we, the world, secrete: what do they want from us?[1]

Native Land, Stop Eject, a 2008 exhibition at Fondation Cartier pour l'Art Contemporain in Paris, curated by Virilio and Raymond Depardon, featured extensive visualisations of qualitative and quantitative data to demonstrate an *Informational Earth-ontology* of generalised mobilisation. Known first as *Exit 2*, to differentiate it from Virilio's curatorial statement, *Exits House*, and then later simply as *Exit*, these indexical, diagrammatic polemics and their immersive environmental staging were realised as a collaboration between statistician-artists, Mark Hansen and Ben Rubin, who developed the physical data display, and architects, Laura Kurgen and Diller Scofidio + Renfro, in collaboration with Stewart Smith,

Robert Gerard Pietrusko, Aaron Meyers, Michael Doherty and Hans-Christoph Steiner, using a projection system created by Bernd Lintermann and managed with Niko Völzow, both of the Center for Art and Media Karlsruhe (ZKM).[2] The result is an iconic, magnificent immersive panorama that works as a cipher for the paradoxical symmetries between various geopolitical emergencies and paradoxes, for example the forced migration of indigenous populations, on the one hand, and the forcible prevention of migration of undocumented persons, on the other. *Exit*, the cosmogram, sees the Earth as digital, or least as a digitisable construct, or perhaps it takes that supposed digital composability as the object of its critique. But what is most urgently at stake, in its rendering of Earth-as-data-in-motion plus Earth-in-motion-as-data, is the *geometry of geography* from which sovereign claims to the planet – and sites upon it, and within its envelope, including our own persons – can be configured. In examining *Exit*, I am interested in a *geophilosophy* of (data) visualisation. We don't have such a resource, or perhaps instead we are drowning in it. We are up to our eyeballs in network visualisations but without sufficient meta-language to make sense of the patterns of the patterns woven from patterns. Or, on the other hand, and in light of recent commentaries by Bruno Latour and Lev Manovich, perhaps the network-images provide an alternative syntax, grammar, vocabulary – even a new anatomical channel of cognition – that make those old meta-languages of meaning meaningless.[3] Is it one or the other? Because Virilio has been one of the most militant and nuanced critics of how the 'grey ecology' of digital information distorts and diminishes the visual field, and with it the scalar integrity of the Earthly horizon, this chapter will draw links between that one and that other. It does so through the example of *Exit*, and its use of complex data visualisation as an auto-pedagogical platform. Through this, we may see how the intensively affective landscape of interactive surfaces, and their liquid digital semiotics, both is and is not constitutive of what Virilio might call *accidents* of perception and the governability of human movement. We can consider a 'Virilian' critique of data visualisation in relation to this exhibition, its ambitions and its insights. Perhaps such critique will validate this particular panorama and perhaps it will not.

Processing: The Relative Motility of the Image of Relative Motility

The voyage stacks space upon space, concrete space upon the space of knowledge, the space of practical communication upon the former two. It therefore stacks map upon map, world-map upon world-map, the uniform space of plains and seas, the space of techniques, the space of knowledges. When the first cycle is exhausted, a second cycle is constituted from it; when the second is finished, a third, and so forth. The voyage is inscribed on several maps at the same time: thus there is a vertical component, thus, interchanges between the world-maps, passages between the maps. There are folds, there are faults, there are breaks, there are passages. (Serres 1975: 175)

I'm nostalgic for the world's magnitude, of its immensity. (Virilio 2010)

The exhibition with two curators and two names has two themes. First, Depardon's *Terre Natale*, 'Native Land', refers to an interest in the loss of 'native' geographies, territories, concepts of space – homelands – through the homogenisation of global grids and their extrinsic, comprehensive, trans-terrestrial perspectives. Just as the global careers of Sanskrit, Latin, French, English endangered and ultimately eradicated tens of thousands of fully formed human languages, mature technologies of expression, so too have telescopes, microscopes, telegraphs, satellites, fibre optics, supply-chain synchronisation protocols, TCP/IP, QR codes, Google Earth, etc. absorbed other possible territories into their master systems. For example, in the exhibition catalogue, Bruce Albert discusses the transformation of 'Yanomami territory' from *urihi pata* ('the whole world') through its translations and encounters with colonial cartographies, up to the present. Spoiler: it gets both smaller and more specific. 'Native spaces', the diversity of human geography, is eaten alive, like native languages, until only network time fills up the Earth. Second, Virilio describes 'Stop Eject' (the English phrase is used[4]) in terms that might suggest a more melancholy version of William S. Burroughs/Brion Gysin's admonition that we, the species, are 'Here to Go'. By that, the innovators of the Cut-Up meant that evolution from one body to the next, from one interior to the next, from one planet to the next is based on a genetic-existential restlessness and desire for flight. For Virilio, the compulsion to movement is instead a kind of absolute inverse incarceration within a total space that requires everyone and everything to live (if to live at all) under the governance of a regime of relative motility. You are not allowed not to move. That is, unless your movement, like that of *sans-papiers*, represents some exact contradiction within a global capital–demand–labour–conflict apparatus that compels migration but punishes and polices its legal representation.

These are the stakes for the exhibition, and specifically for the main showpiece, *Exit*, to exhibit and give representation to the grids that engineer these eradications and compulsions, and, ironically/problematically/purposefully to embarrass and make nude such processes in the real natural language of grid-time itself: the *network visualisation*. So once again, what is network visualisation as a *cosmogram*, or as what Heidegger called a 'World-Image'? I wonder if that is not really the question most at stake as outlined by Virilio for this project? An open question of *planetarity and its portraiture*? After all, what is on display is this logic of display itself. If that is the case, what do we make of the fact that the exhibition suggests no *outside* of this total network space, but only returns that metrical gaze upon itself? Specifically, *Exit* is not one visualisation, but a series of immersive, panoramic cinematic-diagrams conceived, designed and programmed by that extraordinary super-team of artist-coders-architects.[5] (Perhaps soon, that combination of skill-sets will be the norm for any serious work of seeing–inhabiting–analysing, which is to say, 'urbanism'.) Spectacularly in the round, the exhibition screens cinematic visualisations based on data relating to the following (themes as named in the catalogue): *natural disasters, political refugees and forced migration, speechless and deforestation, rising seas, sinking cities, population shifts: cities, remittances: sending money home.* (So that my commentary is not too abstract, the reader should pause from the text now and view still images and videos of *Exit* on the Fondation Cartier channel at <http://www.dailymotion.com/video/xb7pwl_native-land-stop-eject-copenhagen_creation>. For more stills and some commentary on the design, see <http://stewd.io/w/exit> and/or <http://vimeo.com/album/95133>.)

To compose these patterned-events/evental patterns, and to project them as ultimately visual realities, is both timely and fragile. There is a paradox is at work. *Exit*, it would appear, exhibits the information that explicates Virilio's commentary, whereas Virilio and his commentary, it would appear, undermine this innocence of information, and the disposition toward visual translation and exhibition. Insofar as the exhibition and Virilio are neighbours, *in situ*, what does *Exit really* say about Virilio when their conjunction suggests at once the philosopher's commentary as a metatheory of visual culture, or a particular definition of visual culture as information, or an example of that culture, or even perhaps the visual culture of that commentary? How best to account for the works of designer-programmers juxtaposed to the commentary – or to that philosopher's physical person in this case – which are posed as its expressive translation: a visualisation of the argument about visualisation, indeed against even the culture of the visual per se, but which this work is nevertheless itself as an undeniably expert example? At question is the tension between (1) the exhibition of an image of information, a figure which would characterise, distance, challenge the presence of 'information' as world-substance and as an agent of dromocratic mobilisations, and which would serve as analogy to the eschatological condemnation of informationalism in Virilio's texts, and (2) an appearance of the image rendered from information, an immanent diagrammatic constellation of the traces produced by the placement and displacement of connections across time and through space, an indexical smear coded in Processing, OpenGL, drawn from spreadsheets, its rows and columns populated by the accumulated instances of causes, transitions and effects of the forces of relative global motility, from micropayments to megacities, 'every person represented by one pixel'. In this tension, two accidents come into focus: network visualisation as failed cosmogram, and the dissolved subject of data visualisation. More on these below.

From World-Image to World-Visualisation

The coupling of geographic visualisation and remote sensing technologies with ever more accessible gigaflop computing capabilities allows researchers in a broad range of contemporary sciences, from climate modelling and comparative genomics to satellite-based archaeology and population epidemiology, to render intensely vivid representations of worldly processes as 'networks' and to calculate and integrate discontinuous information flows into precise planetary-scale instruments. *Exit* both references critically and exemplifies this coupling. Data visualisation megaprojects are

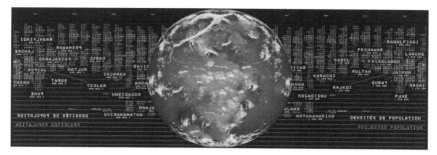

Figure 11.1 From *Exit* (2012), the Earth rolling over the panorama space unfurling data on the projected population of its megacity nodes. Image courtesy of Stewdio.

Figure 11.2 Can you find yourself in this image? From *Exit* (2012), Exhibition attendees viewing a visualisation of the flows of remittances from one country to another. Image courtesy of Stewdio.

not only an increasingly normative means for doing science across disciplines, they often form the basis of general-purpose technologies, letting you and I situate and organise our lives and interests through them or in their image.

For example, the quantified self ('QS') movement evangelises the potential for such transparent feedback systems to improve personal performance and well-being. In the rendering of life as data, our subjectivity is rendered, comprehensively, as the 'User'. A second- or third-order cybernetic architecture is at work: global visualisations (like we see in *Exit*) are composed to sift patterns within landscapes of informational events and actors, which may be already piloting themselves according to more local indexes,

Figure 11.3 'pixels represente . . . ' From *Exit* (2012). Still from amateur video of the exhibition, in which for some visualisations one pixel represents every person.

diagrams and feedback loops (such as the self-accounting regimes of QS), which in turn may also be responding directly to modulations in the global system in which they see themselves as an embedded actor (like the drivers who all refer to the same Google Maps road traffic data updates and switch freeways all at once, effectively causing new traffic jams or even alleviating the snarl from which they tried to escape: the regulatory equilibrium of self-mapping swarms). After all in *Exit*, 'every person is represented by one pixel'.[6] Its global visualisation describes a universal system monitoring particular events, which are, in turn, monitoring themselves in relation to the universal system, and back again. Here the 'global' is not some master abstraction, and the local is not an autonomous thread of events and instances. Instead both are interwoven, mutually embedded scales of assemblage that comprise and delimit one another. As in the *Exit* visualisations, the multiplied accumulation of smaller-scale assemblages (information events such as a single cash remission or cross-border movement) cascades across the plane of the Earth composing the global scale as the pattern-space of these interlocking network flows (as in this case the patterns of the financescape). At the same time, the scale of the global assemblage provides top-down structures (legal, geographic, semiotic) governing and delimiting bottom-up multiplications, and so recomposes forces 'back down' to regional and molecular levels, determining in advance the kind of flows that can and cannot be initiated and sustained. In this architecture, the global and the local are not dichotomous, but are mutually embedded one inside the other.[7] While this is not exactly big news for social theory, it is worth pointing out again for this context in light of, and as a corrective to, some of the current discourses about networks and visualisation. I am specifically referring to Latour's reading of Gabriel Tarde's sociological monadology vis-à-vis data visualisation, which is positioned by him against Durkheim's macrologic abstractions, and leads him to conclude, in characteristically reductive fashion, that there is 'no global' and 'only' nothing but the local at different scales.[8] But instead I find that the sum of parts-that-busily-sum-themselves is always both more and less whole than the whole-which-sums-their-sums. In this recursion – the measurement of phenomena that already order themselves with mechanisms identical to those used to do the measuring – underscores that such planetary information infrastructure and the cultures of a data diagrammatics as a general-purpose epistemological method, is a means not only to scan a world but to *compose* one as well. Data visualisation is, for good or ill, a kind of *worlding*.

However, as Virilio has repeatedly articulated in dozens of different ways in as many books, one persistent irony of modernity's auto-technologisation is that as the capacity for very high-resolution representations of worldly space scales quantitatively, our own individual and collective abilities to comprehend and access the world as a coherent situation correspondingly wane.[9] The modern ethos of disclosure, transparency and enlightenment is channelled into ever higher degrees of informational, diagrammatic density and more operative means to circulate, socialise, represent and instrumentalise these sums, which in their provision of one world and worlding, efface others. They eat languages and territories. This chronic disjuncture between systemic complexity and representational fidelity on the one hand, and the dissipation of meaningful situatedness on the other has been characterised by critical philosophical discourses variously as metaphysical catastrophe, political disorientation and a pervasive precarity of social cognition.[10] In his 1938 essay, 'The Age of the World

Picture', Heidegger lamented the homogenisation of knowledge under the rubric of a techno-science that invests its energies in the construction of increasingly rationalised images of the world, and in the disciplining of these images mistaken for an advanced comprehension of the world (see Heidegger 1982 [1938]: 115). But since then the situation has also changed, has been both radicalised and involuted. The emergence of Information Visualisation as a mature design and scientific discipline is based less on the Enlightenment's curation of carefully harvested bits of precious data points, than as an adaptation to the challenge of an *over-abundance* of information. Its job is to simplify, summarise and attempt to give some narrative to stores of data that come at us too fast and too complex for unmediated interpretation to handle. That is, the answer to a query about the world proves so complicated that another question must be asked of the first answer to make it legible and practical, and so on into further recursion. Our eyes are burned by the light of this abyss, so we shield them with the shade of diagrams. In this cycle, the signal-to-noise ratio of everyday life is at stake. Again, whereas the first modernity of science was predicated on the precious rarity of data coaxed from formal experiment, and the performance of close readings upon it, the second is being designed to manage the oceans of chatter that have resulted from the globalisation of computational surveillance, tracking, monitoring, storage and compositional technologies (and to automate pattern recognition without the depth or prejudice of primate hermeneutics).

Now inside the critical tension of *Exit*, between *image* of *information* ('what is information doing in the world?') and *image* from *information* ('what is the world as information?') is couched another tension between cosmogram and territory as such. The basis of delineation itself is at stake for the contemporary 'world picture' (let's say now 'world-visualisation') now no longer drawn but programmed. No less now than before, the production, display and consumption of the image-territories, constitutes the irresolvability of political geography through the always shifting terms of interiority and exteriority by which one geography is nested inside another by different social actors for different purposes. What is local for me may be global for you. We can ask then: from the age of the world-image to the duration of the world-visualisation, what is delineation within globality, including borders, when as in *Exit*, they are derived both *from* and *as* the programmed image-assemblage of interlocking assembled image-events? Every claim on globality, every cosmogram, is not only a description of what fills space, it is also claim for *the very quality of space* in which it imagines itself to be and into which its politics would ever move. It is not merely that the global, what Jean-Luc Nancy defines as 'an indistinct totality grasped as a whole', is sufficiently vast and objective that it might contain the multiplicity of movements made within it, but that its very positing, position and projection already constitutes a medium of distance and differentiation (see Nancy 2007). Further, for the global, it is not only that its conditions of translation would require visualisation, they are only ever being visualised and re-visualised over and over without resolution, generating the blurred quality of geography by putting it to work, as image, and transforming the world into a territory of *interfaces* specific to its quantifiable characteristics and agendas.[11] This interfaciality is, as I will discuss below, critical for the specific cosmogrammatic claims of *Exit*. And so we must, contra Heidegger et al., entertain the notion then that the chronic disjuncture between information fidelity and phenomenological depth is not a pathology of the modern but a condition of worldliness per se, of the inscription of territorial information as a reductive 'framing of the earth', and as the fundamental basis first of architecture and then of art, of any synthetic identification and projection: of design itself.[12] Or, even, going back to Manovich and Latour, is it a matter of learning another way of thinking through exegetic pattern recognition? But even if we wish to make that particular leap of faith, immanence, even immanence of the emergent diagram, is despite its role in the Deleuzian turn, hardly a fully secular move. For Virilio, the Christian, the global conversion – from Catholic cosmogram and the *axis mundi* that named the temporal immensity of 'the world' to the shrunken, *flattened*, two-dimensional and affectless network time of the 'planet' that fills it up on screen – is an absorption, secularisation and profanation of the divine. He remarks in a recent interview with Sylvère Lotringer on the financial crash, that today's qualities of technology – 'instantaneity, ubiquity, immediacy' – are those 'associated with the divine'.[13] Indeed the classical immanence of the divine in the world is more overdrawn than overthrown by the immanence of the emergent programmed image, appearing in, on, and as the world in the form of recursive data visualisation.

But even so not all parts of Earth are equal. Heidegger obsessed about the ground, but as Catherine Malabou writes, he 'forgot all about the air' (see Galloway 2012). For *Exit*, the emergent, immanent programmed world-visualisation is literally drawn by *lines* extending across a subdivided plane, new longitudes and latitudes cross-segmenting into finer and finer grained grids and alter-grids. This doesn't only segment space, it generates it. In *The Nomos of the Earth* (1950) the infamous, and now posthumously ubiquitous, Carl Schmitt unfolds a European history of such linear partitions as both primordial taking and occupation, and the projection and abstraction of jurisdiction in the image of its territorial division (Schmitt 2003 [1950]). Land and water provided an initial difference between the firm ground as one mode of Earth that is durably occupied and which demands the legal and military claims of the sovereign state, and another liquid surface which was, instead, a vast interstitial commons, dissected by naval strategies and logistical intrigues. The taking to the air, and the ongoing technologisation of aerial warfare (from US Civil War balloons, to World War I Allied/Axis aeroplanes, to the drones over the Durand Line between Afghanistan and Pakistan) floating above land, not on land, somehow not *inside* the land's jurisdictional space, transforms that ungrounded ground into something more like the omnidirectional surface of the open ocean. Virilio's career argument, from *Vitesse et Politique* (1977) to *La Guerre et la Cinéma* (1984) to *L'Horizon Négatif* (1984) to *Open Sky* (1997) bends, extends, reforms and innovates the political theology/geography of Schmitt's Nomos *of the Earth* from the philo-jurisprudence of war toward what replaces it: planetary media as the means without end. The mutability of the spatial segment, both Schmitt's and Virilio's, is not in the past, today it itself accelerates. The line which might partition (and separate) plus the line which might link (and conjoin) is also the line of velocity. This explosion of subdivision, the emergent image of planetary subdivision and this abstraction through deep materialisation of the unfolding of the real events of network time (radio spectrum allocation, air rights provisioning, micropayment targeting, minority language extinctions) is what *Exit* demonstrates and what it literally *does*. This is what *Exit* repeats in miniature upon its panorama, this globality composed in the first instance by the primordial taking and abstraction of network visualisations of an unequal Earth in motion and *of* motion.

Cosmograms That Show Something, Cosmograms That Do Something

The last chapter of the *Native Land/Stop Eject* catalogue book is called 'Animated Maps: Data Sources'. It provides a basic bibliography of the sources from which the *Exit* design team drew the raw data with which they composed their visualisations. The datasets themselves are not made available, nor the exact methodology employed to express them, nor the source code of the programs running along the panoramic wall, all disclosures that might be expected by the disciplinary norms of peer-reviewed science. This transparency is there to ensure the reproduction of results and the reliability of knowledge produced. Bad data sources ensure bad visualisations, regardless of the honourable methodologies executed upon them. But the expectations for data and art, or data and philosophy, or data art that seeks to explicate philosophy, as in this case, are less defined. The bibliographic inclusion of legitimate sources is more a gesture toward responsibility than an invitation to replicate their results. What would that even mean anyway? What is the result, true or false, of the explication and expression of a philosophical intervention? Where the title card next to a work of art in a museum might normally describe its source materials, date of completion, dimensions and so forth, when and how should it communicate or verify or directly make available in some way the source data so that, for other criteria, we might be able to guarantee the quality of the work? Does data intensive art-design demand a different kind of peer review? Does it resist it? Does it instead stage that transparency as a kind of seductive truth-affect? In the dispositions of art (and design, architecture, philosophy) do we even know what to do with information other than to stare at it? Or as put bluntly by Gayatri Chakravorty Spivak in her lecture, 'Imperative to Re-imagine the Planet', 'globalization takes place only in capital and data. Everything else is damage control. Information command has ruined knowing and reading. Therefore we don't really know what to do with information' (Spivak 2012: 1).

Now this may be because many of our methods of knowing and reading require revision and yet are hesitant, to say the least. For example, while the real history of worldwide quantification, the statistical imaginary, of managerial numeracy, probabilisation, stochastic accounting, etc. is substantial, it is not as well philosophically developed as it might be, Frankfurt School dismissals of bureaucratic rationalism notwithstanding. (In addition to Foucault's work on the history of population medicine, key histories of the quantification of society might include *Governing by Numbers: Figuring Out Democracy* (1991) by Nikolas Rose and *The Taming of Chance* (1990) by Ian Hacking. There are many others, but, to Spivak's point, Theory is playing catch-up.) As Manovich points out, statistical modelling has long been based on the selective sampling of representative data points and the inference of general patterns from them. Sampling is a function of both the efficiency of reductive synthesis and of the difficulties (technological, communicative, conceptual) in gathering all points in a given data set. In this, the statistical imaginary is designed to favour the regularisation of data points and the establishment of mathematical norms across fields of samples. Averages and means organise and structure statistical enquiries, and this is how the statistical imaginary framed its subject and subject matter: average patient, typical voter, ergonomically normal user. But under conditions of data abundance, and even population comprehensiveness, when every point in a field can be accounted for and represented, where n of sample = n of population, then the modality of pattern shifts off-centre from one of reductive average to other emergent, shifting, plural clusters of likeness, difference, relation, proximity and inferred causality (Manovich 2011). Multiple and unlike queries of one set are more easily expressed, such that one data point might be more or less significant depending on what is asked about the entire population as a whole. The mean is no longer the spine of the diagram, but instead the possibility of a less final form of incremental variation within an open field without centre.[14] Because of that plurality, the seeing and recognising of patterns within diagrams becomes a more contingent and partial reading delimited as much by the textuality of enquiry as by the materiality of the enquired-upon. Imagine the superimposition and stacking of multiple, layered visualisations of the same information, diagramming different distributions, each the result of differing enquiries (models really) upon its matrix of data points. Eventually the accumulated diagrams become absolute, opaque, over-coded, hyper-imposed within one another; all points made to appear according to some possible model: pattern not as mean or median but as torque. That arc toward a heterogeneity of response tilts away from spinal averages and toward the opposite of information (noise) and the inverse of pattern (the plainness and openness of the well-blackened canvas).

As indicated, Latour's interest in data visualisation is closely linked to his invocations of Gabriel Tarde's *Monadologie et Sociologie* (1895), which was already invested in the rising tide of statistical science.[15] Tarde wondered,

> if statistics continues to progress as it has done for several years, if the information which it gives us continues to gain in accuracy, in dispatch, in bulk, and in regularity, a time may come when upon the accomplishment of every social event a figure will at once issue forth automatically, so to speak, to take its place on the statistical registers that will be continuously communicated to the public and spread abroad pictorially by the daily press. (Quoted in Latour 2010)

Today we might recognise that statistics don't just fill newspapers, they are the actuality of news and newness. Not only are statistics an important rhetoric of civic truth-telling, but data-driven diagrammatic-instruments (what we call *interfaces*) are the permanent frames through which embedded systems announce their state conditions and through which we in turn act upon them. As we have in *Exit*, the statistical image-as-diagram, or cinematic diagram, cannot be finally separated from the diagram-as-interface. Just as for software, there are numbers which *mean something*, which we call data, and there are numbers that *do something*, which we call programs and instructions and algorithms. Here there are *images* that mean something, which we call visualisations, and images that do something, which we call *interfaces*. Between and across the two, number and image, is an architectonic of the diagram within the abstract time of computation. In turn, governance through statistics (and statistical visualisation) is itself not finally separable from the frame and discipline of the interfacial image. Statistics is by its very operation a reductive *abstraction* of a larger landscape of information, and this capacity to reduce and render pattern from otherwise unreadable datasets is what allows statistics to draw lines across the axes of a graphic plane or, as for *Exit*, the planar geography of the planet. While the interfacial image may be graphically indistinguishable, it instead activates the diagram by making it into a tool and putting it to work back upon the events or data that it represents (another cybernetic recursion of representation and the represented). In doing so, the interface-

instrument repeats the reductive abstraction of the statistical visualisation, but does so not only in the synthesis of what patterns are
to be figured, but also in the array of which possible actions can be
undertaken with interface as it shuttles intention back down into
the system. With the accumulation of layers and windows into its
specialised regime, the interface begins to unfold and unpack its
reductions and abstractions, demanding and training finer grain
expertise on the part of its users, to manage and manipulate data
closer to the bone. In short, the interface not only graphically
frames and synthesises what it itself can do as an interface, it also
reduces and abstracts what the machine that it describes can do. In
that interfaces are a data visualisation of the technical affordances
of systems, interfaciality is the actual medium of the map-and-user
recursion between the global and the local.

   In *Exit*, the actual character of the globe itself is weird, as is its
interfaciality. There are more than one globe, but each is in its
way total. The flattened landscape is the ground on which a round
planet Earth rolls, like a master pinball in a tracked groove. But
as it rolls, the Earth-figure activates and reveals the key diagrams
and visualisations on the dioramic screen. As recognised in the
interface discussed above, we see here not Earth as limit horizon
or absolute address, but *Earth as cursor*. We see the earth un-
peeling across the screen, delaminating itself in the round, as the
panorama shifts away from a virtual satellite photographic perfec-
tive toward a horizontal command and control array. Earth is a
dog carrying its own leash, stripping for some curious observer.
A forensic confession. Of what? Of an ambition for the interface
as both tool and *cosmogram*, more than just a collapse of tool
into ground, as for any landscape architecture, but a collapse of
technology into the image-of-the-world that would locate ground
in the first place. Now we could say that the world is always, for
those of us doing the looking, dependent on its capacity to qualify
imagery. Alphonso Lingis makes this point, when he says that he

set out to recognize that the things themselves engender 'images' or
doubles of themselves – shadows, halos, the images of themselves they
project on water, on the glass of windows – and also on the surfaces of
the eyes of mammals, birds, fish. For example, the puddle of water that
appears shimmering on the surface of the road ahead in a hot day is not
'subjective,' produced by the mind; it is engendered by the road and the
sun and everybody in the car sees it. (George and Sparrow 2012)

Images *are*, not images *of*. Image immanence above all. As we've seen, some discourses on diagrammatic data visualisations make that distinction differently, and perhaps not as well. On the one hand, it is said that such diagrammatic visualisations are the direct expression of the underlying data, the unmediated presentation of the monadological networks of the real. Latour at times veers himself toward this conclusion. On the other, the image itself is valorised as a highly flexible, mutable representation of a network condition out there in the world, an external pattern that we can now see and coordinate through its diagrammatic appearance to us. Our life is given pattern by its appearance as a data point in that image, as both the subject and object of its emergence. But here, for *Exit*, such slippages are suspended and staged in the posture of Earth-as-cursor. It is not only a figure, it is at least rhetorically, an interface, but for whom does the Earth display itself in this way? Who is the 'user' of this cosmic interface? Is it one of the lives rendered in the visualisations here now recognising herself as one of 7 billion drifting pixels? Or instead some transcendental entity? By scale, we might presume that the user is not only situated at some Archimedean outside, but is literally floating in outer space surveying the vast Earth machine (Edwards 2010). I wonder about the Marvel Comics characters, the Silver Surfer and Galactus, the latter of which marauds through the cosmos looking for planets to eat. Should the Surfer have had to prepare a convincing, thoughtful business plan on the suitability of Earth for this appetite, would it look like *Exit*?

What We Do is Secrete

Virilio has much to say about the psychic life of the 'user' (perhaps in lieu of a three-dimensional theory of the subject), and in the sense described above, *Exit*'s exhibition of his philosophy of mobility, displacement and globalisation hinges on its construction of the user as a core component of its pedagogy. Virilio is, of course, extremely gloomy in his assessments of what digital media does to people and their self-identities. My interest is in thinking with and against both *Exit* and Virilio (not the same thing) about the conditions of the appearance and disappearance of the user, of each of us, in Virilio's theory of visual–digital culture, which might provide some progress toward a more lasting answer to Neil Denari's initial question.

Appearance and disappearance both show up and go away at strange times and in strange ways. I wonder, not without some perverse pleasure, what Virilio might make of my friend and colleague, Larry Smarr's near decade-long interest (obsession, some might say) with the rational self-quantification and observation of data pertaining to the health of his biological person. Originally a mathematician and astrophysicist, Smarr is now Director of Calit2, the California Institute of Telecommunications and Information Technology, the University of California system's flagship IT research institute, in La Jolla. Smarr was the founder of NSCA, the National Center for Supercomputing Applications, which among other things brought forth Mosaic, the web browser that became Netscape. He is among the key pioneers in cyberinfrastrucure, scientific visualisation and what he calls 'planetary scale distributed computing'. But as of late, the information platform that has captured his most intense interest is his own body. While the quantified self movement, championed in California, has many precedents, Smarr's own quest reminds me most of Buckminster Fuller's own notebooks, called the 'Dymaxion File', in which he recorded every single activity. The personality type of those who see the design of planetary technologies as their daily vocation seems to suggest an interest in modelling the activities of the day itself as if it were a problem of astrophysics. For others in the quantified self scene, the pursuit may instead have more to do with narcissism, or an unhealthy internalisation of neoliberal evaluative criteria of systems performance and benchmarking applied to the existential void of the office park. Smarr and I have discussed this at some length and it's clear to me that his interest is much larger and far less individualistic than that, and his regime more holistic. Smarr tracks his health at a fine-grain level that most of us could probably not manage, even or likely want to.[16] It demands forms of data-mining that he is uniquely prepared for (he diagnosed himself in adult-onset Crohn's disease years before doctors confirmed this). His blood is drawn and analysed according to a dizzying array of tests every few weeks, he has monitored and quantified his food intake for years, he's had his personal genome mapped at a resolution few others ever have, and perhaps more interestingly he has also done the same for his microbial gut biome, the ecology of microscopic life that inhabits our body and does much of the work necessary to keep each of us alive. The genome of the microbial biome inside our guts has evolved over millions of years in line

with the human species (sometimes beneficially, sometimes patho-
logically) and without it our bodies would crash. Over the course
of our individual lives, our bodies provide selection pressures on
how our individual microbial biomes change and evolve inside
us. What we eat, in particular, can fundamentally alter the alien
ecology in our gut, for better or worse. Smarr's current focus on
the microbial biome as a key to his personal medicine is unusual
in that the focus is shifted from the self-regard of his own purified
somatic body toward the curation and gardening of his internal
microbial civilisation. That shift is based in Smarr's intellectual
project for the establishment of digital medicine at a systemic level
which envisions the co-embodiment of information at the scale
of 7 billion humans and unfathomable zillions of genes, environ-
mentally bound molecules, proteins, microbes. This is planetary
biocomputation. It suggests the explosion of traditional, individuated patient models into pluralised software platforms in which
everyone's genomic, nutritional, neuronal, microbial, environmental data would be systematically aggregated into an information
commons where new kinds of analysis and pattern recognition
would dissolve the individuation of the singular patient, into alternative patterns of biological plasticity, and which would surely
deform our definitions of 'disease' along with them. Synthetic
biology turns that commons into a toolkit, and in the larger
context of massively transparent digital biology, what's a 'doctor'?
Artificial intelligence systems might be designed to interpret the
exabytes of real-time and historical data, and produce interpretive
causal models, images of emergent patterns, that startle us. What
we surely would realise in this bright digital future is that causality
and pathology zigzag across scale from microbe to bioregions and
back again in utterly surprising ways, and that our basic conceptions of organ, body, group, collective, etc. are available to alien
re-categorisations, ones which when revealed in patterns of data
will appear as self-evident, but which we can today scarcely antici-
pate.[17] Fast-forward into the light.

To be sure, the biopolitics therein are ambiguous, paradoxical, dangerous and weird.[18] Our at-hand ideas about sovereignty,
transparency, therapy, jurisdiction, privacy, etc. are unreliable
tools to model a cosmopolitanism of biocomputation based on
the composite information that each of us secretes. This is part of
what makes *Exit* utterly incomplete in its premature gestures to
totality. What is required is less a textualisation of the informa-

tion trace, than a protocol politics of the stigmergic smear, not so unlike the Earth-figure-cursor rotating its way around the panoramic territory of its own location, leaving a trail of data visualisations along its path. With this in mind, it should also be noted that Smarr collects his own shit, and has it expertly analysed. Doing so is the best way to keep tabs on the state of his gut microbes, and in some ways on the general state of his own health. Grandparent toilet-bowl stool diviners, you were right. Considering the density of DNA from microbes, from one's own internal fluids, and from the DNA of the remaining foodstuffs one ate, the human stool is one of the most information-rich, information-dense substances you're likely to regularly encounter. Bit by bit, your stool is far more information-dense than your iPhone. All metaphors aside, we secrete more information than we constitute as static entities. In their aggregation, are our shadows more substantial than what casts them? If so, can we imagine a social bioethics for which the refusal to submit our data trails to holistic ecological monitors and models, and to refuse to participate in the care of the larger biological population that each of us is inevitably both consuming and secreting at once, is analogous to today's noxious stunt of refusing a vaccine? Put another way, when systems and individuals become indistinguishable, not to mention redundant, in such radically transparent environments, we can well wonder if the accountability of individuals, as the subject-users of such digital regimes can remain a viable criterion.

Now with regard to the discussion of *Exit* and Virilio, that question should be qualified by the juxtaposition with Gayatri Spivak's remark, from her lecture on *planetarity* mentioned above, that, 'the most pernicious presupposition today is that globalisation has happily happened in every aspect of our lives. Globalisation can never happen to the sensory equipment of the experiencing being except insofar as it always was implicit in its vanishing outlines' (Spivak 2012: 2). I take this to mean that 'globalisation', which for Spivak, as for us, is but one version of planetarity, does in fact 'happen' to the sensory equipment of the experiencing being exactly through making the outlines of that being disappear. Virilio's take on Smarr's odyssey of self-quantification might suggest that before that disappearance there must first be the making-appear of the cybernetic subject position of the 'user', and that making of the world, even the direct experience of the embodied self as such, into an interactive platform. Here we pinpoint a critical oscillation between appearance and disappearance that characterises the cultural resonance of Big Data. First, the fine-granular composition of data turns techniques of verification and measurement born of big-box supply chains and reassigns them to making heretofore unseen patterns visible, knowable, action-able as interfacial diagrams. Positions, subjects, agents, effectors are drawn and strongly interpolated, as discrete image-objects of knowledge. Users are given firm and visible outlines that convince us and them of their stable contiguity. This is an updating of the Lacanian mirror-stage for the exabyte ego, and in this, Spivak has it wrong. Globalisation, in the sense that she defines it here as the planetary career of electronic capital as ubiquitous grid, is very much experienced at the level of sensory equipment precisely because it, at least initially, makes possible and over-traces their outlines as the validation of a subject produced in their image. But finally, as shown in the example of the exploded quantified self, the ultimate effect of the inclusion of information from extrinsic (if also internal) sources into an economy of identity also has the opposite effect, and exactly the one Spivak names: the vanishing of outlines. To the extent that the composition of the 'user' as a bio-political subject also includes vectors of data – genomic, microbial, microeconomic, meta-ecological, etc. – into the living diagram of interpolation, then the site of the subject is seen as so infused and overcome with extrinsic flows of multiple scale, that the coher-ency, stability and confidence previously invested in the visual outline of the quantified self quickly perforates and liquefies. The somatic ego of *homo economicus*, especially the one reflected in the mirror of Big Data, burns brightest in its extinguishment. Capitalism, as ever, fabricates subjects, even universalising them as transhistorical actors, only to melt them down as the raw mate-rial of another project.[19]

Conclusion: 'Planetarity' and the Database Aesthetics of Disappearance

The same, to a degree, goes for planets. At the cusp of the 1960s and 1970s (the high-water mark of modernity, some say) the 'Earth rise' images from Apollo and the 'blue marble' photographs of the singular planet against a ground of black metaphysical void concretised the idea of Earth as a synchronic ecology, as one single thing separate and stranded. This surely did much to support the pop-Copernican conception of the Earth as an astro-object delineated not just by an Archimedean master perspective from the air, or of the permeability of the horizon, but by an *outside* and an outline, an icon. That imagined outline in turn made the programme of ecology as self-evident as the unknown, unmapped zones of colonial maps had once made geography. But at the same time, just as for the user, the misrecognition of a prematurely singularised body is at work here. Earth is no less multiple than any other body, rather more so in fact. Latour and Sloterdijk compete to agree more emphatically than the other that the image of the globe has also provided the detours that mis-think globalisation as a top-down conclusion that coheres all networks and spheres, in turn, into a falsely coherent abstraction.[20] But my point is not theirs. While indeed the images from Apollo promise exactly the *Apollonian* programme of comprehensive closure of a singularised, bound domain, this comes at the expense of what? The Dionysian promiscuity of interwoven, multiversal points and edges? I don't believe so, if that is taken to mean a geophilosophy in Nietzsche's or Schelling's Romantic tradition of the grounded horizon, however cosmically inspired it might be. Instead the inverse of Apollo, the more radical Copernicanism, requires yet another rotation from the residual 'Ptolemaic' subject-as-centre/centre-as-subject positions. Reza Negaristani locates 'geophilosophical realism' in the promise of concluding and extending the Copernican rotation in this way: the 'remorseless displacement of the unthought that thinks it is a center into the exploded, perforated horizon of the universal *open*' (Negaristani 2011). For that rotation, the Earth, as such, cannot be presented as the natural ground from which our senses of velocity, duration, embodiment are deranged, and on whose behalf we are, like Virilio, supposed to be permanently scandalised. Nor can it stop at the scopic outline of the absolutely synchronic subject of literally world-scale closure, nor the claustrophobic territory of the screen which stands both for the scale of the diagram, the grid of the data-to-be-diagrammed, and the temporal register of its unfolding. These are neo-Ptolemaic Earths for misplaced users.

As such, the digital Earth described and signalled by *Exit* enjoys enough elasticity that its panorama (and cursor) can unfurl diagrams of worldly flow that appear to suggest a generic universality. Any bit, sign or exchange within the field is already accounted for before it even collapses from wave into pixelated particle. However, this closed genericity is, as should be clear, only a simulation of the universality for which it stands. In this, *Exit* well *performs* the logical closure of the worldly network that both Virilio and Spivak have spent their very different careers tilting against. A parallel observation can be made regarding (or against) the master concept of *plasticity* in the work of Catherine Malabou. Malabou makes the comprehensive and emphatic (for that awkward) distinction between, on the one hand, *plasticity* as the absolutely generic capacity of the world to be made anew, and in essence, to hold its form just long enough to provide sufficient resistance that history can actually take shape, and on the other, *flexibility*, that is, the bad momentum of fast capitalism to absorb, immolate, disassemble and recombine everything within its general economy of rearrangements within production and consumption cycles. But as others have noted, it's not clear finally where plasticity starts and flexibility stops (perhaps that boundary is itself plastic!) (again, see Galloway 2012).

Now leaving *Exit* on behalf of our specific geophilosophical question, one for which *the plasticity of planetarity* as such is really the crux of matter (along with what can and cannot count as a centre: user, mean/median, line of sight), perhaps this chapter has identified three possible open hinges around which that question teeters, and which we'll have to leave even more ajar than we found them.

Appearance/disappearance. The capacity to collect, sort, pattern and display the *secretion* of world-as-data, in near real-time, has the effect of first, over-subscribing and over-delineating the simulation of single subjects (bodies, persons, planets), and second, the criss-crossing of data into and over the site of that corpus to fragment it to the point of dissolution and disappearance.

Closed recursive spaces/open formal universality. The point of differentiation between the plastic and the merely flexible may rest on the quality and openness of the world that is undergoing change and staging the emergence of new things. The flexible prefers closed loops and the exploration of the phase space of possible state conditions of a finite set of binary resources, like the board of Go. The plastic, on the other hand, presumes that the table of the elements and alphabet of proteins is but a sample of the ultimately available building blocks of things and worlds.[21] Its ethics of otherness rests not on the novelty of innovation but, as Negaristani writes, on absorbing new *traumas* coming our way from the absolutely extrinsic, abyssal scale of the universal.

Present centre/absent centre. To visualise this point, consider it by way of Copernicus's revision of the Ptolemaic cosmogram that shifted the Earth from the natural centripetal centre, and replaced it with the royal Sun.[22] Today any cosmogrammatic idea is complicated by the preponderance of dark matter and dark energy, expanding space, and these sorts of all-but-incomprehensible evidences. But thinking more locally, our neighbourhood, the Milky Way, is composed of curving arcs, logarithmic spirals filled with millions of stars around which countless little planets twirl. At the centre of our teeming local whirlpool, at the core of the Milky Way, is what we call the galactic centre. Current astrophysics suggests that the galactic centre is a black hole. A real, carnivorous *void* is what holds it all together. And so, to close, it's not about de-centring exactly. There *is* a centre that gives shape and weight and distance to all that encircles it. However, the centre is precisely *absence*.

Exit has it backwards, but in an interesting way. I doubt very much if this describes more clearly what it is that Virilio's philosophy looks like, but it may go some way toward describing what it sees.

Notes

Internet links last accessed 18 July 2012.

1. Yes, the title puns 'What We Do Is Secret', EP, The Germs, Slash Records (1981).
2. For full credits please refer to Stewdio's own site, <http://stewd.io/w/exit>.
3. Some recent theoretical initiatives discover a positive programme for this emergent digital granularity, and see for it a shift in the complexity of the visual field, the activity of networks, and even the objectivity of interpretive analysis, e.g. Manovich (2011) and Latour et al. (2011).
4. The thematic metaphor ('stop/eject') is drawn from the old mechanical interface for magnetic tape cassettes (it is unclear from Virilio's conversation with Depardon in the catalogue if the anachronistic quality of the reference is intentionally meaningful).
5. The official credits from the catalogue are as follows. Exit (2008). Installation using Java, OpenGL, and Processing software. 12′ (370 cm) high, 29′ (8.8 m) diam. Diller Scofidio + Renfro (USA, est. 1979), Laura Kurgan (American, born South Africa 1961), Mark

Hansen (American, born 1964) and Ben Rubin (American, born 1964) in collaboration with Stewart Smith (American, born 1981) and Robert Gerard Pietrusko (American, born 1979).

6. From an online interview with Stewdio's Stewart Smith, one of Exit's programmers, <http://stewd.io/w/exit>.

7. Manuel De Landa's work on assemblage theory articulates this recursion between scales most clearly (see De Landa 2006). It should be said that the principle of the systemic reflexivity for the subject who possesses an incomplete diagram of the social structure in which he or she is acting yet who acts recursively in relation to that diagram, is not dissimilar to that described by Anthony Giddens et al. and the thesis of reflexive modernisation (see, for example, Giddens 1991).

8. See Latour's comments in O'Hanian and Royoux (2005: 223–40), and his re-enactment of the Tarde/Durkheim debate with Bruno Karasenti and Louis Salmon, which can be viewed online at <http://www.bruno-latour.fr/node/354>.

9. In this paragraph I am paraphrasing my own essay, 'On Geoscapes and the Google Caliphate' (2009).

10. For example, Heidegger's 'World Picture', Fredric Jameson's 'cognitive mapping' and Ulrich Beck's 'risk'.

11. Once again, this idea is discussed in Bratton (2009: 340–1).

12. The connotation of 'framing' is inspired by Elizabeth Grosz's Deleuzian-Darwinian usage (Grosz 2008).

13. Virilio remarks, 'in this case too, if time is money, speed is power. This is why we are constantly in a race. What is a race? It means taking hold of power by getting there first. And at the same time we are on horseback, on foot or driving a car. It's very clear that speed=power, and power=speed, and instantaneity, ubiquitousness and immediacy are the prerogatives of the divine.' from 'Itineraries of the Catastrophe', an interview with Sylvère Lotringer, 2008.

14. One or many wolves spimes?

15. Translated as *Monadology and Sociology* (2012). For a Deleuzian appreciation and critique of Tarde, see Alliez (2004).

16. On Larry Smarr's regime, see Cohen (2012).

17. On the use of artificial intelligence to analyse large quantities of health data, see Lee Hood's research group at the Institute for Systems Biology, <https://www.systemsbiology.org/hood-group>.

18. Brian Massumi (2009) calls this military ambition a 'full spectrum line of sight'.

19. The overdetermination of the quantified self is a condition analogous

to the blackened canvas, overwritten with all possible diagrammatic images of the same data, defeating the spine of the mean. It is also another telling of the parable of the Ship of Theseus, all its components replaced one-by-one, and yet it retains that same identity.

20. Again, see Latour's argument in O'Hanian and Royoux (2005).
21. The NASA astrobiologist, Lynn Rothschild, disagrees. She argues that based on analyses of materials found on asteroids, it's quite likely that the elements we know are all that there are, at least within our galaxy. Her comment to this effect was made at the Google/Arctic/Mars symposium co-organised by Geoff Manaugh, Ed Keller and myself at Columbia Architecture, Studio-X, 8 May 2012.
22. In some ways it is Copernicus's essential promoter, Rheticus, who should be credited (see Danielson 2006).

References

Alliez, Éric (2004), 'The difference and repetition of Gabriel Tarde', *Distinktion, Scandinavian Journal of Social Theory* 5(2): 49–54.

Bratton, Benjamin H. (2009), 'On geoscapes and the Google caliphate: Reflections on the Mumbai attacks', *Theory, Culture & Society* 26(7–8): 329–42.

Cohen, Jon (2012), 'The patient of the future', *MIT Technology Review* (March/April), <http://www.technologyreview.com/featured-story/426968/the-patient-of-the-future/>.

Danielson, Dennis (2006), *The First Copernican: Georg Joachim Rheticus and the Rise of the Copernican Revolution*, New York: Walker & Co.

De Landa, Manuel (2006), *A New Philosophy of Society: Assemblage Theory and Social Complexity*, London: Continuum.

Edwards, Paul N. (2010), *A Vast Machine: Computer Models, Climate Data, and the Politics of Global Warming*, Cambridge, MA: MIT Press.

Galloway, Alexander (2012), *Catherine Malabou, or the Commerce in Being*, French Theory Today pamphlet documenting a seminar at the Public School New York, <http://cultureandcommunication.org/galloway/FTT/French-Theory-Today.pdf>.

George, Bobby and Sparrow, Tom (2012), 'Interview with Alphonso Lingis', <http://singularum.com/interviewwithalphonsolingis>.

Giddens, A. (1991), *The Consequences of Modernity*, Palo Alto: Stanford University Press.

Grosz, Elizabeth (2008), *Chaos, Territory, Art: Deleuze and the Framing of the Earth*, New York: Columbia University Press.

Heidegger (1982 [1938]), 'The age of the world picture', in *The Question Concerning Technology, and Other Essays*, New York: Harper Torchbooks, pp. 115–54.

Latour, Bruno (2010), 'Tarde's idea of quantification', in Mattei Candea (ed.), *The Social After Gabriel Tarde: Debates and Assessments*, London: Routledge, pp. 145–62.

Latour, Bruno, Jensen, Pablo, Venturini, Tommaso, Grauwin, Sébastian and Boullier, Dominique (2011), 'The whole is always smaller than its parts: A digital test of Gabriel Tarde's monads', <http://www.bruno-latour.fr/sites/default/files/123-WHOLE-PART-FINAL.pdf>.

Manovich, Lev (2011), 'From reading to pattern recognition', <http://manovich.net/DOCS/reading_patterns.2011.pdf>.

Massumi, Brian (2009), 'National enterprise emergency: Steps toward an ecology of powers', *Theory, Culture & Society* 26(6): 153–85.

Moyer, Michael (2012), 'Is space digital?', *Scientific American*, 17 January.

Nancy, Jean-Luc (2007), *The Creation of the World, or Globalization*, Albany, NY: State University of New York Press.

Negaristani, Reza (2011), 'Globe of revolution: An afterthought on geophilosophical realism', *Identities: Journal for Politics, Gender and Culture* 17: 25–54.

O'Hanian, Melik and Royoux, Jean-Christophe (2005), *Cosmograms*, Berlin: Lukas & Sternberg.

Schmitt, Carl (2003), *The Nomos of the Earth, in the International Law of Jus Publicum Europaeum*, Candor, NY: Telos Press Publishing.

Serres, Michel and Malanchuk, Maria (trans.) (1975), 'Jules Verne's Strange Journeys', *Yale French Studies*, 52, Graphesis: Perspectives in Literature and Philosophy, pp. 174–88.

Spivak, Gayatri Chakravorty (2012), *An Aesthetic Education in the Age of Globalization*, Cambridge, MA: Harvard University Press.

Tarde, Gabriel (2012 [1895]), *Monadology and Sociology*, ed. and trans. Theo Lorenc, Melbourne: Re:Press.

Virilio, Paul (1977), *Vitesse et Politique*, Paris: Galilée.

Virilio, Paul (1984), *L'Horizon Négatif*, Paris: Galilée.

Virilio, Paul (1984), *La Guerre et la Cinéma 1: Logistique de la Perception*, Paris: Cahiers du Cinéma.

Virilio, Paul (1997), *Open Sky*, London: Verso.

Virilio, Paul, Depardon, Raymond, Diller Scofidio + Renfro, Hansen, Mark, Kurgan, Laura and Rubin, Ben (2010), *Native Land/Stop Eject*, Arles: Actes Sud.

12

Relics of Acceleration: A Field Guide

Gair Dunlop

Figure 12.1 The Centrifuge Pit in Lab 2, AWRE Orford Ness (2006).

Notes Towards an Artist's Genealogy of Spaces

Scale, mass, solidity and haunting bulk are factors that are una-voidable when thinking about twentieth-century military and experimental scientific structures. Whether sites of state science or defence, they have many aspects in common: secrecy, a cultivated sense of unknowability and a paradoxical relation between intangibility of subject and solidity of structure.

This chapter reflects on some of these places as key sites in the modern history of speed in the UK. Acceleration takes on different guises in each. The specific historical contingency of these sites also leaves space for re-imaginings and alternative possibilities to be considered without the pessimistic inevitability that a focus on contemporary military futurism would yield.

Sombre relics of a techne that we are invited to believe became too heavy for civil society to bear, we can sense the aura of Easter Island on the abandoned runways and test facilities. Defensive in terms of their meaning as well as their accessibility, many such sites have their origins in a definitively analogue relation to the external world. Having said that, digital networked communications and feedback systems can largely be said to originate from such locations and the overlay is often uneven or paradoxical. For example, at RAF Coltishall, during flight simulation systems' evolution from mimetic to immersive/responsive, the resulting 'electronic false day' (Virilio 1991: 14) enabled surprising new (albeit temporary) forms of nostalgia as well as a more immediate training and surveillance regime.

Artists, if they can use wit and critical awareness in the face of seduction by the ruinous charms of such sites, can deploy a wide range of techniques to probe and transmit atmospheres, residues and consequences. Among the many advantages of their position is an ability to sidestep the commonsensical and enter into questioning dialogue with the rational approaches of other specialists such as geographers, archaeologists, etc.

Experiencing them as workplaces – albeit unusual ones – enables contact with the motivations and rationalisations of those on site. Experiencing them at a remove, after abandonment – as nature reserve or on the fringe of a 'heritage zone' – offers Ballardian pleasures akin to those of Jefferies *After London* (1885) or Rose Macaulay's wartime feral Eden in *The World my Wilderness* (1992 [1950]).

Contemporary exchanges between contemporary arts practices and techniques of information-gathering and presentation more associated with reportage and media contexts – what Alfredo Cramerotti calls 'Aesthetic Journalism' (2009) – offer ways in which artists can access sites, engage in dialogue with staff and use their presence to explore context and authority. This raises awkward questions about the limits of circulation of information, given that the circulatory power of the artwork is seen as a narrower channel than mass media. Citing artists such as Hito Steyerl, Luke Fowler, Walid Raad and the Atlas Group, Cramerotti begins from the observation that more and more material in the realm of art circulation takes forms of, repurposes and opens to question investigative journalism's tropes and methodologies. He locates this thrust as a response to 24-hour news agendas and an increasingly thin focus on the 'breaking news' concept, where a near instantaneous obsession with the latest information squeezes out all analysis and context from the onrushing information flood. Contemporary events are reduced to a sequence of action-comment/response/contradiction/next event, losing any sense of relation. The consequent emptying of depth from media/broadcast time can be seen as a consequence of its acceleration. We could conceptualise the movement of meaning-construction into the field of art as a re-crystallisation of discourse in the vacuum left by this acceleration. Parallels with Virilio's information bomb are inevitable; the rush of air back into the blast area.

> A witnessing experience is centred on the issue of time. Art is one of the few realms in which time is still a negotiable term . . . More than ever, we need a witness attitude in art, for it might inspire a witness attitude in journalism; a kind of knowledge looking beyond what is immediately visible, a latency, so to speak, an imaginative reading of what is not directly accessible to the senses. (Cramerotti 2009: 104)

The following 'field guide' framework brings together sites, technologies, social actors and techniques for artists' engagement. From specific observations, there follows a 'theory toolkit' for artists and collaborators to make a new kind of sense of such places.

Code: Station X

The Turing Test and Alan Turing's personal trajectory are well known; the founding mythos of computer theory distils down to a few English eccentrics in small huts. Nearby, the railway line connects Oxford, Cambridge and Whitehall. Intercept information arrives day and night from outstations in the Home Counties, East Anglia and from up the Great North Road. Watling Street is half a mile away, Roman Road connecting the secret to deep history.

As a twenty-first century Heritage Site, Bletchley Park today plays up to the hieratic tradition: newly renovated wooden huts, a faded manor house, an ideal wedding or conference venue.

On the edge of the site, and downplayed in both guided tour and interpretation material, Blocks D, F and G represent the logistical consequences of the huts: code-breaking on an industrial scale.

The development of the Colossus computer represented a

definitive acceleration of information: 5,000 characters per second, paper tape racing over optical sensors, confined initially to a singularity; one machine in one room. The first truly digital programmable computer – albeit with no memory – Colossus was developed to break Lorenz teleprinter ciphers, and was functioning by December 1943. Ten machines were functioning by the close of the war, accelerated time and attention now spread through utility architectures across several acres. This technology was one of the best-kept secrets of the war. The speed of the rest of the associated network was still that of the motorcycle courier or the train.

The end of World War II meant that important decisions had to be made on where the destiny of British computing would lie: to expand publicly outwards into industry, thus socialising the emergent technology – or to remain in the closed world. The imperatives of secrecy won. All machines on site were broken up; selected elements disappeared into the realm of Signals Intelligence (now functioning against Warsaw Pact rather than Axis code). Henceforth it would generally be assumed that the American ENIAC (Electronic Numerical Integrator And Computer) was the first of its kind; the unknowability seemed more important than national pride. American claims to be the originators of program-mable computing were left unchallenged. Bletchley Park thus represents a state-induced wilful reversal of fortune: knowledge systematically removed from the realm of the public.

The normative concept of the military–industrial complex assumes the active presence of military logics and architectures pushing outward, permeating the formerly civil industrial and technological environment. Bletchley shows us the absences and missed chances generated by militarily technological imperatives when they are seen from the perspective of a declining power, sensing its own weakness and aware that it has been infiltrated. A chance to advance is removed from the public realm and shut into the closed world. The reception area of Block D now gives access to the National Computing Collection; rooms full of derelict equip-ment, manuals and obsolete storage systems. A sense of eternity: dusty but not yet eroded. It's an irony that so much technological debris has come to rest here, where the ideas were created but the manufacturing was stillborn. We can map out a particularly British version of stunted progress, in the same manner as Tom Nairn posits a stunted polity based on a semi-fulfilled political

Figure 12.2 First Floor Room, Block G, Bletchley Park (2008).

maturing during the 1688 'Glorious Revolution' which was choked off by the restoration of monarchy (Nairn 1988).

Bletchley is also a signpost to the future destinations of the New Elizabethans: cold, isolated, unacknowledged outposts of a secret knowledge. Or a plane to America for the educated and ambitious . . . down the 'brain drain'.

Something strange happened at Bletchley after the war: a willed forgetting. The cable ducts and ghost signage of its subsequent occupiers – a GPO systems training school – do not entirely dissipate its atmosphere. An artist's strategy for this site is direct and simple: wander, drift, break up the space and ignore the boundaries between the official site of memory and the now 'peripheral' surrounding blocks. Embrace the tearoom. Remember the true nature of the achievement: an information factory.

Orford Ness

A cold shingle spit, the Ness is separated from the Suffolk town of Orford by a boat ride to a formerly guarded landing stage. A few miles up the coast lies Sizewell nuclear power station and Aldeburgh, where Benjamin Britten and Peter Pears tried to insulate themselves from the sounds of Cold War aircraft manoeuvres. When the noise became unbearable, they would periodically decamp to Horham. To the north, Walberswick, birthplace of Humphrey Jennings, visual poet of technology.

Originally designated as the Central Flying School's Experimental Flying Section airfield in 1913, it has been a zone for flight experimentation, bomb testing and countermeasures ever since. Acres of abandoned drop zones and cryptic foundations for unrecorded structures litter the flat centre of the gravel-fringed peninsula. The northern section contains the power-station bulk of the World Service/diplomatic service transmitter station, and the fan-like immensity of Cobra Mist, a never-to-be-successful over-horizon 1960s' radar scatter station. To the south-east fringes of the site are the extraordinary pagodas of the Atomic Weapons Research Establishment.

The acceleration here was chemical, physical and implosive; the handling qualities of the coyly named 'physics package' were tested in a variety of laboratory conditions. Maintenance of the UK independent deterrent called for guaranteed delivery systems, carrying a perfectly synchronised inwardly focused detonation to trigger criticality. Shaken, spun, dropped, heated, moistened and frozen, nuclear and thermonuclear bomb components were treated as roughly as possible on a lonely Suffolk shore. The first time I stood in a room with a nuclear bomb was here, in the former control room. The effect was intense; an object of detestation and fear, now hollowed out and presented on a trolley in its white scientific coat.

Now under the control of the National Trust, the site is a stricter than usual nature reserve: limited numbers of visitors who arrive by boat are strongly advised to stick firmly to the paths due to the amount of munitions secreted among the gravels. Among the abandoned scrap, there are still objects to raise a frisson in the experienced Cold War flâneur; a ramshackle trolley suddenly takes on new significance when it is identified as the transport cradle for Blue Danube, the first UK 'independent' deliverable atomic weapon.

Artist's strategy for the site: reverberation

Orford Ness as a physical visual environment is impossible to compete with. The sheer scale, strangeness and unique nature of the structures and their disposition make any visual intervention or attempt at alteration void. Sound is a constant element of experiencing the Ness; shingle, wind, birds; natural sounds through unnatural structures. Sound therefore became the key to a major site-specific artwork by Louise K. Wilson on the Ness in August 2005. Wilson has been using sound (recording and resituating) in an ongoing project to explore the cultural and architectural heritage of the Cold War. She is particularly interested in the presence of reflected (reverberant) sound. This springs from a desire to ask how far we can 'archive' the atmosphere of a place. Previously she has visited a number of military test sites in both the UK and Australia and made work that features samples, recordings and measurements of these locations alongside dialogues with ex-employees.

A mixture of helpful coincidence – such as the regular summer choral workshops held on the Ness by the Exmoor singers – and rigorous field recording led to a range of sonic interventions in the site. Observation and test facilities became transformed into listening posts, a sometimes visceral reminder and reaffirmation of the dark purposes of the zone. Perhaps the project is best summarised through the intervention in Lab 2, former site of the massive centrifuge which was used to test the first UK nuclear weapon 'Blue Danube'. The centrifuge itself was transferred to Aldermaston and is still in use. Lab 2 is a crumbling wreck (see Figure 12.1). After protracted negotiations, Wilson recorded the sounds of the centrifuge and resituated them.

> In the crumbling shell of Lab 2, where the heart of the building was once ripped out, the centrifuge begins to pound again. The hangover throb of machinery vibrates through the body, as two enormous infra-bass sub-woofer speakers blast out the memory of air being forced around a drum at 100rpm ... It's an exercise rich in paradox: the sound of a machine simultaneously present and absent; and echo of the past that is incontrovertibly current, recorded only weeks ago. (Palmer 2006: 113)

The second time I stood in a room with a nuclear bomb, I didn't notice it for a while.

Dispersals

Figure 12.3 Wall Painting, 6 Squadron Offices, RAF Coltishall (2007).

RAF Coltishall, a historic RAF base in rural Norfolk, was closed in 2008. A team of three artists, invited in by English Heritage, observed the two-year process of 'drawdown'.

The demise of the base was due to simple redundancy; acceleration measured and found wanting. Intercept response time of the ageing Jaguar aircraft was no longer relevant. The site in its slow closure embodied high Cold War history counterpoised with the rural idyll, the air knights of old and England's Dreaming.

This closure involves the last extension of national geophysical limits, where logics of interception are thrown to the far edges of the national territory. East Anglia cannot fulfil a spatial function in relation to the symbolic Russian threat. Its remaining cluster airbase at Marham is not focused on interception. Even RAF Leuchars in eastern Scotland has been marginalised, and will be closed as an airbase in 2013. A few precious minutes closer to Murmansk, Kinross remains as the sole and vigilant outcrop; the Arctic Wall. The consequences of this acceleration and interception logistic are inescapable and have had strong economic and social effects.

On the day of closure, blessings and speeches paused. Eyes scanned the horizon. Dots appeared, and suddenly a wave of noise and vibration swept the field. A formation of low-flying aircraft had gone, almost before fully seen. Cameras and binoculars wobbled uncertainly. The skyfull of roaring silver metal was too big to register. (Dunlop and Schofield 2012)

Agreeable terror and the art of display

Concepts of 'the Sublime' as a category of experience derive from aesthetic theory, in particular Romantic Landscape conceptions of beauty, wildness, excess and fear. The 'Technological Sublime' is a concept elaborated by David E. Nye (1994) from an original idea by Leo Marx. Events or sites evoking this emotion become important elements in national identities: the flypast, the dam opening, the bomb test. RAF Coltishall, as the last of the original World War II fighter stations, embodied some interesting paradoxes concerning the technological sublime in an age of mechanical obsolescence. In the case of the Coltishall closure parade, there was a chronological paradox, in that the sense of immensity was generated by obsolete machines. Preceded by a Hawker Hurricane and escorted by a Typhoon Eurofighter, a 'Diamond nine' formation of Jaguars hurtled over the parade ground and into history. The past and the future – represented by World War II aircraft and the 'new' Eurofighter – bookended their farewell.

Differing approaches to the site involved analysis and comparison between the mirror partners in the Cold War, and also mirroring between the reality of the airfield and the virtual airbase as represented in the flight simulator. The former raised unsettling questions of equivalence and interdependency between the two military blocs, while the latter raised issues of the coexistence of ideal and everyday place. Interesting insights arose from the 'green world' versus 'closed world' opposition elaborated by Northrop Frye (1965) in literary criticism.

Green-world drama contrasts with closed-world drama at every turn . . . Borders and limits, where they exist, constitute temporary problems rather than absolute confinements . . . Green-world drama has the character of a heroic quest rather than that of a siege; its archetype is the Odyssey . . . Green-world iconography is that of the frontier and the inner spiritual journey.

Closed-world protagonists pit their own rationality, their reflexes, and their technical expertise against a dominating system and its technology from within. (Edwards 1996: 310–11)

Useful tools to develop insights are here: the role of the ideas of 'mastery' and 'character' in reconciling individuals to roles, the way in which idyll and conflict – particularly in the context of the endlessly deferred conflict – coexist in the mind.

The venue for my second close encounter with a nuclear bomb took place as a result of the Coltishall work. Working with Angus Boulton on his film that mirrored Western and Warsaw Pact facilities, we found ourselves waiting at RAF Marham for access to the Hardened Aircraft Shelters (HAS). We were invited to pass some time in the 'history room'. Much as expected, cases and tables bore a historical weight: models, photographs, goggles, parts of aircraft and assorted trophies. Among the scatter of bits, a We177 nuclear freefall bomb, similar to the one at Orford but this time in its olive drab military coating. It appeared normal, innocuous. The astonishment at 'not noticing' was almost as intense as the feeling of shock on my original encounter.

Filming completed, we return to Coltishall and the slumbering lanes of deeply rural England. The technological obsolescence of Coltishall enhanced the sense of idyll, which coexisted with the vigilant alertness posture. The 'green world' and the 'closed world' seemed closely linked. The green world of rurality, the ideal, harmony and resolution coexisted with the closed world of games theory, Manichean conflict, zero sum calculations and mutually assured destruction.

Coltishall's role as a centre for flight did not cease with the withdrawal of aircraft. The last surviving access to homely Coltishall persisted in the flight simulator, long after the hangars were cleared and equipment was removed from the control tower.

Artist's strategy for the site: mirroring (simulation)

The digital computerised simulator was housed in the same building as the original analogue simulator, where a huge warehouse-sized building was filled with a model terrain of North Norfolk, traversed by miniature cameras on a servo-based wire network. This fed back to a medium-resolution projection screen in front of the simulator cockpit. Enough electricity for a small town was required to light the set adequately; realism and sense of immediacy was tenuous. The replacement simulator used new technologies of real-time computer rendering, fed to synchronised and blended digital video projections. Any airfield, any theatre of war, any technical failure, weapons option or attack scenario was digitally stored and could be played into a 180-degree projection dome. Landscape was meticulously mapped in contour and form, and wrapped with landscape textures generated on the fly. (This led to surreal and sometimes hilarious imagery; mountainous hilltops wrapped with the texture of gentle field and village.)[1]

The Jaguar pilots saw out the last months of their aircraft based at RAF Coningsby, and drove down to Coltishall for simulator training. They insisted on 'flying' from Coltishall during these virtual missions. The 'electronic false day' (Virilio 1991: 14), represented by the pilots' ability to cling to the enduring virtual structure, thus became a paradoxical locus for nostalgia and a sense of play among the pilots. They would drive across the grass, squeeze through impossible gaps between various buildings and fly through as many bridges as possible on their way to 'wars'. Once finished, they would remove their NBC flight suits and drive north to Coningsby again. The virtual Coltishall, where squadron badges still appeared on buildings, was the last place where the pilots of these exhausted aircraft could feel at home.[2]

Dounreay

Figure 12.4 The Dome of Discovery, 1957 and 2010 (2011). Digital film still.

Artist's strategy for the site: mirroring (temporal, split, simultaneous)

Acceleration regime: subatomic, measured in doubling time – the opposite of half-life. This doubling time gives an indication of the strength of the evolving nuclear criticality, and also a reasonable

measure of the time available to invoke safety procedures in the
event of an accident.

There is also a second, more political meaning of the concept:
the required time for a fast breeder reactor to generate enough
fissile material to seed the next reactor in a chain. This in practice
works out at around 10 years. The two full-scale Dounreay reactors operated from 1959 to 1977 and 1974 to 1994 respectively.

In addition, a small test reactor facility operated between 1958
and 1969. Two military reactors, of the type in UK nuclear sub-
marines, are also operated at a separate facility on site by Rolls-
Royce. Vulcan Naval Reactor Test Establishment is likely to be
closed and decommissioned in 2015.

Understanding the call of modernity in the Dounreay context is
crucial. Some of the tone of the call to participation in the technocratic British nuclear state can be sensed in the quasi-Audenesque
tones of a British-sponsored documentary:

> The sound of the moment of atomic fission is a thin compulsive music;
> the indefinable orchestration of immense invisible forces, disciplined
> inside a kind of terrible elegance. The powerhouses of the nuclear age
> are quiet and clean, stark and sterile. This country has many of them,
> spread across the land; at Berkeley and Bradwell . . . (*Today in Britain*
> 1964)

The tones of lost modernity assume some surprising forms: a
quasi-futurist voice-over, a carefully coached vox pop, and the
recycling of limited footage to various purposes. There's a particular dark humour for the workers on site – talk of the SCRAM
button being an acronym for 'safety control rod axe man' being a
good example. The idea of the original SCRAM button – the emergency evacuation alert switch – being named after an early safety
procedure at Harwell where a technician stood over the strings
holding the safety rods with an axe to cut them and drop the shut-
off gates is both urban legend and irresistible to the mind's eye.
Similarly, the revelatory qualities of film footage from inside the
reactor facility are severely compromised by its reuse with different
voice-overs in different films. The same neutral shot of a technician entering a lab and operating the 'robot arms' is first filmed in
1964 to show local people with a chance to advance. By 1966, the
footage is recycled to explain that these dedicated scientists have
forgone the bright lights of southern cities to pursue the greatest

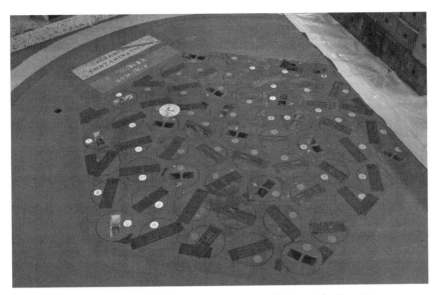

Figure 12.5 Sample Holding Area, Dounreay Materials Test Reactor (2011). Originally used for testing reactor parts and assemblies, later used for production of medical isotopes. Shut down in 1969.

goal in modern science. This material self-generates a critique of the concept of truth in film and is key to a use of simultaneity in approaching this material.

The tones of confidence within the nuclear adventure have now faded; their echoes can give valuable clues to governmental imperatives as they impact specific places. The poignant turn to the tone of certainty, the pleasures of the archive and the challenge of the debased but hopefully redeemable real world are the subjects of 'Atom Town: life after technology'. The future is a product not only of the tangible physicalities, the new infrastructures, the demographics of a rural population doubling and mutating into a scientific powerhouse; it's inside our minds. When the actual future has rolled on by, and slower rhythms of a country town reassert themselves, the idea of the future lingers on. The vestiges become rusty but somehow sharper as signs.

Caithness as a county has long been sustained by the experimental reactor establishment; schools, transport infrastructure and housing were all expanded for the arrival of 'The Atomics' in the late 1950s. Atomic fission has ceased. 'The Atomics' remain.

The sound of the aftermath of atomic experiment is the

'clipclops'. Ceaseless beta gamma and neutron detectors constantly proclaim their readiness across the site. It's a peculiarly insistent sound, but a lot of the Dounreay staff don't even hear it anymore; they just notice very very quickly if it stops. Air pressurisation systems howl and hiss. It's not quiet in there.

Going over the barrier for the first time is a frightening experience. A long bench runs across a room; all one has to do is get the protective layers on without touching the ground on the inside. The oversuit you've been issued with suddenly seems impossible to figure out. Wobbling, unbalanced, teetering, trying to get the overshoes on without touching the floor. Scanned in, scanned out.

Entry to the facilities is via claustrophobic screening cabinets, smaller than a phone box; it is necessary to adopt the correct positions when prompted by an automated voice.

All around other people are cracking jokes, relaxed, as if it's normal life. And of course, it is. It's a taster of what life might have become for many more of us, if the trans-uranic economy had fully taken off. It's also strangely intimate. Dust, gases, splinters, particles, all to be kept from the body.

It induces an extraordinary sense of vulnerability. It feels like the moment before a long climb. You don't really want to think about what will happen if the scanners go off on your way back out.

Artists, Rationality and Magpie Methodologists

Philosophical positions can be seen as tools rather than belief systems for practising artists. There follow brief summaries of a set of insight-tools which have come in useful in these explorations.

The Incidental Person

The British artist John Latham (1921–2006) coined the expression the 'Incidental Person' (IP) to qualify an individual who engages in non-art contexts – industry, politics, education – while avoiding the 'for/against', 'you vs me' disposition typically adopted to resolve differences. The IP, Latham argued, 'may be able, given access to matters of public interest ranging from the national economic, through the environmental and departments of the administration to the ethical in social orientation, to "put forward answers to questions we have not yet asked."'[3]

This concept, applied in the pioneering work of the Artists Placement Group, was originally used to define a positional ideal for an artist on becoming involved in a company or organisation. It can gain traction in seemingly unlikely contexts. Sites and activities formerly secret are particularly suitable for an approach where the artist enters with some sanction but no particular brief from the controlling organisation. Abandoned places and sites of ongoing decommissioning or heritage packaging are often most revelatory in dialogue with just the right person. Artists' approaches are therefore subject to all the randomness, good/bad luck and unrepeatability that conventional methodologies shun.

Supermodernity and postmodernity

Marc Augé's conception of supermodernity (1995) is a very useful field tool,[4] avoiding the claustrophobia of the postmodern diagnosis while acknowledging the collapse of the 'progress' motif in modernism. In common with Virilio, he emphasises the emergence of Speed, communications networks and new relations between the human and the spatial. The concept of the 'non-place' – airport, station and transit zone – can equally be applied to zones where conflict is held in suspension. The feeling of excess, concentration and increasing weight of the 'super-' prefix describes the weightiness and the pressure on the imagination that these places produce. Instead of the idea of 'supplanting' that the word postmodern implies, 'supermodernity' implies intensification, pressure, baroque involution and the potential for a sociopathy of modernity: Ballard as tour guide. Modernity is not replaced or overcome; it evolves. The promise of modernity becomes the cracked façade; entropic modernism. The spatial mirroring implied by the non-place (departure lounges require corresponding arrivals halls) implies mirroring in geographical terms of the world-object: development and delivery, East and West Bloc. A conceptual mirroring also takes place in our blindness to the dark side of modernism, the way in which the canonical histories structure the dynamics of architecture around the white galleries, curtain wall office skyscrapers and heroic individualism. Atkins, Skidmore Owens Merrill, Laing: all seen via the bright and shiny. The anonymous, secret, massive structures they built are elided from our vision.

The world-object

> By world-objects I mean tools with a dimension that is com-
> mensurable with one of the dimensions of the world. A satellite
> for speed, an atomic bomb for energy, the Internet for space,
> and nuclear waste for time . . . these are four examples of world-
> objects. (Serres 2006)

Michel Serres's concept of the 'world-object' enables us to
get beyond the urban/rural, military/civil, centre/periphery
distinctions, which limit our thinking about space, and our
responsibilities in time.

World-objects dropped into isolated or formerly remote locations reveal a great deal about the logics of power in different
times.

> From the nature we used to speak about, an archaic world in which
> our lives were plunged, modernity casts off, in its growing movement
> of derealisation. Having become abstract and inexperienced, devel-
> oped humanity takes off toward signs, frequents images and codes,
> and, flying in their midst, no longer has any relation, in cities, either to
> life or to the things of the world. (Serres 1995: 120)

World system or world-object, the siting of military and scientific facilities in remote or secluded areas opens a dual perspective
on their lived meaning: reverie, pastoral stillness, mirror of alertness. Northrop Frye's concept of drama, which conceptualises
'green world versus closed world' settings, offers another perspective that may be useful. Modernity, with its assumption of
a technocratic polis, is by definition incapable of considering the
non-human, and therefore incapable of reacting to nature or the
world per se. Monitoring of growth, cybernetic systems and economic feedback are all indicators that have replaced meaningful
assessment. Virilio's concepts of space territory and velocity act in
a sphere both expanded and virtualised; this is the source of their
unreachability from 'civil' society.

Can we experience the test grounds of apocalypse rationally?
How did their staff and crew experience themselves, make sense of
their role and integrate it with a positive sense of the future? We
might think of a fragmented self, living simultaneously in a narrative of progress and a historic tale of triumph and idyll.

The process of experiencing these ideas *in situ* is a kind of 'feral scholarship', which enables new insights. The privilege of allowing irrationality and contradiction into the discourse can be productive. Bipolar places (loci which generated despair and euphoria in equal measure), sites which in their media selves were referred to in educational films, news features, propaganda films and speculative film and fiction carry social force as influencing machines.

Bunker archaeology is contemporary archaeology

Territory, limit, derealisation and disappearance; we are used to such radical negations in Virilio's work. A return to some of the sites that enabled such radical disconnection of the experiential sensorium from social systems is sometimes shocking, sometimes banal and sometimes shot through with absurdist black comedy.

Archive material gives us a connection with those living in the logistical and administrative aftermath of Manichaean believers, and the network of assumption and belief that sustained them. Cold War ideologies created and sustained these sites, although many of the staff involved may have held highly ambivalent rationales and beliefs in those positions. In understanding a multifaceted sense of belonging and sense of place, using archive material is key. Displayed alongside and sometimes in contradiction to contemporary material, different conclusions can be reached by different viewers. Simultaneity is posited as an investigative strategy and as a display methodology that foregrounds the past and present – or the real and virtual – as two poles of experience which the viewer is constantly pulled between and is invited to formulate his or her own synthesis.

Site-specific and site-based artists can grasp some interesting freedoms. Heritage zones, military or test facilities and relics of scientific advance offer loci for reflection and recontextualising the common sense of 'progress'.

Virilio more than most thinkers reminds us that the role of theory is not necessarily to act as factual proof or a reliable guide to a pre-existing reality but exists as a mythopoetic catalyst or signal.

On looking at the remnants of acceleration embodied by these selected sites, a strong intuition develops that this sort of speed and response is now decisively elsewhere. These sites, which once were planned at geographically specific sites for logistical or

Figure 12.6 Runway 04, RAF Coltishall (2008).

safety reasons, now point to a sense that acceleration is no longer a national concern. Whether virtualised or experienced through transnational alliance, Acceleration has been an early (the very first?) subject of globalisation for the UK, and has been effectively outsourced.

All of these sites represent (super) modernity as a form of recruitment to a silent, technocratic, specifically twentieth-century citizenship, the atmospheres and motivations of which can be approached through a use of multiplicity in display. The viewer can be empowered as an active participant in the construction of meaning.

Notes

1. For further still and video images of the Jaguar flight simulator, see <http://www.atomtown.org.uk/html/gairspace/htm/dispersals.htm> (accessed 23 July 2012).

2. An extended discussion of this phenomenon is contained in Dunlop (2008).
3. Latham, John, *The Artist as Incidental Person: new role vis-à-vis government*, John Latham Archive (JLA) 13/4231, Folder 335. A recent summary and re-invigoration of the concept took place during 'The Incidental Person' exhibition. Curated by Antony Hudek at Apexart, Manhattan, New York, 6 January to 20 February 2010, <http://www.apexart.org/exhibitions/hudek.php> (accessed 21 January 2012).
4. The particular relevance of this concept in understanding zones of conflict and contested meaning is explored in Gonzalez Ruibal (2008).

References

Augé, Marc (1995), *Non-Places: Introduction to an Anthropology of Supermodernity*, London: Verso.

Cramerotti, Alfredo (2009), *Aesthetic Journalism: How to Inform Without Informing*, Bristol: Intellect Books.

Dunlop, Gair (2008), 'The War Office', *Cultural Politics* 4(2): 155–60.

Dunlop, Gair and Schofield, John (2012), 'Art, landscape and the "technological sublime": An investigation at RAF Coltishall (Norfolk)', in press with Imperial War Museum, London.

Edwards, Paul N. (1996), *The Closed World: Computers and the Politics of Discourse in Cold War America*, Cambridge, MA: MIT Press.

Frye, Northrop (1965), *A Natural Perspective: The Development of Shakespearean Comedy and Romance*, New York: Harbinger Books.

Gonzalez Ruibal, Alfredo (2008), 'Time to destroy: An archaeology of supermodernity', *Current Anthropology* 49(2): 247–79.

Jefferies, Richard (1885), *After London*, <http://www.gutenberg.org/ebooks/13944> (accessed 23 July 2012).

Macaulay, Rose (1992 [1950]), *The World My Wilderness*, London: Virago.

Nairn, Tom (1988), *The Enchanted Glass: Britain and its Monarchy*, London: Radius.

Nye, David E. (1994), *American Technological Sublime*, Cambridge, MA: MIT Press.

Palmer, Judith (2006), 'Echoes of destruction', in Louise K. Wilson, *A Record of Fear*, Ely: Commissions East, pp. 97–118.

Serres, Michel (1995), *The Natural Contract*, Ann Arbor: University of Michigan Press.

Serres, Michel (2006), 'Introduction to *Revisiting The Natural Contract*', translation of a paper presented by Michel Serres to the Institute of the Humanities at Simon Fraser University (Canada) on 4 May 2006, <http://www.ctheory.net/articles.aspx?id=515> (accessed 17 January 2012).

Today in Britain (1964), 35 mm colour/sound film, 26 minutes. Director Peter Hopkinson. Script by James Cameron. Sponsors: Foreign Office, Commonwealth Relations Office, Colonial Office, Central Office of Information.

Virilio, Paul (1991), *Open Sky*, London: Verso.

13

The Production of the Present

Ian James

I

> Our vision is a battlefield in which the movement of our culture towards nothingness and disappearance is concealed in the obvious. (Virilio 2005: 38)

The concluding paragraphs of Virilio's foreword to *Negative Horizon* strike what might seem to be, to some of his readers at least, a characteristically apocalyptic note. The desertification of culture, its slide towards nothingness and disappearance, the possible ruin and degradation of our worldly milieu, all these motifs may appear to testify to an outlook dominated by an overwhelming presentiment of impending catastrophe. Such an apocalyptic or catastrophic tone might also confirm the view of some of Virilio's more critical commentators that his is a rather conservative view of contemporary culture, and specifically in its negative assessment of the visual culture produced by mass media and digital communications technologies.[1] According to this view, Virilio's account of the contemporary is far too dominated by an all too nostalgic attachment to the values of immediacy and presence as well as to those of situated and grounded bodily experience. This apocalyptic outlook and the conservative tendencies that underpin it could be attributed to his Catholic humanism on the one hand and to his residual attachment to the phenomenological account of presence and embodiment on the other.[2]

That Virilio is highly critical of contemporary culture can hardly be doubted. That he perceives tendencies within the present that he believes may have potentially disastrous consequences for the future is more than confirmed by the epigraph given above. Yet it may be rather too hasty to conclude from this that he is simply a cultural conservative with an overly apocalyptic bent, unable to free himself from the pre-deconstructive and pre-postmodern prejudices of immediacy and presence. It could be immediately noted, for instance, that, in the same sentence that warns against 'the movement of our culture towards nothingness and disappearance', the faculty of vision is framed quite unambiguously as a battlefield. Vision here is a site of struggle and conflict and not simply or solely a field understood to be declining into a virtuality marked by desertification, loss and absence. By the same token the concluding pages of 'The Enterprise of Appearances', and indeed the entirety of the foreword to *Negative Horizon*, frame the struggle that takes place within this battlefield of vision as a struggle between sameness and difference and not, as Virilio's critics might think, between presence and absence. This is not a struggle waged in the name of a recuperation of a plenitude or immediacy of presence and against the empty virtuality of a denatured experience. Throughout the opening pages of *Negative Horizon*, as even the most cursory reading will reveal, it is far more a question of a hierarchy of vision that imposes pre-formed structures of perception and, against these, the attempt to seek out and reveal the in-between, the marginal, the concealed, the new and the different (Virilio 2005: 31).

Virilio sums this up very succinctly in the following terms: 'Today we are no longer truly seers of our world, but already merely reviewers, the tautological repetition of the same, at work in our mode of production (i.e., industrial production), is equally at work in our mode of perception' (2005: 37). For all that he here evokes the value of 'true seeing' and the loss or erosion of that value, he also quite clearly opposes this to a mode of vision which is 'merely' repetition. More specifically and more importantly perhaps, this mode of vision as 'repetition of the same' results from a contingent work of production or creation, one in which the industrial production of contemporary culture is profoundly interwoven with a dynamic of perception. At stake here, therefore, is not the value of presence, but more directly and insistently the value of the present and of its production. More importantly it is a question of the specific logic that underpins or informs the production of the present: that of a totalising and hierarchising domination of the same on the one hand and that of a diversifying and de-hierarchising force of differentiation and difference on the other. The opposition here is between a logic of cultural vision that obliterates the singularity and richness of experience and one that actively produces a diversity of singularities and intensities, a diversity which would be irreducible to the 'repetition of the same'. Seen from this perspective, Virilio's outlook and emphasis appear less catastrophic and apocalyptic and far more polemical, conflictual, but also crucially, affirmative and creative. The dominant tone of the concluding paragraphs of 'The Enterprise of Appearances' is arguably characterised far less by the warning of a cultural 'movement towards nothingness' than it is by the affirmation that: 'it is necessary to endeavour positively to reinvent our vision of the world' (2005: 38).

II

any theory of painting is a metaphysics (Merleau-Ponty 2004 [1961]: 303)

'The Enterprise of Appearances' is ostensibly a rather anecdotal and autobiographical account of Virilio's experiments with, and meditations upon, painting. As such it represents a key moment of engagement, within the Virilian corpus as a whole, with one particular genre or technique of visual culture. Yet, as the preceding introductory discussion might suggest, the apparently anecdotal account of his experiments in painting have far-reaching implications for Virilio's broader critical understanding of vision and visual perception, and for the cultural politics of vision that can be seen to inform his work as a whole. Indeed his discussion of transparency, figure and ground, form and antiform, of tropism and hierarchies of perception, are all highly theoretical and arguably represent one of his most important critical-philosophical engagements with the question of visual perception and with the fundamental position it enjoys within his writing. Specifically, and although no direct references are made, the foreword to *Negative Horizon* represents a key critical engagement with the phenomenological account of seeing and visual perception and marks decisive ways in which Virilio differs, or takes his distance from the phenomenological perspectives of both Husserl and Merleau-Ponty. This difference or distance, it will become clear, provides the key to understanding Virilio's affirmation of vision and visual culture as a battlefield, and his affirmative project of a production of the present.

Husserl: self-evidence versus tropism

The reference to phenomenology in Virilio's writing is most explicit in texts such as *The Insecurity of Territory* (1993), *The Lost Dimension* (1991) and *The Vision Machine* (1994). The phenomenological reference is nowhere more decisive, of course, than in *Polar Inertia* (2000), where the characterisation of the concept of polar inertia itself is derived from a reading of Husserl's short 1930s piece 'The Earth does not Move'. This piece, together with 'The Origin of Geometry', which is also cited, are satellite texts of *The Crisis in European Sciences and Transcendental Phenomenology* (Husserl 1970). Despite the decisive importance of the Husserlian reference in *Polar Inertia*, Virilio's descriptions of visual experience in 'The Enterprise of Appearances' are in stark contrast to the fundamentals of perceptual consciousness such as they are conceived by Husserl in *The Crisis* and related texts. As was indicated earlier, no explicit mention of these texts is made here, but from the outset there are echoes and resonances as when, for instance, in the second sentence of the foreword Virilio affirms: 'I have always been resistant to the formulas of mathematics but open to the figures of geometry and geography' (Virilio 2005: 26). This immediately resonates with Husserl's critique, throughout *The Crisis*, of abstract mathematical formalism and its methods or techniques, and also with his interest (in 'The Origin of Geometry' in particular) in recovering the original historical life-world and lived field of perception in which geometrical forms and knowledge were discovered in the first instance. Both Husserl and Virilio are deeply concerned with a more fundamental or originary layer of visual perception that penetrates accumulated layers of handed-down and habitual knowledge or tradition; they wish to pursue, respectively, an 'inquiry back into the most original sense in which geometry once arose' (Husserl 1970: 354) and an enquiry into 'the silent appearance of objects, of things, of figures', into a 'legacy concealed within everyday vision' (Virilio 2005: 27, 31).

Yet what each encounters once those accumulated layers of knowledge and tradition have been peeled away are entirely different deep structures of vision and perception. In posing the question of the beginnings of geometry Husserl's key concern is to demonstrate the way in which universal, abstract idealities and forms both arise from and are discovered within contingent historical life-worlds. His concern, then, is to challenge what he sees to be a 'ruling dogma of the separation between epistemological elucidation and historical . . . explanation, between epistemological and genetic origin' (Husserl 1970: 370). In order to avoid the collapse of the universal, abstract idealities of geometry into mere relativistic and historically contingent 'values', Husserl has to locate, within the deepest layer of perceptual experience, a constant, invariant and indubitable possibility of originary self-evidence. At its heart Husserl's phenomenological method relies on a very specific and extended use of the Cartesian *cogito*. Once everything contingent is stripped away or 'bracketed-off' there remains an indubitable and primordial presentation to consciousness, a fundamental structure of phenomenological seeing, which is endowed with an absolute and invariant certainty. Throughout the pages of 'The Origin of Geometry' Husserl refers to this as 'self-evidence' and defines it in the following terms: 'Self-evidence means nothing more than grasping an entity with the consciousness of its original being-itself-there . . . in this self-evidence, what has been realized is there originaliter, as itself' (1970: 356). Just like the Cartesian *cogito* Husserlian self-evidence is a non-negatable and irreducible presence to consciousness and, for Husserl, this self-evidence is one of visual perception, or one in which phenomenological consciousness itself is figured in terms of vision and seeing. Thus beneath the contingent surface of lived historical worldly experience lies a primary and very stable field of vision that the Husserlian phenomenological method can recover:

> we have removed every bond to the factually valid historical world . . . This freedom, and the direction of our gaze upon the apodictically invariant, results in the latter again and again – with the self-evidence of being able to repeat the invariant structure at will – as what is identical, what can be made self-evident *originaliter* at any time, can be fixed in univocal language as the essence constantly implied in the flowing, vital horizon. (375)

So not only can original self-evidence be recovered, also 'what has been realized originaliter, as itself', can, on the basis of this recovery, be restored to consciousness in its 'most original sense' (354), its 'strictly unassailable self-evidence' and its 'absolute supratemporal validity' (354, 373). Husserl's perhaps rather exorbitant use of the Cartesian cogito deployed in the form of the originary apodictic self-evidence of phenomenological seeing secures a domain of visual forms, and, indeed, a domain of primordial vision that is absolutely stable and invariant, and upon which the universal abstract idealities of geometry (and by extension all science) find their ground. Thus original geometrical intuitions can be secured through 'careful a priori explication' (375).

A clearer affirmation of phenomenological presence could not be more explicitly made. And yet how different this is from Virilio's account of forms and antiforms in the opening pages of *Negative Horizon*. When Husserl describes the originary presentation to perception of geometrical forms there is a clear sense that, in their self-evidence, a specific foregrounding of their essentially ordered essence is taken as being inevitable and goes unquestioned:

> First to be singled out from the thing-shapes are surfaces – more or less 'smooth,' more or less perfect surfaces; edges, more or less rough or 'fairly' even; in other words more or less pure lines, angles, more or less perfect points; then, again, among the lines, for example, straight lines are especially preferred, whereas totally or partially curved surfaces are undesirable for many kinds of practical interests. (Husserl 1970: 376)

'Pure lines', 'perfect points', the preference for the straight or partially curved, all these present themselves to the phenomenologically reduced gaze as a function of the purity, invariance and ideality of the geometrical forms that emerge. In stark contrast, Virilio speaks of a 'double dynamic' of perceptual form, one internal, one external, which between them generate or produce fundamental perceptual forms or shapes in an unstable, supple and variable manner:

> The dynamic of things seemed to me to double . . . on the one hand, an internal dynamic that assured the material reality of the object . . . or, in the case of a drawn figure, that assured on the paper the geometrical reality of the circle, of the roundness within the circumference, and, on the other hand, an external dynamic that induced the void, the transparence, that gave form and value to absence. The surface of the object, the line of the drawing, the outlines, served two purposes: one of internal individuation that established it was a case of a circle or a square, the other of external information that produced a field. When one brought a second figure alongside the first, the external fields

would meet each other and the antiform would arise and show itself. (Virilio 2005: 32–3)

The interrogation of the primordial forms of vision carried out in the name of painterly experimentation directly opposes itself to Husserl's attempt to uncover a bedrock of self-evidence and apodictic invariance. At the heart of the most fundamental and original possibility of vision or visual perception, there is, for Virilio, an unstable dynamic of lines and surfaces, of figure and ground, presence and absence, form and antiform. Husserl recognises only the first 'internal dynamic', that which 'assures geometrical reality' and guarantees its self-evidence, apodictic invariance and therefore, ultimately, its universal ideality. In recognising a second dynamic and the production of mobile and variable 'fields', Virilio introduces a dynamism, instability and mutability into the most primordial layer of phenomenological seeing and visual perception. This suggests quite clearly that, at its most fundamental level of articulation, Virilio's account of seeing and the visual in no way affirms an originary presence, self-presence or self-identity. Nor, therefore, can it affirm a nostalgia for such an originary presence. Rather it affirms an originary dynamism of production, and originary transformability, or plasticity of presentation.

It is in this context that the importance Virilio accords to the motif of 'tropism' can be understood. From the moment that his painterly interrogation reveals to him that the fundamental forms of visual perception are constituted or produced in a double dynamic (the internal form, and the external field) then the deliberate juxtaposition of fields can, as indicated above, generate, if only momentarily, the perception of an antiform. Here, a different relationship between the line or surface of the figure and its formative 'field' is perceived and a different and hitherto hidden form is revealed to perception. It is this instant or site of switching from the perception of one figure to that of an entirely different figure that Virilio calls a 'tropism'. More specifically he speaks of: 'the tropism of the point where the form and the antiform oscillated' (Virilio 2005: 33). The tropism is significant here not only because it introduces a dynamism, instability, transformability and plasticity into the fundamentals of visual perception. In introducing such dynamism and instability it also and in the same stroke introduces politics into perception. More precisely, it makes of perception a site of politics, a site of political relationality which has a historical, social and cultural dimension. In discovering the possibility of generating antiforms, Virilio remarks, 'I had taken on the goal of making visible the invisible . . . the antiforms that I exhumed here or there were nothing other than a series of edges . . . whoever paid attention to such figures?' (33). Again the contrast with Husserl's formulations is stark. Husserl, it will be recalled, spoke of geometrical figures emerging on the basis of 'preference' being given to 'pure' or 'perfect' lines, surfaces, points, etc. The self-evidence, ideality and universality of geometric forms are more than enough, for Husserl at least, to guarantee the rationality and certainty of such perceptual 'preferences'. Yet, by Virilio's account such preferences would be nothing other than a form of cultural prejudice, the prejudice of a European and Eurocentric culture that rejects 'the ground, margins, difference' (32). Virilio's exhumation of a 'series of edges' carries a heavy cultural-political weight, therefore, since the answer to his question is obviously that no one has paid attention to such figures for the precise reason that our culture has trained their perception to ignore and marginalise them. So where for Husserl the project of returning to the origin of geometrical forms leads us to the supra-historical invariants and the 'the essential structure of what is generally human' (Husserl 1970: 378), for Virilio the interrogation of originary forms reveals a culturally determined 'hierarchy of perception' and leads him to the conclusion that 'there are probably as many perspectives as there are visions of the world, of cultures, of ways of life' (Virilio 2005: 35).

What these points of contrast and opposition between Husserl and Virilio should by now have made abundantly clear is that the Virilian account of visual perception is in no way anchored in a phenomenological affirmation of originary presence. It is anchored in an understanding of the presentation or production of the present as being fundamentally dynamic, mobile, transformable. The notions of transparency and tropism give 'form and value to absence' and suggest that the oscillation between presence and absence is fundamentally constitutive of the visual. It is only on the basis of this ultimately groundless, mutable and plastic structure of visual perception that historical contingency and cultural value can be admitted into the fundamental ordering of the way we come to see and only on this basis can Virilio conclude that 'our vision is a battlefield'.

Merleau-Ponty: what can a body do?

While Virilio's decisive distance from the Husserlian account of phenomenological presence is hard to deny, his greater proximity to the Merleau-Pontean account of visual perception may be a more complex issue to resolve. Again the stakes here relate directly to the way in which Virilio responds critically to contemporary visual culture and to the seemingly negative assessments he makes. If it can be conceded, for instance, that his critical evaluation of the culture of virtual reality is not anchored in a nostalgia for Husserlian presence, might it nevertheless be plausible to suggest that such an evaluation is deeply suffused with an attachment to Merleau-Ponty's account of the 'body proper' and of the grounding of visual perception in the immediacy of situated bodily experience? Certainly, if 'The Enterprise of Appearances' can be shown to be implicitly very critical of Husserl, it nevertheless appears to be far more closely aligned with Merleau-Ponty's work. More specifically, the interest in relating painting to the fundamentals of perception is the central preoccupation of Merleau-Ponty's last finished essay 'Eye and Mind' (2004 [1961]). Similarly the interest in figure, ground and the perception of forms provides a central point of focus for his major early work *Phenomenology of Perception* (1962), deeply influenced as it is by the experimental work carried out by Gestalt psychologists in Germany in the first half of the twentieth century.

One of Virilio's most important references to Merleau-Ponty can be found in *The Vision Machine* where the phenomenologist is cited without the reference itself being sourced:

All that I see is, in principle, within my reach (at least within the reach of my gaze), it is registered on the map of what 'I can do'. In this important phrase, Merleau-Ponty precisely describes that which is ruined by a teletopology which has become ordinary. The essentials of what I see are no longer, in effect or in principle, within my reach and even if it is within reach of my gaze it is no longer necessarily inscribed on the map of what 'I can do'. (1994: 7)

In fact the quotation is drawn from 'Eye and mind' and there is, without question, a clear invocation of a ruination and loss brought about by the detachment of visual perception from the situated and spatially orientated field of bodily experience. The

teletopological structure of seeing brought about by the technologies of contemporary visual culture detach us from our bodily
capacity, from a richness and density of a material existence
'within my reach'.[3] The judgement here of teletopological vision
is clearly very negative and clearly grounded in a positive evaluation of the account of situated and embodied visual perception
that informs Merleau-Ponty's thinking about painting in 'Eye and
Mind'.

Yet there are important differences to be marked between
Virilio and Merleau-Ponty, which are similar to those that have
been highlighted in relation to Husserl. Once again these differences suggest that the Virilian account of visual perception is
rather more complicated than his explicit references to phenomenological thought might suggest. Once again it is a question of
what may be discovered once the phenomenologist has penetrated
into the deeper, more primordial ordering or structure of perception. As has been indicated, for both Merleau-Ponty and Virilio it
is the gaze of the painter that operates as a privileged figure of this
more fundamental order of vision. In this context Merleau-Ponty's
discussion in 'Eye and Mind' of the technical prosthesis of the
mirror and its representation in Dutch painting is very revealing.
The specular image, he remarks, 'anticipates, within things, the
labour of vision', and he continues:

> Like all other technical objects, such as signs and tools, the mirror
> arises upon the open circuit that goes from seeing body to visible body.
> Every technique is a 'technique of the body'. A technique outlines and
> amplifies the metaphysical structure of our flesh. The mirror appears
> because I am seeing-visible, because there is a reflexivity of the sensi-
> ble: the mirror translates and reproduces that reflexivity. My outside
> completes itself in and through the sensible. (Merleau-Ponty 2004
> [1961]: 300)

Here is an account of vision structured in a reflexivity, reciprocity
and fundamental unity of the seeing and the seen in which embodied visual perception results from an entwining, mutual imbrica-
tion and completion of flesh in the world, or of flesh *as the* world.[4]
The metaphysical structure of flesh is ultimately characterised by
this reciprocity and reflexivity and therefore by a fundamental
symmetry, continuity and unity. The 'vision machine' of the mirror
does nothing but reveal this metaphysical structure. Arguably this

unified or unifying structure of 'flesh' is a more philosophically mature and complex development of Merleau-Ponty's thinking of the 'Gestalt' in his earlier work, *Phenomenology of Perception* (1962). Here he called upon the concept of 'Gestalt' to account for the way in which visual perception is always structured according to a unified organisation of figure and ground that gives the whole of a visual form, so that vision is not simply the result of atomised sense data and their subsequent or a posteriori organisation. In each case, for both the early and the late Merleau-Ponty, it is the unity or the unifying dynamic of figure and ground, of seeing and seen (in the Gestalt form and in 'flesh' respectively) that underpins the fundamental structure of visual perception.

Once again this can be seen to be in stark contrast with Virilio's account of figure and ground in 'The Enterprise of Appearances'. As was the case in the analysis of Husserlian perception above, it is clear that the Virilian motif of the tropism, and the instability, mobility and mutability of figure and ground that the tropism articulates, is not consistent with Merleau-Ponty's emphasis on unity, wholeness, reflexivity and reciprocity. The mobility of 'fields' and their susceptibility to being variably juxtaposed enable oscillations between forms and antiforms. To reiterate, such mobility constitutes the visual as a fundamentally plastic and mutable field. This is not at all compatible with the unified structuring of figure and ground that is at work in the Merleau-Pontean Gestalt. Once again, and as was the case with Husserl, we encounter a logic of stability or unity operating in the most fundamental ordering of visual perception. In the case of Merleau-Ponty, this logic of unity or wholeness constitutes the body and embodied vision as a home or originary site of belonging. The seeing body with its logic of the 'reflexivity of the sensible' is 'both natal space and the matrix of every other existing space' (Merleau-Ponty 2004 [1961]: 307). The body is a primordial projection of the space of the visible whose metaphysical structure the technicity of the mirror reveals, but which, crucially, *remains untouched* by that technicity. There is a sense here that visual and teletopological technologies would certainly be able to superpose themselves on the primordial vision of the Merleau-Pontean body. However, that primordial vision – the 'seeing-seen' which opens up a natal space which in turn is the matrix of all other existing spaces – always has the capacity to be uncovered and therefore recovered or recuperated, if only due phenomenological care and attention is given. The very mutability, instability and plasticity of primordial visual perception in Virilio mean that it is not, ultimately a 'natal space' that can provide the matrix for all other existing spaces. Primordial visual perception here is eminently susceptible to the 'clandestine voluntarism' of cultural prejudices and contingently determined ways of seeing (Virilio 2005: 36). Moreover, in its susceptibility to contingent, historical and material forms, vision is always primordially and already permeable or permeated by techniques, technicity or technical prosthetics. This simply cannot be the case for Merleau-Ponty for whom the 'natal space' of the body is pre-technical, a unified circuit of the seeing and the seen which technical objects 'arise upon'. Put bluntly, where for the phenomenologist 'Every technique is a "technique of the body"', for Virilio, *every body is a body of technique*.

III

those who perceive transparence know well that nothing is immobile (Virilio 2005: 26)

Reading 'The Enterprise of Appearances' as a twin critique of both Husserlian presence and the Merleau-Pontean 'body proper' yields an important twofold perspective on Virilio's approach to contemporary visual culture. First, his critical assessments of visual culture in no way presuppose originary presence or ground, nor any unified ordering of a structured whole. Rather the fundamental plasticity of visual forms presupposes an originary absence of ground or foundation. Here, a logic of the fixed presence gives way to a transformable dynamic of the production or presentation of the present. It is in this context that the final, seemingly obscure, lines of the foreword to *Negative Horizon* can really make sense:

He who dreaded that the sky would fall, he who feared the liquid mass and movements of the ocean, tore apart a logical structure of vital importance, an essential continuity between the solid and the liquid, between the gaseous and the mineral, between presence and absence: he destroyed the relativity of the instant of vision. (2005: 38)

The figure evoked here, the figure of he who dreads mutability, permeability and the oscillation between apparently opposed instances, could so easily be the Husserl of *The Crisis*; this is to say, the Husserl who, as has been shown here, seeks the self-evidence and apodicticity of an invariant and supra-temporal phenomenological seeing that penetrates beneath the changing surface appearances of historical worlds. Granted, Virilio's untying of Husserlian presence here is not as technical, patient and philosophically sophisticated as Derrida's early deconstructive work. Yet it is perhaps no less forceful and decisive for all that.

Second, and just as decisively, the absence of ground and foundation within visible forms means that they are, from the beginning and, as it were by way of or 'out of' that absence of ground, always already inhabited by technicity, and technical prosthetics or objects. There is no homely origin of a seeing body in Virilio; if teletopological technologies can have such a powerful impact on 'the map of what "I can do"', that is because that map has already and from the beginning been charted out in an originary technicity of bodily life.

Virilio, then, should not be aligned with a conservative cultural agenda that yearns for the restoration of a lost presence or the recuperation of the capacities of the 'body proper'. He needs to be aligned much more with contemporary thinkers such as Bernard Stiegler whose deconstruction of phenomenology via a thinking of technical prosthetics is carried out in the name of a struggle to liberate our culture from the levelling and deadening effects of mass consumption or economic production and exchange (see Stiegler 1998, 2009, 2011). So when it comes to the question of where Virilio might lead his readers in their engagements with visual culture, the necessity of pursuing a very specific kind of struggle is critical. As Stiegler puts it in his analysis of the symbolic misery of contemporary culture, it may be a question of '*identifying forces, tendencies, processes and energies against which a struggle must be led*' (2005: 14). If Virilio singles out particular forms of art for rather harsh criticism, he does so precisely in order to identify and oppose certain contemporary forces or tendencies. In such cases it is less a matter of a politics of immediacy or presence and their diminution and far more a matter of specific economies of affect, those of the commodification and marketisation of experience, as when, for instance, he talks about video and concept art in *Art and Fear*:

from VIDEO ART onwards, no one can hear talk of CONCEPT ART without hearing the background noise of the mass media concealed behind the words and things of the art market. (Virilio 2003: 77–8)

The problem with an artform that is intimately tied up with the logic of mass media is that it necessarily standardises or homogenises collective vision and so produces a flattening of collective intensities or affects and a wasting of libidinal engagement with the materials of cultural production. In this sense any cultural politics that might be inspired by theoretical meditations on the visual (and on what one might call the 'technicity of seeing') will be a politics that will be resolutely ordered according to the primordially technical and prosthetic nature of our collective vision. It will, at the very same time, seek to affirm and produce singular intensities of libidinal attachment to the objects of cultural production rather than the flattened and standardised affects of mass consumption. It will be a question, ultimately, of the way the material and technical articulations of visual culture are produced and to what ends. There is a sense here that, without in any way being prescriptive or predetermining in advance the specific form of a new visual culture, Virilio's writing demands that we seize hold of the technicities of cultural production in order to produce different economies of affect, to produce singularities and intensities of experience.

Seen from this perspective, Virilio's apocalyptic warnings or catastrophic presentiments can be understood as a series of rhetorical weapons in the service of just such a demand. This is a rhetoric of cultural warfare, an ongoing struggle for the perception of the real. The struggle here, waged on the battlefield of vision, is not so much a struggle for what we may have lost in our contemporary visual culture. Rather it is a struggle for the 'relativity of the instant of vision' and for a future of plurality, diversity and richness of ways of seeing. It is a struggle, ultimately, for future and as yet unknown productions of the present.

Notes

1. See, for instance, Douglas Kellner who judges Virilio's understanding of technology and of contemporary technological culture as being : 'excessively negative and one-sided' and as ignoring 'the empowering and democratizing aspects of new computer and media technologies' (Armitage 2000: 103).

2. Virilio was very much influenced by the 'personalist' doctrines of Emmanuel Mounier who founded the review *Esprit*. On this, see James (2007: 94).

3. For a more developed discussion of 'teletopology' in Virilio, see James (2007: 48).
4. Merleau-Ponty's account of 'flesh' as a way of thinking bodily perception of the world as being also fundamentally and reciprocally part of the world is central to his last unfinished major work, *The Visible and the Invisible* (1968).

References

Armitage, J. (ed.) (2000), *Paul Virilio: From Modernism to Hypermodernism and Beyond*, London: Sage.

Husserl, E. (1970), *The Crisis in European Sciences and Transcendental Phenomenology*, trans. David Carr, Evanston, IL: Northwestern University Press.

James, I. (2007), *Paul Virilio*, London: Routledge.

Merleau-Ponty, M. (1962), *Phenomenology of Perception*, trans. Colin Smith, London: Routledge and Kegan Paul.

Merleau-Ponty, M. (1968), *The Visible and the Invisible*, trans. Alphonso Lingis, Evanston, IL: Northwestern University Press.

Merleau-Ponty, M. (2004 [1961]), 'Eye and mind', in Thomas Baldwin (ed.), *Maurice Merleau-Ponty: Basic Writings*, London: Routledge, pp. 290–324.

Stiegler, B. (1998), *Technics and Time 1: The Fault of Epimetheus*, trans. Richard Beardsworth and George Collins, Stanford: Stanford University Press.

Stiegler, B. (2005), *De la misère symbolique 2: La Catastrophè du sensible*, Paris: Galilée.

Stiegler, B. (2009), *Technics and Time 2: Disorientation*, trans. S. Barker, Stanford: Stanford University Press.

Stiegler, B. (2011), *Technics and Time 3: Cinematic Time and the Question of Malaise*, trans. S. Barker, Stanford: Stanford University Press.

Virilio, P. (1991), *The Lost Dimension*, trans. Daniel Moshenberg, New York: Semiotext(e).

Virilio, P. (1993, second edition), *L'insécurité du territoire*, Paris: Galilée.

Virilio, P. (2000), *Polar Inertia*, trans. Patrick Camiller, London: Sage.

Virilio, P. (1994), *The Vision Machine*, trans. Julie Rose, London: British Film Institute.

Virilio, P. (2003), *Art and Fear*, trans. Julie Rose, London: Continuum.

Virilio, P. (2005), *Negative Horizon*, trans. Michael Degener, London: Continuum.

Index

Illustrations are indicated by page numbers in italics.

242